European Handboc

AUSTRIAN RAILWAYS

LOCOMOTIVES, MULTIPLE UNITS & TRAMS

FIFTH EDITION

The complete guide to all Locomotives, Multiple Units & Trams of the Railways, Tramways and Metro Systems of Austria

Roland Beier & Brian Garvin

Published by Platform 5 Publishing Ltd.,
3 Wyvern House, Sark Road, Sheffield S2 4HG, England.

Printed in England by Berforts Information Press, Eynsham, Oxford.

ISBN 978 1 902336 94 7

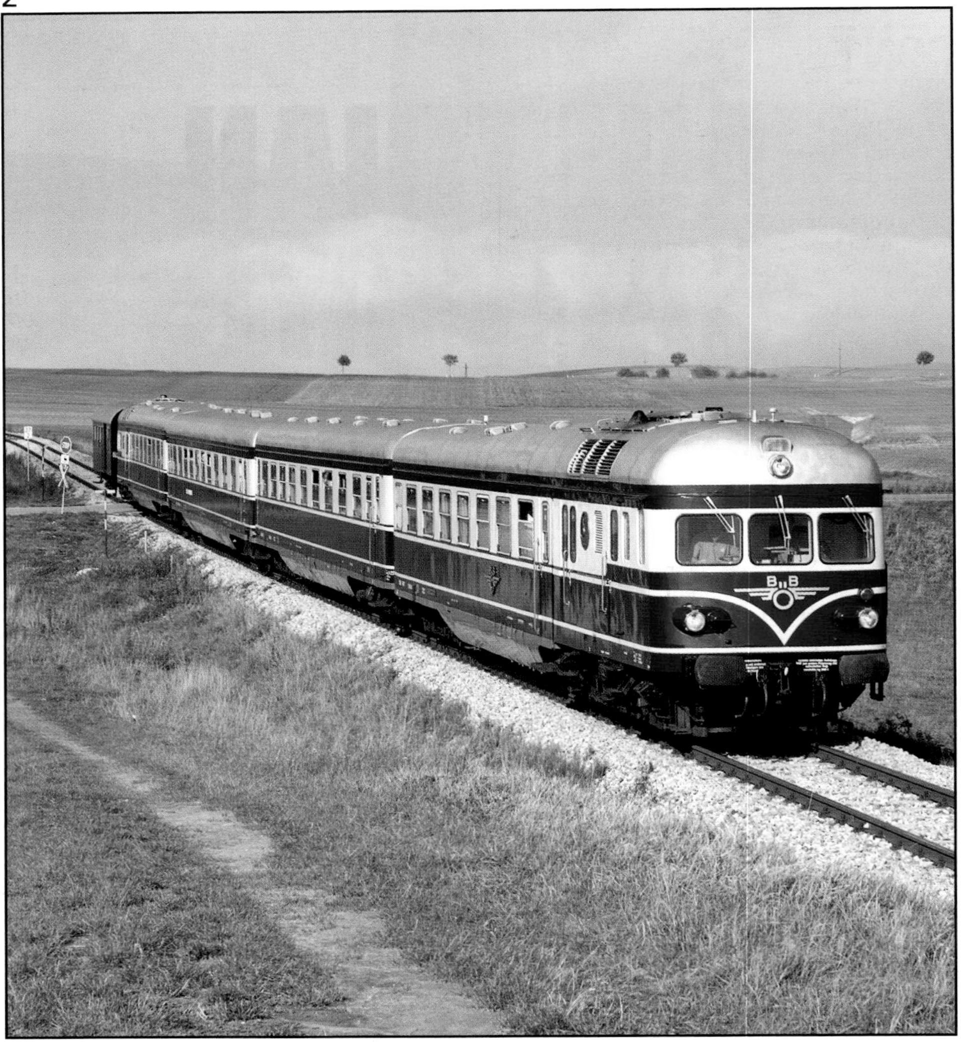

Above: Originally built as Class 5045 for long distance services in the 1950s and subsequently rebuilt and reclassified, all remaining examples of ÖBB Class 5145 have now been withdrawn. Several units have been preserved, including 5145 001 and 5145 011 at Eisenbahnmusem Strasshof. Here they are seen en route to Ernstbrunn near Naglern-Simonsfeld on 30th September 2007.

Front Cover: Railjet is ÖBB's premium express passenger service, operated using fixed formation push-pull coaching stock and Class 1116 Taurus electric locomotives, sporting a distinctive dark red/black/grey livery. 1163 213 leads a Railjet service at Unter Oberndorf on 28th April 2012. **Raimund Wyhnal**

Back Cover Top: It took Stadler a while to have the new GKB Class 5063 GTW DMUs fully commissioned. On 16 June 2011 5063 009 was seen on a train to Graz near Oisnitz.

Back Cover Bottom: The only active ex-ÖBB Class 2092 is operated by SLB. On 13 July 2010 Vs 51 stands at Tischlerhäusl depot.

CONTENTS

INTRODUCTION TO THE FIFTH EDITION

Welcome to the fifth edition of **Austrian Railways**. It contains details of all motive power of *Österreichische Bundesbahnen* (ÖBB) and of independent railway companies acting either on their own infrastructure or on the ÖBB network under open access rules. Details of tram and metro operators are included as well as details of preservation societies and their rolling stock. Data is updated to May 2012.

Since the last edition of this handbook was published in 2005 more open access operators have appeared on the rail freight market bringing the overall market share of new entrants to 15% in 2011. The first open access passenger operator was City Airport Train (CAT) in 2003 providing a fast service from Wien Mitte to Schwechat airport. This company is part owned by ÖBB, however. In December 2011 the first "real" new entrant started passenger services between Wien and Freilassing via Salzburg; WESTbahn Management GmbH is 26% owned by SNCF, the other shares being owned by private investors. Other independent operators also have passenger services, but either on their own infrastructure or in co-operation with ÖBB.

ÖBB's freight arm, RCA, has expanded into neighbouring countries by taking over MÁV Cargo (now Rail Cargo Hungaria) and by establishing subsidiaries in Romania, Slovenia and Italy. ÖBB Personenverkehr is now operating EC trains from München to Verona and beyond together with DB and Italian independent operator Trenord.

Another recent development is the privatisation of branch lines. This started with selling the Zell am See-Krimml line to SLB and the Schafberg rack railway to SKGB. At the end of 2010 more than 600 km of branch lines were transferred to NÖVOG which is a new railway undertaking owned by Land Niederösterreich. Most of these branch lines had lost traffic several years ago and have now been formally closed, but the narrow gauge lines in Niederösterreich such as the famous Mariazellerbahn are now operated by NÖVOG. Similar steps may follow in Land Oberösterreich where ÖBB want to get rid of several branch lines.

ÖBB have renewed their motive power significantly; the Taurus family (classes 1016/1116/1216) now has a total of 382 locomotives. This has led to the withdrawal of many older electric locomotives. 100 new diesel locomotives of Class 2016 helped to reduce the number of active Class 2043 and 2143 locos although some are still in use. New EMUs (classes 4023/4024/4124) have also been introduced as well as new DMUs (Class 5022). Independent railways have also had their share of new motive power; Stadler delivered several GTW multiple units to GKB and StLB and new EMUs for the NÖVOG operated Mariazellerbahn will be delivered in 2013.

New entrants in rail freight have also obtained additional locomotives. These are of various types including second hand locomotives from ÖBB as well as new locomotives built by Bombardier and Siemens.

To keep this book up to date, subscribe to **Today's Railways Europe**, the monthly magazine from Platform 5 Publishing which contains updates of Austrian train fleets plus details of usage, news and other useful information.

A BRIEF HISTORY OF AUSTRIA

Österreich, the German name for Austria, has its origins in the territory known as the Ostmark (Eastern March), established by Charlemagne in the Donau (Danube) valley in 803 AD. When Charlemagne died the Magyars overran the Ostmark. In 955 the Hungarians were defeated by Otto I and the Ostmark re-established. From 996 the Ostmark was referred to as *Ostarrichi* which eventually evolved into the name *Österreich*.

For several centuries from the Middle Ages until 1918, Austria was ruled by the Habsburg Empire (also known as the Austro-Hungarian Empire as it also included Hungary until the declaration of Hungarian independence in 1848).

1918 saw the end of World War I and of the Habsburg Empire, and the following year the treaty of St. Germain defined Austria's borders. In 1920 a new constitution was drawn up which established the Republic of Austria. After an attempted Nazi coup in 1934, 1938 saw the *Anschluss* (annexation) of the country and incorporation into Germany by Hitler. Austria then once again came to be known as the Ostmark.

After World War II Austria regained its former borders and was occupied by Soviet, British, French and American forces. All four of these signed the Austrian State Treaty in 1955 which established Austria as an independent and neutral country. Since 1995 Austria has been a member of the EU and is also a signatory to the Schengen Agreement, meaning an end to border controls for travellers between Austria and all its neighbouring countries.

The heritage of the Austro-Hungarian Empire is still present in the capital city of Wien, which has 1.8 million inhabitants. This figure compares to 9 million inhabitants for the whole of Austria of which the majority live in the eastern parts. The cities of Graz, Linz, Innsbruck and Salzburg are much smaller than Wien. Central and western Austria have high mountains and a beautiful scenery, whilst lakes can be found all over the country from Bodensee at the borders with Switzerland and Germany to Neusiedlersee at the border with Hungary.

Austria being a mountainous country some of its railway lines are curvy and hence severely speed-restricted, since they have to go up, down, around and through mountains. Because of this, journey times between some centres can be long for the distances involved, but the scenic views are magnificent. On the other hand the Wien-Linz line has already been quadrupled in some sections with more to follow in December 2012. These lines can be traversed at speeds of 200 km/h and many long distance trains (Railjet, ÖBB EC and WEST) are already travelling at this speed. The same applies for the new Wörgl-Baumkirchen tunnel line which has been designed for 230 km/h operation and is due to open to traffic in December 2012. Maximum speed on other main lines is usually 140 to 160 km/h apart from some mountain sections.

COMMON TERMS IN ENGLISH & GERMAN

German is spoken all over Austria; it is the native language of the Austrians. There are minorities in Burgenland who speak Croatian and others in Kärnten who speak Slovenian. English is the lingua franca in tourism but especially in rural areas you cannot expect locals to speak English.

English	*German*
cancelled	ausgefallen
class (of ticket)	die Klasse
class (of vehicles)	die Baureihe
compartment	das Abteil
couchette car	der Liegewagen
delayed	verspätet
depot	die Servicestelle
diesel loco	die Diesellok
DMU	der Dieseltriebwagen
driver	der Lokführer*
driving trailer	der Steuerwagen
electric loco	die Elektrolok
EMU	der Elektrotriebwagen
freight train	der Güterzug
guard	der Zugführer*
lateness	die Verspätung
locomotive (loco)	die Lokomotive (Lok)
main station	der Hauptbahnhof
marshalling yard	der Verschiebebahnhof
narrow gauge	die Schmalspur
passenger coach	der Reisezugwagen
passenger train	der Reisezug
platform	der Bahnsteig
railbus	der Schienenbus
restaurant car	der Speisewagen
scheduled, timetabled	fahrplanmässig
shunting	der Verschub
sleeping car	der Schlafwagen
station	der Bahnhof (abbreviated to Bhf)
steam loco	die Dampflok
ticket	die Fahrkarte
timetable	der Fahrplan
track	das Gleis
tramway	die Straßenbahn
works	das Ausbesserungswerk

(*Note: these terms also have feminine forms, i.e. die Lokführerin, die Zugführerin)

TICKETS AND PASSES

Single tickets may be bought at ticket windows, automatic ticket machines and via the Internet. Please note that tickets may be bought on board of a train only if this is a long distance train and even then a surcharge applies. When boarding a regional or local train service you MUST have a valid ticket, otherwise you will be fined 70 Euro. There are some exceptions to this rule on minor branch lines where there are no automatic ticket machines at some stations and then you can buy a ticket on board the train, either from the driver or at a ticket machine. Please note that ticket machines accept cash, credit and debit cards but change is given only in coins up to an amount of €9.90. So if you buy a ticket worth € 9 you cannot use a €20 bank note!

Fares are lower than in Germany or Switzerland and there are a lot of bargain offers such as SparSchiene. These are available for a certain number of seats on a train and are restricted to a specific train service. Almost the whole of Austria is covered by integrated tariff areas, where you will not get an ÖBB ticket but a ticket issued by the regional tariff authority. Usually these tickets are slightly cheaper than the regular ÖBB tickets.

There is no pass covering the whole of Austria except for the ÖsterreichCard which is valid for one year and costs €1790 (second class) and €2420 (first class). Several regional passes are on sale, most of them within the integrated tariff areas. Urban and suburban rail services are usually integrated into urban tariff systems so you can normally use a tram or bus ticket also on the urban sections of the rail network. Full details can be found in the annual Rail Pass Guide published in spring of each year in **Today's Railways Europe**.

GETTING THERE FROM GREAT BRITAIN

By Rail

Getting from the UK to Austria by train is quite time consuming and involves a lot of train changes. Wien has direct train services to München (Railjet), Frankfurt (ICE), Zürich (Railjet), Praha (EC) and Budapest (Railjet). Salzburg has Railjet services to München and Zürich whilst Innsbruck can be reached from Zürich (Railjet), München (EC) and Verona (EC). Fast trains to Slovenia are less frequent and there is only a solitary overnight train from Wien via Salzburg to Venezia. Most of the Railjet, ICE and EC trains operate at intervals of two hours.

If you take the train from Britain to Austria it takes 16 hours or more either via Paris and Zürich or via Paris, Stuttgart and München. However, if you combine a visit to Austria with a trip to Germany or Switzerland you may use one of the frequent Railjet or ICE trains for your onward journey.

By Air

There are direct flights from several British airports to Wien Schwechat, Salzburg and Innsbruck. Wien Schwechat airport is rail connected.

LAYOUT OF INFORMATION

For each class of vehicle, technical and historical information is given followed by a list of individual vehicles arranged as follows:

(1) Number.
(2) Previous number in parentheses (if any).
(3) Livery code (if applicable) – in bold condensed type.
(4) Sector code (if applicable)
(5) Detail difference notes (if applicable).
(6) Depot allocation code.
(7) Name (if any).

FOREIGN MOTIVE POWER IN AUSTRIA

Austria is a transit country for freight and also has good passenger train links to neighbouring countries. Austrian train operators often have operating agreements for international train services with railway companies from abroad. Locomotives often do not change at the borders, especially at those with Germany, but instead work through. This involves Austrian locomotives working into neighbouring countries as well as foreign locomotives working into Austria. For the latter we give a short overview on the types used. In addition foreign locomotives reach the following border stations inside Austria: Kufstein, Salzburg (Germany); Gmünd, Retz (Czech Republic); Marchegg (Slovakia); Spielfeld-Strass, Bleiburg (Slovenia).

GERMANY

DEUTSCHE BAHN

DB Regio is operating the whole passenger service Garmisch-Partenkirchen-Reutte-Pfronten-Steinach on behalf of Land Tirol. International long distance passenger trains often use DB locomotives in Austria and the same applies for international freight trains.

Class 101: Salzburg-Graz, Salzburg-Linz.
Classes 110 and 111: weekend tourist charters Salzburg-Villach and Kufstein-Landeck.
Class 111: Mittenwald-Innsbruck.
Class 185: Freight trains Passau-Linz-Wien-Hegyeshalom.
Class 189: weekend tourist charters Kufstein-Brenner and Salzburg-Villach-Tarvisio.
Class 411: Wien-Passau and Kufstein-Innsbruck.
Classes 425 and 426: Garmisch-Partenkirchen-Reutte.
Class 628: Simbach-Linz
Class 642: Pfronten-Steinach-Reutte.

▲ TX Logistik operates a fleet of German registered Class 182.5 and 185.5 locomotives and Italian registered Class E412 from parent company Trenitalia, that can often be found operating on the Austrian railway network. 185 538 plus two FS Class E412 are pictured heading a Brennero bound intermodal train on 24 July 2008 near Schwaz.

LOKOMOTION

Lokomotion is based in München, Germany and has a safety certificate for working in Austria. Lokomotion operates freight trains in Austria using its **Class 139, 185, 186 and 189** locos on the following lines:
Kufstein-Brenner, Salzburg-Villach-Tarvisio/Jesenice, Salzburg-Hegyeshalom, Salzburg-Wien-Breclav.

TX LOGISTIK

TXL has a subsidiary in Austria called TX Logistik Austria. This subsidiary is responsible for operating TXL trains in Austria using **Class 182, 185 and 189** locomotives owned or leased by the parent company. TXL freight trains can be seen on the following lines:
Kufstein-Brenner, Passau-Wien-Hegyeshalom, Passau-Wels-Graz-Kalsdorf.

OTHER GERMAN OPEN ACCESS OPERATORS

Locomotives of other German open access operators can often be seen on freight trains operated in co-operation with Austrian railway companies. These include mostly **Class 182, 185, 186 and 189** locomotives as well as **SBB Cargo Class 482** on hire to German operators. Amongst these are ERS, HGK, EVB/MWB, OHE, RTB and LOCON.

HUNGARY

MÁV

Class 5342 EMUs (same as ÖBB Class 4124) are used on Hegyeshalom-Wien passenger trains. **Class 470** (former MÁV Class 1047, same as ÖBB Class 1116) are used on Hegyeshalom-Wels RoLa trains and on some Hegyeshalom-Wien West fast trains.

SWITZERLAND

SBB

Class Re 421 is being used on fast trains St.Margrethen-Bregenz-Lindau.

SLOVENIA

SZ

Class 541 (same as ÖBB Class 1216) are used on fast trains Jesenice-Villach and on freight trains Jesenice-Villach-Salzburg-Linz.

ACKNOWLEDGEMENTS

I would like to thank all who helped me compiling and updating the information contained in this book, especially Alexander Binder, Brian Garvin, Karl-Arne Richter and all the staff of ÖBB and independent railways who provided information. All photographs are my own unless otherwise stated.

Roland Beier, Wien, Austria **May 2012**

▲ ÖBB Class 1014 locomotives are now stored and see only occasional use for trials. On 29 July 2009 ÖBB 1014 015 was still in regular service on a passenger train near Gramatneusiedl.

▼ ÖBB 1216 025 achieved a world record speed of 357 km/h, at the time carrying number 1216 050, and now carries a unique livery to commemorate the achievement. On 18 May 2009 it is seen piloting 1116 241 on a Wien–Villach IC train leaving Wien Süd.

MAPS OF THE AUSTRIAN RAILWAY NETWORK

The following pages contain basic maps of the Austrian Railway network. We have tried to show as clearly as possible the entire ÖBB network, plus lines operated by independent railways and heritage lines. Different electrification systems are denoted by colour and narrow gauge lines by thickness of line. Freight only lines and lines currently out of use are shown as well as main stations, depots and some other topographical features.

Whilst we hope these maps will prove very useful to readers of this book, we would refer readers looking for more detailed maps to the comprehensive atlases produced by Schweers and Wall, details of which are below.

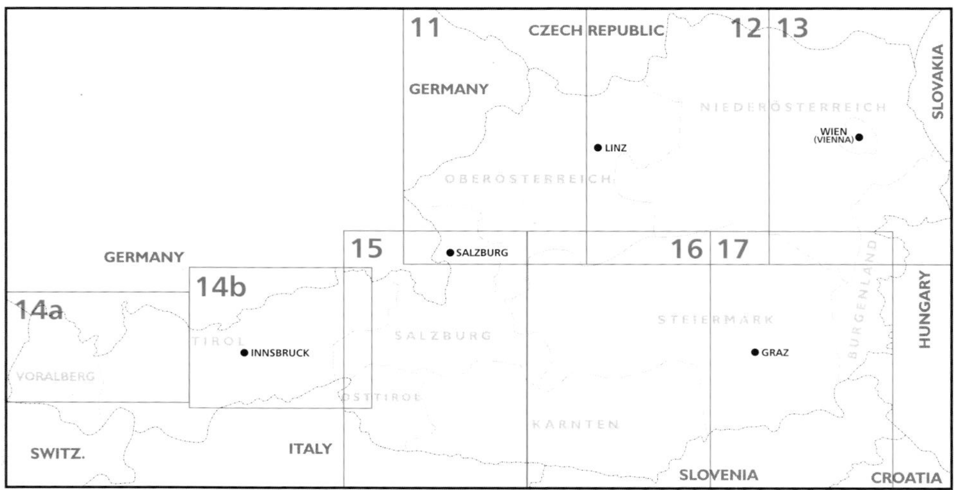

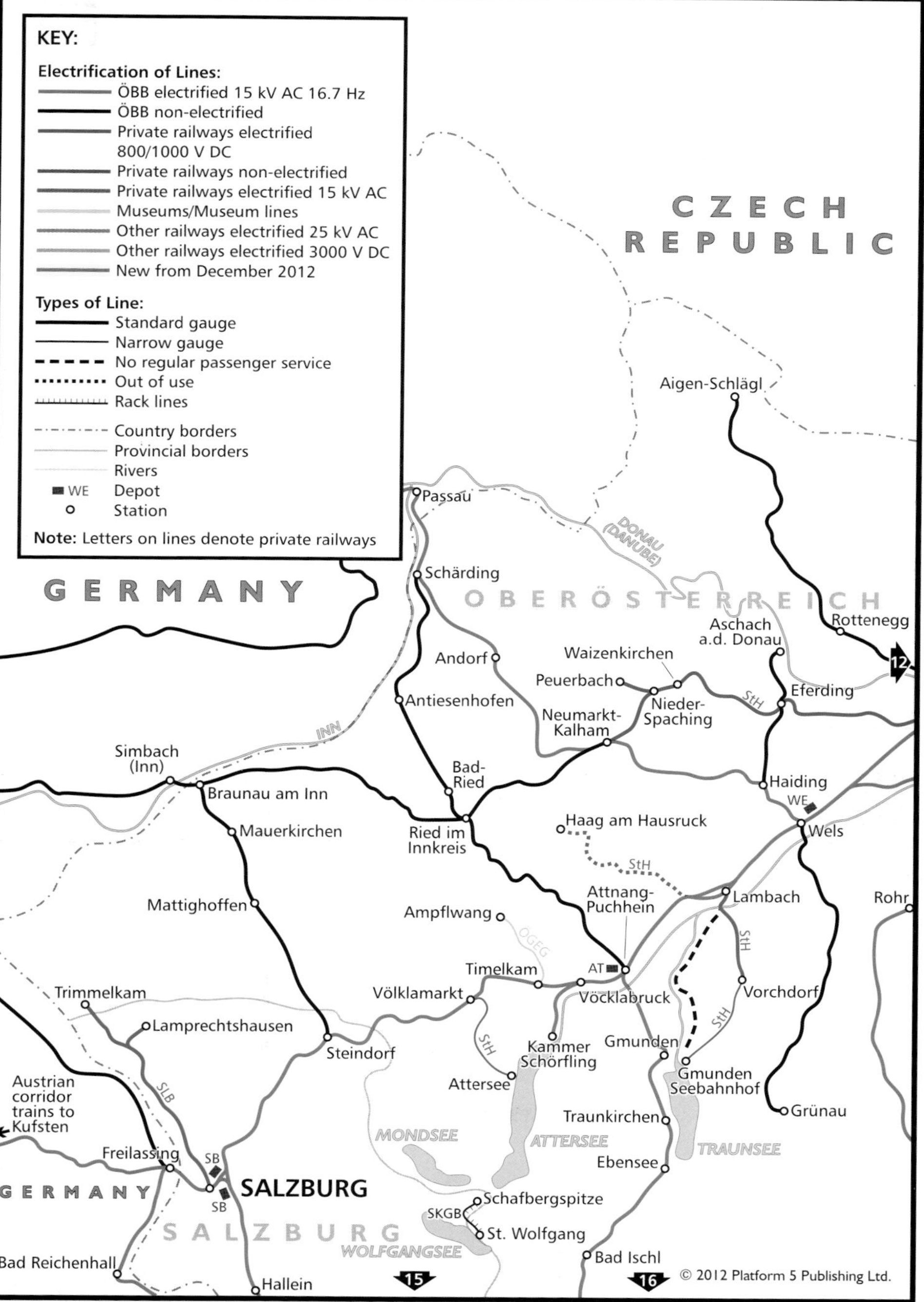

KEY:
Electrification of Lines:
ÖBB electrified 15 kV AC 16.7 Hz
ÖBB non-electrified
Private railways electrified 800/1000 V DC
Private railways non-electrified
Private railways electrified 15 kV AC
Museums/Museum lines
Other railways electrified 25 kV AC
Other railways electrified 3000 V DC
New from December 2012
Types of Line:
Standard gauge
Narrow gauge
No regular passenger service
Out of use
Rack lines
Country borders
Provincial borders
Rivers
WE Depot
Station
Note: Letters on lines denote private railways
CZECH REPUBLIC
GERMANY
OBERÖSTERREICH
DONAU (DANUBE)
INN
Aigen-Schlägl
Passau
Schärding
Rottenegg
Aschach a.d. Donau
Andorf
Waizenkirchen
Peuerbach
Nieder-Spaching
StH
Eferding
Antiesenhofen
Neumarkt-Kalham
Simbach (Inn)
Braunau am Inn
Bad-Ried
Haiding
WE
Mauerkirchen
Ried im Innkreis
Haag am Hausruck
Wels
Attnang-Puchhein
Lambach
Rohr
Mattighoffen
Ampflwang
OGEG
AT
Timelkam
Vorchdorf
Völklamarkt
Vöcklabruck
Trimmelkam
Lamprechtshausen
Kammer Schörfling
Gmunden
Steindorf
Attersee
Gmunden Seebahnhof
SLB
Austrian corridor trains to Kufsten
Traunkirchen
Grünau
MONDSEE
ATTERSEE
TRAUNSEE
Freilassing
SB
Ebensee
SALZBURG
Schafbergspitze
SKGB
St. Wolfgang
WOLFGANGSEE
Bad Reichenhall
Bad Ischl
Hallein
15
16
12

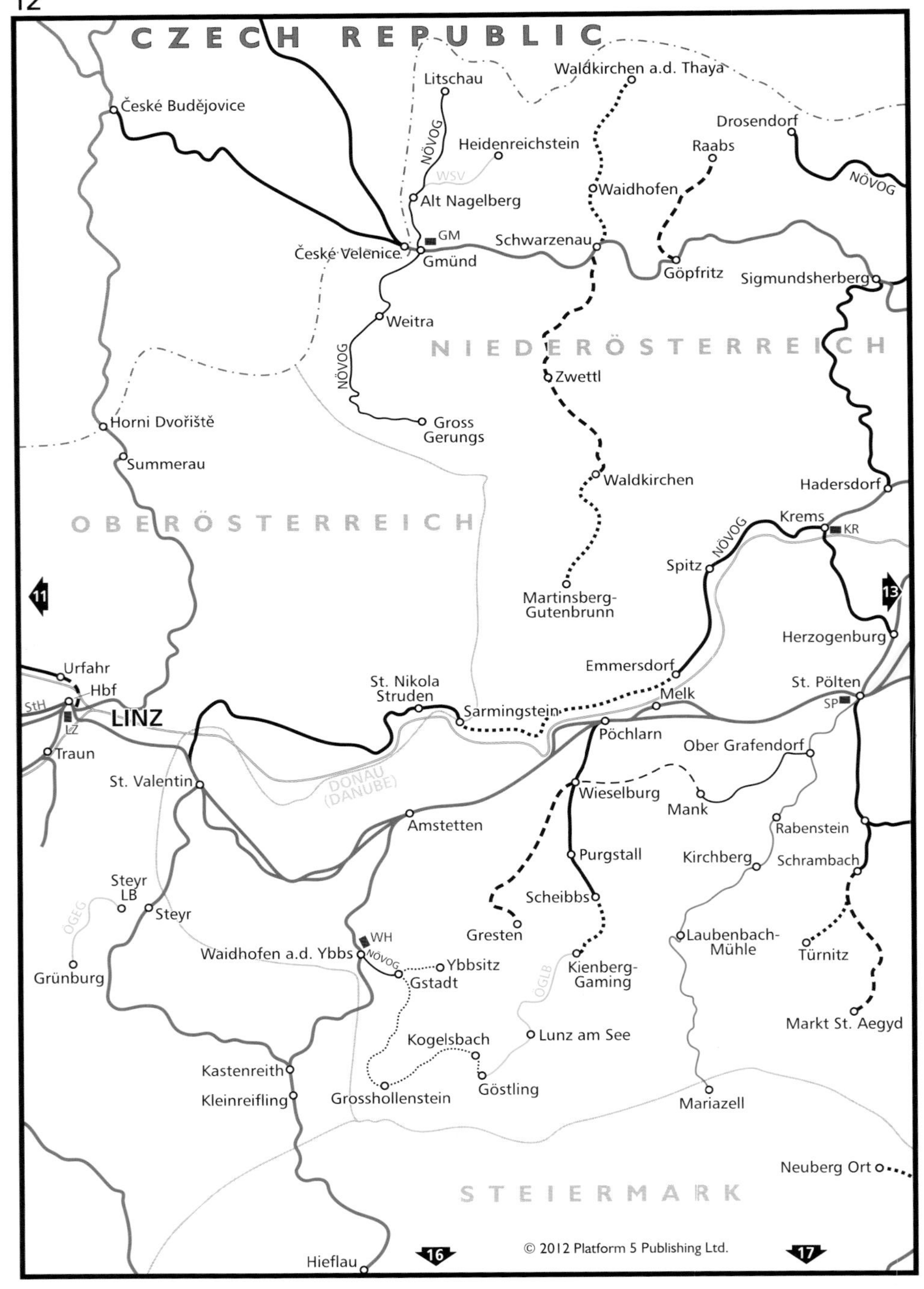
CZECH REPUBLIC
České Budějovice
Litschau
Waldkirchen a.d. Thaya
Drosendorf
NÖVOG
Heidenreichstein
Raabs
WSV
Waidhofen
Alt Nagelberg
GM
České Velenice
Gmünd
Schwarzenau
Göpfritz
Sigmundsherberg
Weitra
NIEDERÖSTERREICH
Zwettl
Horni Dvořiště
Gross Gerungs
Summerau
Waldkirchen
Hadersdorf
OBERÖSTERREICH
Krems
KR
Spitz
11
13
Martinsberg-Gutenbrunn
Herzogenburg
Urfahr
Hbf
StH
LZ
LINZ
St. Nikola Struden
Sarmingstein
Emmersdorf
Melk
St. Pölten
SP
Pöchlarn
Ober Grafendorf
Traun
St. Valentin
DONAU (DANUBE)
Wieselburg
Mank
Amstetten
Rabenstein
Purgstall
Kirchberg
Schrambach
Steyr LB
Steyr
ÖGEG
Scheibbs
Gresten
WH
Waidhofen a.d. Ybbs
Ybbsitz
Gstadt
Laubenbach-Mühle
Türnitz
Grünburg
Kienberg-Gaming
ÖGLB
Markt St. Aegyd
Kogelsbach
Lunz am See
Kastenreith
Kleinreifling
Grosshollenstein
Göstling
Mariazell
Neuberg Ort
STEIERMARK
Hieflau
16
17

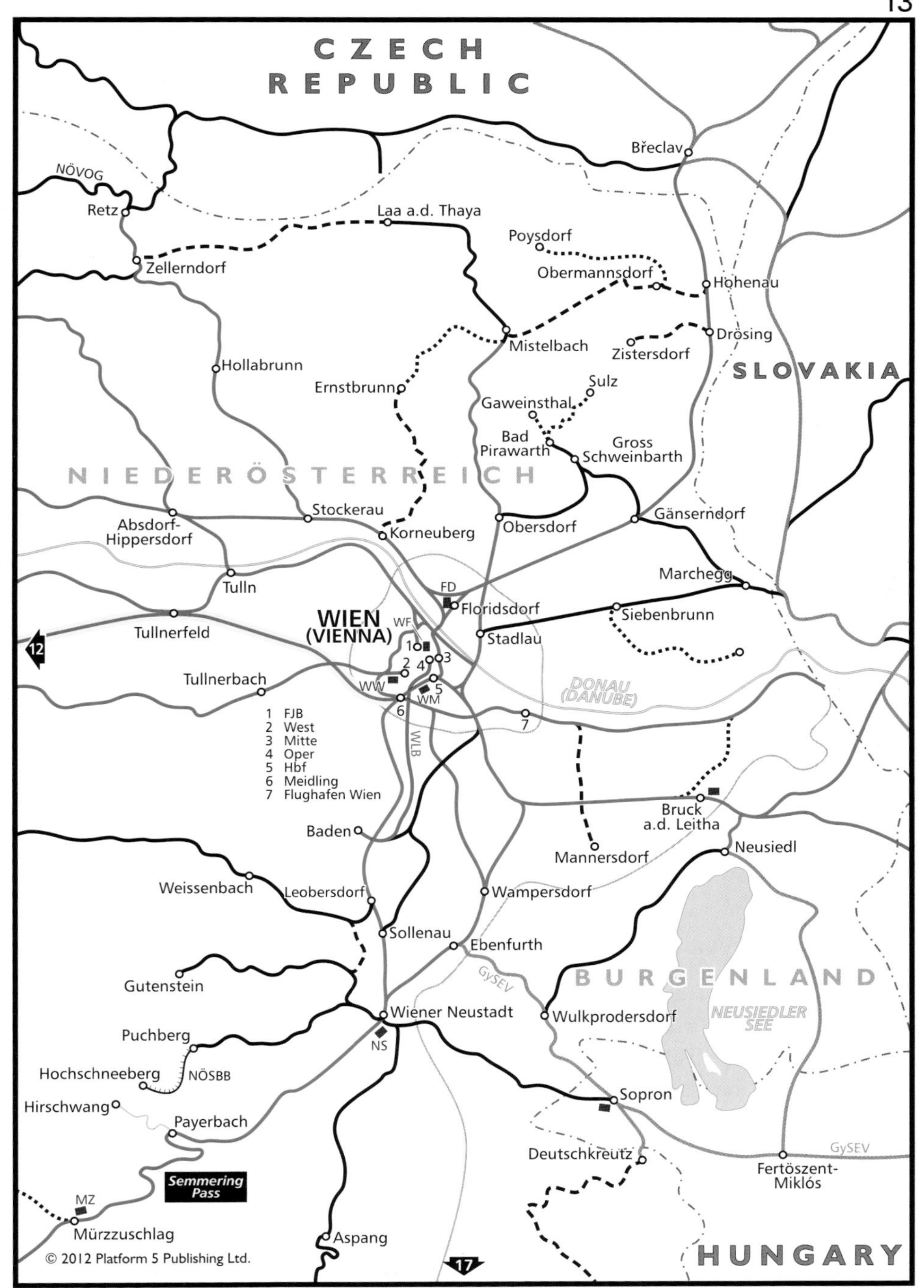
CZECH REPUBLIC
SLOVAKIA
NIEDERÖSTERREICH
BURGENLAND
HUNGARY
NÖVOG
Retz
Zellerndorf
Laa a.d. Thaya
Poysdorf
Obermannsdorf
Hohenau
Břeclav
Mistelbach
Drösing
Zistersdorf
Hollabrunn
Ernstbrunn
Sulz
Gaweinsthal
Bad Pirawarth
Gross Schweinbarth
Stockerau
Korneuberg
Obersdorf
Gänserndorf
Absdorf-Hippersdorf
Tulln
Marchegg
FD
Floridsdorf
Siebenbrunn
WIEN (VIENNA)
WF
Tullnerfeld
Stadlau
12
Tullnerbach
WW
WM
DONAU (DANUBE)
1 FJB
2 West
3 Mitte
4 Oper
5 Hbf
6 Meidling
7 Flughafen Wien
WLB
Bruck a.d. Leitha
Baden
Mannersdorf
Neusiedl
Weissenbach
Leobersdorf
Wampersdorf
Sollenau
Ebenfurth
Gutenstein
GySEV
Wiener Neustadt
Wulkprodersdorf
NEUSIEDLER SEE
NS
Puchberg
Hochschneeberg
NÖSBB
Sopron
Hirschwang
Payerbach
Deutschkreutz
Fertöszent-Miklós
Semmering Pass
MZ
Mürzzuschlag
Aspang
17

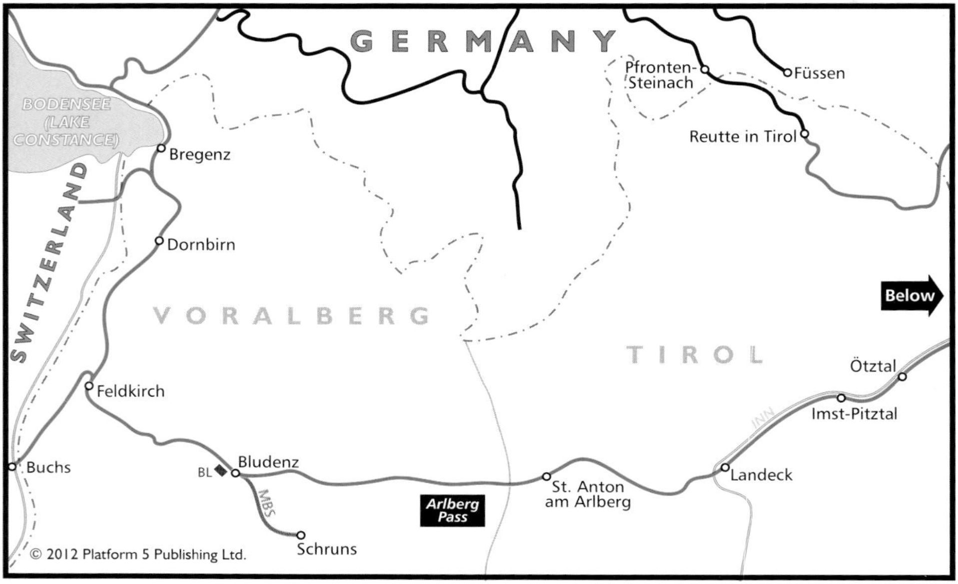

GERMANY
Pfronten-Steinach
Füssen
Reutte in Tirol
BODENSEE (LAKE CONSTANCE)
Bregenz
SWITZERLAND
Dornbirn
VORALBERG
Below
TIROL
Ötztal
Imst-Pitztal
INN
Feldkirch
Buchs
BL
Bludenz
MBS
Schruns
Arlberg Pass
St. Anton am Arlberg
Landeck
© 2012 Platform 5 Publishing Ltd.

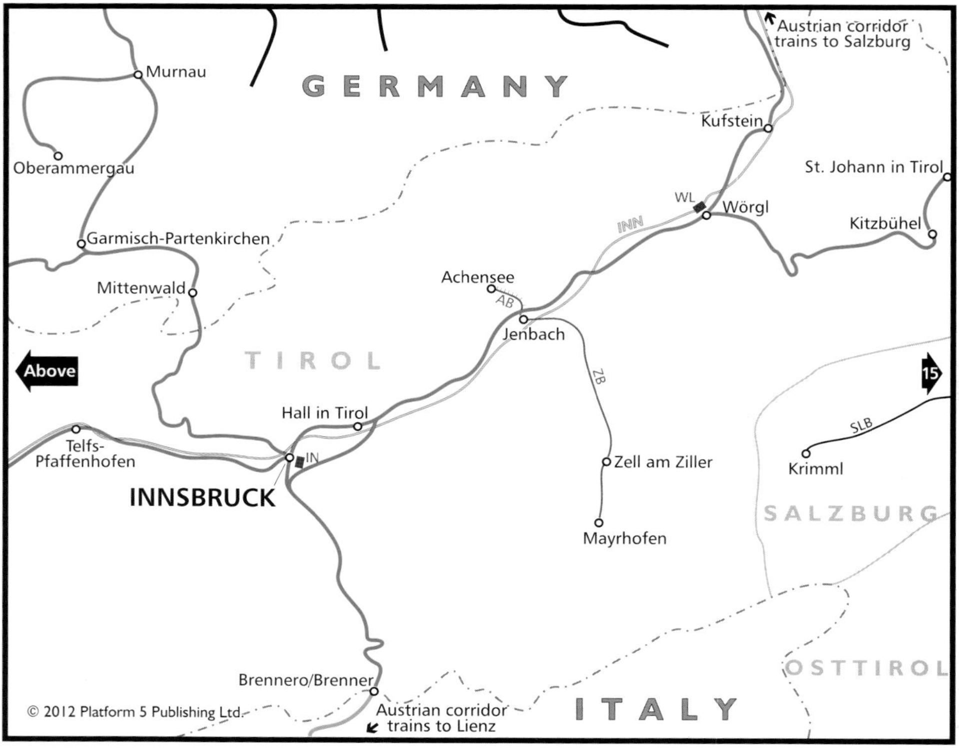

Austrian corridor trains to Salzburg
Murnau
GERMANY
Kufstein
Oberammergau
St. Johann in Tirol
WL
Wörgl
Kitzbühel
INN
Garmisch-Partenkirchen
Achensee
AB
Mittenwald
Jenbach
Above
TIROL
ZB
15
SLB
Hall in Tirol
Telfs-Pfaffenhofen
IN
INNSBRUCK
Zell am Ziller
Krimml
SALZBURG
Mayrhofen
OSTTIROL
Brennero/Brenner
Austrian corridor trains to Lienz
ITALY
© 2012 Platform 5 Publishing Ltd.

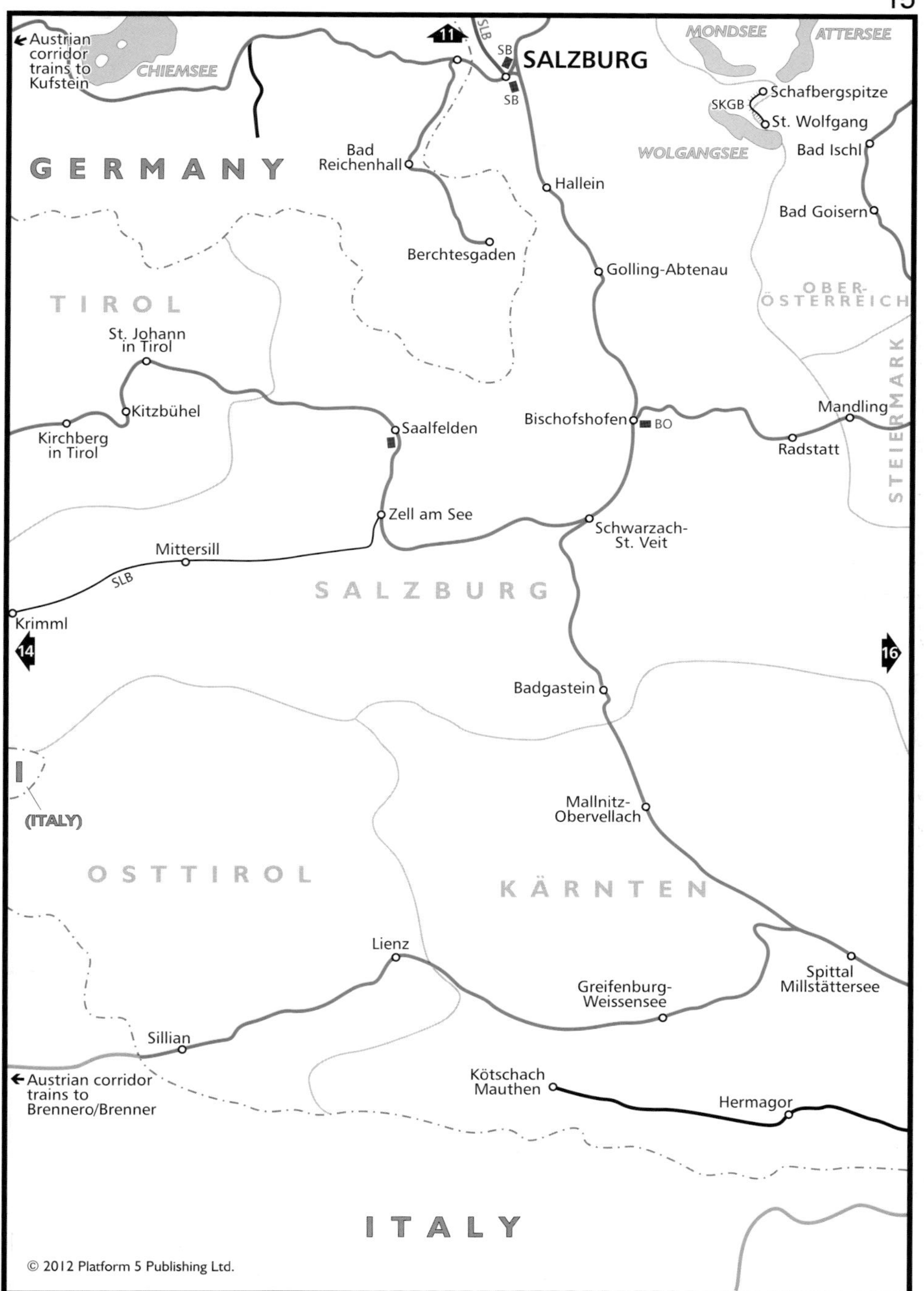

Austrian corridor trains to Kufstein
CHIEMSEE
11
SLB
SB
SALZBURG
SB
MONDSEE
ATTERSEE
Schafbergspitze
SKGB
St. Wolfgang
WOLGANGSEE
Bad Ischl
GERMANY
Bad Reichenhall
Hallein
Bad Goisern
Berchtesgaden
Golling-Abtenau
OBER-ÖSTERREICH
TIROL
St. Johann in Tirol
STEIERMARK
Mandling
Kitzbühel
Bischofshofen
BO
Saalfelden
Kirchberg in Tirol
Radstatt
Zell am See
Schwarzach-St. Veit
Mittersill
SLB
SALZBURG
Krimml
14
16
Badgastein
I
(ITALY)
Mallnitz-Obervellach
OSTTIROL
KÄRNTEN
Lienz
Spittal Millstättersee
Greifenburg-Weissensee
Sillian
Austrian corridor trains to Brennero/Brenner
Kötschach Mauthen
Hermagor
ITALY

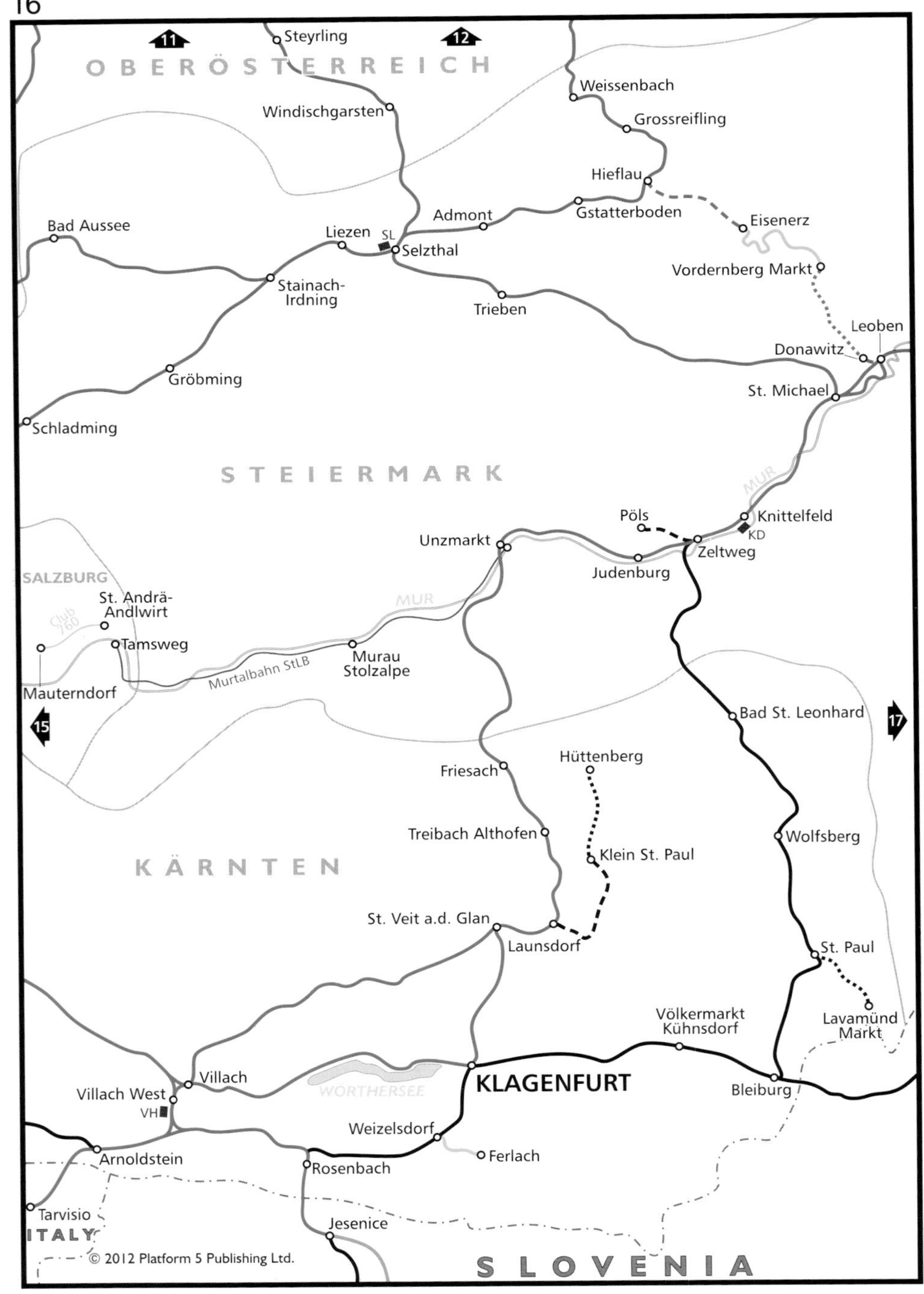

11
12
OBERÖSTERREICH
Steyrling
Windischgarsten
Weissenbach
Grossreifling
Hieflau
Eisenerz
Admont
Gstatterboden
Bad Aussee
Liezen
SL
Selzthal
Vordernberg Markt
Stainach-Irdning
Trieben
Leoben
Donawitz
Gröbming
St. Michael
Schladming
STEIERMARK
MUR
Pöls
Knittelfeld
KD
Unzmarkt
Zeltweg
Judenburg
SALZBURG
St. Andrä-Andlwirt
Club 760
MUR
Tamsweg
Murau Stolzalpe
Murtalbahn StLB
Mauterndorf
15
Bad St. Leonhard
17
Hüttenberg
Friesach
Treibach Althofen
Klein St. Paul
Wolfsberg
KÄRNTEN
St. Veit a.d. Glan
Launsdorf
St. Paul
Völkermarkt Kühnsdorf
Lavamünd Markt
Villach
KLAGENFURT
Bleiburg
Villach West
VH
WORTHERSEE
Weizelsdorf
Ferlach
Arnoldstein
Rosenbach
Tarvisio
Jesenice
ITALY
SLOVENIA

12
13
Payerbach
Semmering Pass
Neuberg Ort
Semmering
MZ
Mürzzuschlag
NIEDERÖSTERREICH
Edlitz
Aspang
Oberloisdorf
Kindberg
Friedberg
STEIERMARK
Kapfenberg
Bruck a.d. Mur
MUR
StLB
St. Erhard
Birkfeld
Rohrbach
Oberschützen
Rechnitz
Mixnitz
Club U44
Hartberg
Oberwart
FROWOS
SRB
Oberfeistritz
Grosspetersdorf
Frohnleiten
StLB
Weiz-Stadt
Weiz
Bad Waltersdorf
Übelbach
StlB
Peggau
StLB
BURGENLAND
Bad Blumau
Gleisdorf
Judendorf
GRAZ
Lassnitzhöhe
Fürstentfeld
GZ
Köflach
16
GKB
Studenzen-Fladnitz
Flughafen Graz-Feldkirchen
Feldbach
Jennersdorf
Szentgotthárd
Fehring
MUR
Lieboch
StLB
Werndorf
Bad Gleichenberg
Stainz
Preding
Deutschlandsberg
GKB
Wettmannstätten
Leibnitz
Bad Radkersburg
Spielfeld-Strass
Wies-Eibiswald
MUR
Maribor
SLOVENIA
Ormož
CROATIA

1. ÖSTERREICHISCHE BUNDESBAHNEN (ÖBB) (AUSTRIAN FEDERAL RAILWAYS)

THE AUSTRIAN RAILWAY SYSTEM

ÖBB is the incumbent railway undertaking which owns most of the Austrian railway network. Total track length is 5241 km, of which 2046 km are double track and 3715 km are electrified at 15 kV 16.7 Hz AC using overhead catenary. To comply with EU regulations on future structure of railways, ÖBB was reorganised in 2004 by separating infrastructure from train operating. Interestingly two infrastructure companies were established, one for operating and maintenance (ÖBB Infrastruktur Betrieb AG) and one for major construction works (ÖBB Infrastruktur Bau AG). There were also two train operating companies: ÖBB Personenverkehr AG for passenger and Rail Cargo Austria (RCA) for freight transport. These two jointly owned two more companies: ÖBB Traktion GmbH (providing locomotives and drivers) and ÖBB Technische Services GmbH (for maintenance of rolling stock).

2010 REORGANISATION

In 2010 another reorganisation came into effect. The two infrastructure companies have been merged into ÖBB Infrastruktur AG and ÖBB Traktion GmbH changed its name to ÖBB Produktion GmbH. The reason for changing the name was the idea to transfer shunting activities from ÖBB Infrastruktur to ÖBB Produktion, although this has not happened so far for various reasons. The parts of the organisation that mostly affect traction etc. are shown below with other departments/organisations omitted.

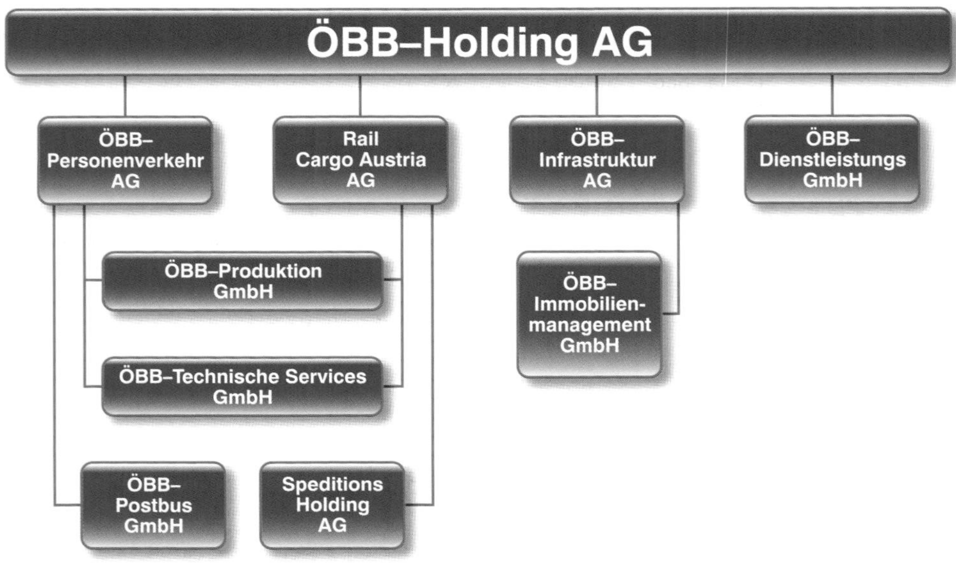

ÖBB-PRODUKTION GMBH

It is Produktion's job to supply the passenger and freight businesses with locomotives and drivers etc for their trains. Produktion also includes shunting staff as they couple locomotives to trains, detach vehicles etc. Where radio controlled locomotives are concerned shunters are in effect often the drivers. Most traction "depots" are at the same locations as Technische Services but there are additional locations where drivers are based which can be counted as sub-sheds and locomotives and multiple units are likely to stable there. With effect from 11 December 2011 all locomotives have been formally allocated to either ÖBB-PV or to RCA. Loco dispatchers from both companies should use their "own" locomotives if possible although some common diagrams still exist for greater synergy.

Produktion is no longer divided into areas. For the older classes loco diagrams are still bound to a certain depot but the new widespread classes such as 1016 and 1116 work in diagrams covering the whole of Austria and locos are even serviced at the nearest depot if required and not at the "home" depot. Therefore these locos can be found anywhere in Austria despite their actual allocation.

DEPOTS

A list of depots and codes is given in Appendix 2 on page 172.

ÖBB TECHNISCHE SERVICES GMBH

This is the maintenance arm and covers not only the main workshops but also what are the repair and maintenance facilities at depots and wagon shops. The main workshops are now referred to as Werke and the depots as Servicestellen.

WORKSHOPS

Werke	*Function*
Jedlersdorf	EMUs, wagons.
Knittelfeld	Snowploughs, OBW, MTW, special vehicles, wheelsets.
Linz	Electric locomotives plus Class 2016 diesels.
St. Pölten	Diesel locomotives (except Class 2016), DMUs and carriages.
Simmering	Carriages.
Wörth	MBW, internal fitting and components.

AUSTRIAN TRAIN SERVICES

In recent years ÖBB and its competitors have introduced some new categories for their trains. Current classifications are as follows:

RJ	Railjet (ÖBB premium express train).
ÖBB EC	ÖBB Euro City train. An EC but with better quality stock and services.
ÖBB IC	ÖBB Inter City train. An IC but with better quality stock and services.
ICE	Inter City Express (DB ICE in Austria).
EC	Euro City. International quality express train.
EN	Euro Night. International sleeping car train.
IC	Inter City.
CAT	City Airport Train.
WEST	WESTbahn fast train.
D	Fast train.
REX	Regionalexpress – semi-fast train.
R	Regionalzug – regional train.
S	Schnellbahn – suburban train.

LOCOMOTIVE & RAILCAR NUMBERING SYSTEM

The present ÖBB numbering scheme dates from 1953 when the former DRB system was replaced. ÖBB locomotives and multiple units had, until recently, a two-part number. The first part was of four digits and referred to the class of vehicle. It was separated by a full-stop from the second part which was the serial number within the particular type. Variations within a type were often given running numbers in a separate hundred. eg: 1042.01, 1042.501.

Early in 1985 the scheme was amended for use with computers. The running number part is now always 3 digits and there was an additional check digit suffix, e.g. 1016 026-5. The class number and serial number are separated by a space.

The class coding system refers to the type of vehicle & its use as follows:

1st digit – Traction Code

0 Steam
1 Electric Locomotives
2 Diesel Locomotives
3 Steam Railcars
4 Electric Multiple Units
5 Diesel Multiple Units
6 Driving Trailers (6000-6499 for EMUs, 6500-6999 for diesel railcars)
7 Intermediate Trailer
8 (Not used)
9 Tenders

2nd digit – Origin Code

0–5 Austrian or German standard types. (0 was not carried on steam locomotives).
6–8 Pre-DRB types
9 Various Foreign types

This system was later amended for electric traction:

0–7 AC Electrics
8 AC/DC Electrics
9 DC Electrics

The second digit is also increased by 1 to represent developments of types. Thus Class 1116 is a development of Class 1016. 1216 is a further development of the same.

3rd & 4th digits – Utilisation Code

Steam Locomotives
01–39 Passenger Tender
40–59 Freight Tender
60–79 Passenger Tank
80–96 Freight Tank
97 Rack Fitted
98–99 Narrow Gauge

Electric Locomotives
01–19 Express
20–39 Heavy Freight
40–59 Mixed Traffic
60–69 Shunter
70–89 Spare, but used for old types
90–99 Narrow Gauge

Railcars
01–19 Express
20–59 Local
60–79 Baggage
80–89 Light Railbus
90–99 Narrow Gauge

Diesel Locomotives
01–19 Express Passenger Locomotive over 2000 h.p.
20–39 Heavy Freight Locomotive over 2000 h.p.
40–59 Mixed Traffic Locomotive 1000-2000 h.p.
60–64 "B" wheel arrangement locomotive under 1000 h.p.
65–69 "C" wheel arrangement locomotive under 1000 h.p.
70–79 "D" wheel arrangement locomotive under 1000 h.p.
80–89 Free (was rack fitted locomotive) later used for self-propelled snowplough.
90–99 Narrow Gauge Locomotives

After the running number there is a computer check digit which double checks that all the preceding digits are correct. It is arrived at by multiplying the class and running number digits alternatively by 2 and 1. The resulting digits are added together and the sum deducted from the next whole ten gives the check digit.

As these check digits are no longer carried on all locomotives and units they are not included in this book.

European Vehicle Numbers (EVN)

In 2007 European Vehicle Numbers were introduced for locomotives, railcars, multiple units and departmental stock. Whilst wagons and coaches have carried such numbers since 1972 based on UIC regulations which were later adopted by the EU, the above mentioned types of rolling stock were numbered according to various national and even local numbering systems. Some countries like Austria had used 12 digit numbers for their locos and railcars by simply putting "93 81" in front of the 8 digit computer number. This had the advantage of getting the same control digit for both variants of the vehicle number. Some independent railways had their own "country" codes assigned by UIC: 34 –StLB, 35 –StH, 37 –WLB, 39 – MBS, 43 – GySEV and 45 – GKB. These were mostly used for wagons and coaches but sometimes also for locos and railcars by putting "9x yz" in front of the 8 digit computer number. X was chosen in a way that the control digit remained the same.

When the new EVN regulations were published by the European Union in the Technical Specifications for Interoperability (TSI) on operations these things changed. On one hand special "country" codes for independent railways were given up, the owner is now identified by the vehicle keeper marking (VKM) added to the vehicle number. In fact several letters are added, such as "A-OBB". A identifies the country where the vehicle is registered, this need not necessarily be the country where the owner comes from. OBB identifies the owner. Therefore special "country" codes for independent railways are no longer necessary.

Another new feature is that the second digit of the 12 digit number identifies the type of loco or railcar:

90 Miscellaneous traction – mostly used for steam locomotives
91 Electric Locomotives faster than 99 km/h
92 Diesel locomotives faster than 99 km/h
93 High speed EMUs
94 EMUs
95 DMUs
96 Loose trailers
97 Electric shunting locomotives or electric locomotives with maximum speed less than 100 km/h
98 Diesel shunting locomotives or diesel locomotive with maximum speed less than 100 km/h
99 Departmental vehicles

By introducing this numbering system ÖBB locomotives received different control digits for 12 and 8 digit numbers. To avoid confusion these vehicles carry the 12 digit EVN on the side walls whilst at the front ends they carry their "short" vehicle number without control digit. Class numbers of ÖBB vehicles have not been changed except for departmental stock, but most locos and multiple units of independent railways commissioned for use on the ÖBB network have now received a 12 digit EVN and for this purpose some new class numbers have been introduced. Only some ÖBB classes (1016, 1116, 1216, 1044, 1144, 2016 and the most recent 5022) have so far received the new EVNs as there is a transition period and national numbers may continue to be used inside a member state.

The situation with independent railways is similar. Some vehicles received new EVNs in line with TSI requirements, others retain their old own "country" codes and some which are used only on own infrastructure retain the particular numbering system of their owner.

This situation is reflected in our lists. If applicable we show the EVN in the way it is actually written on each vehicle, whether it is in line with the latest TSI regulation or not.

1.1. ELECTRIC LOCOMOTIVES

CLASS 1014 Bo-Bo

A dual-voltage locomotive intended for working around Wien and into the Czech Republic, Slovakia and Hungary. Due to limited availability of spares they are all now stored and may be sold. Four locos are serviceable and are being used occasionally for trials requiring low axle loads.

Built: 1993–94.
Builder – Mech. Parts: SGP.
Builder – Elec. Parts: Elin.
One Hour Rating: 4300 kW.
Maximum Tractive Effort: 190 kN.
Wheel Diameter: 1150 mm.
Weight: 64 tonnes.
Length over Buffers: 17.50 m.
Maximum Speed: 170 km/h.
Systems: 15 kV AC 16.7 Hz/25 kV AC 50 Hz.
EVN: 93 81 1014 xxx-c
Non-standard liveries:
A Rail Cargo Austria.
N Red with white lower bodysides, colours reversed on cab.

1014 001	**N**	C	WM (Z)
1014 002	**N**	C	WM (Z)
1014 003	**N**	C	WM
1014 004	**N**	C	WM (Z)
1014 005	**N**	C	WM (Z)
1014 007	**N**	C	WM (Z)
1014 008	**N**	C	WM (Z)
1014 009	**N**	C	WM (Z)
1014 010	**N**	C	WM (Z)
1014 011	**A**	C	WM
1014 012	**N**	C	WM (Z)
1014 013	**N**	C	WM (Z)
1014 014	**N**	C	WM
1014 015	**N**	C	WM
1014 016	**N**	C	WM (Z)
1014 017	**N**	C	WM (Z)
1014 018	**N**	C	WM (Z)

CLASS 1016 TAURUS Bo-Bo

Disappointed with Class 1012 (all now withdrawn), ÖBB shopped around and eventually turned to Siemens for a new main line locomotive type to be known as Taurus. The design chosen was the Siemens Eurosprinter which was proving popular at the time with exports to Spain, Portugal and Germany (DB Class 152 is based on this series). In September 1999 ÖBB ordered 50 Class 1016 and 25 Class 1116, the latter to be dual-voltage. The first three 1016s were built in München by Siemens Krauss Maffei but part of the deal with ÖBB was for a certain amount of local input. For the remainder the bodywork was fabricated in München and then taken to the ÖBB works in Linz where the locomotives were actually assembled with cabs coming from the ÖBB works in Knittelfeld and bogies from the Siemens plant in Graz (the former SGP works). Most electrical equipment came from the Siemens plant in Erlangen, Germany. After a while ÖBB decided that the 1116 version met their needs very well so no more 1016s were ordered. Besides working all over Austria the 1016s also work to München in Germany.

Built: 2000–01.
Builder – Mech. Parts: Siemens-Krauss-Maffei, ÖBB TS Linz, ÖBB TS Knittelfeld.
Builder – Elec. Parts: Siemens.
One Hour Rating: 6400 kW.
Maximum Tractive Effort: 300 kN.
Wheel Diameter: 1150 mm.
Weight: 85 tonnes.
Length over Buffers: 19.28 m.
Maximum Speed: 230 km/h.
EVN: 91 81 1016 xxx-c
Non-standard livery:
A 1016 023 is in blue livery "KYOTO EXPRESS ÖSTERREICHS GRÜNE SCHIENE".

1016 001		P	SB
1016 002		P	SB
1016 003		P	SB
1016 004		P	SB
1016 005		P	SB
1016 006		P	SB
1016 007		P	SB
1016 008		P	SB
1016 009		P	SB
1016 010		P	SB
1016 011		P	SB
1016 012		P	SB
1016 013		P	SB
1016 014		P	SB
1016 015		P	SB
1016 016		P	SB
1016 017		P	SB
1016 018		P	SB
1016 019		P	SB
1016 020		P	SB
1016 021		P	SB
1016 022		P	SB
1016 023	**A**	P	SB
1016 024		P	SB

1016 025	P	SB
1016 026	P	SB
1016 027	P	SB
1016 028	P	SB
1016 029	P	SB
1016 030	P	SB
1016 031	P	SB
1016 032	P	SB
1016 033	P	SB
1016 034	P	SB
1016 035	P	SB
1016 036	P	SB
1016 037	P	SB
1016 038	C	SB
1016 039	C	SB
1016 040	C	SB
1016 041	C	SB
1016 042	C	SB
1016 043	C	SB
1016 044	C	SB
1016 045	C	SB
1016 046	C	SB
1016 047	C	SB
1016 048	C	SB
1016 049	C	SB
1016 050	C	SB

CLASS 1116 TAURUS Bo-Bo

This is the dual-voltage version of Class 1016 with the first locomotive built in München and all others at Linz in a similar way to the 1016s. ÖBB ordered a large fleet of Taurus locomotives (400 altogether) and preferred the dual-voltage version as there was hardly any price difference to the single voltage locos. However certain plans did not come to pass and as locos were also needed for working into Italy and Slovenia where there is 3000 V DC electrification ÖBB cancelled the last 68 1116s and instead ordered 50 tri-voltage Class 1216 – the version with 3000 V DC equipment. The 1116s are real multi-purpose locomotives which now work deep into German territory getting as far north as Hamburg and Bremen. The 1116s also work into Hungary and the Czech Republic. Both MAV and GySEV have small batches of 1116s designated as Class 1047 and these locos work deep into Austria with the MAV locos reaching Wels whilst the GySEV locos reach Wien Kledering yard on freight trains. The nickname Taurus reflects the strength of the locomotive but they could also be called Doh-Ray-Mee-Fahs due to the electrical noises when starting up! 1116 058–061 and 1116 063–065 are leased to GySEV for a period of 20 years, whilst other examples are leased to ÖBB's Hungarian subsidiary Rail Cargo Hungaria which uses these locos all over Hungary but also in Romania.

Built: 2000–06.
Builder – Mech. Parts: Siemens-Krauss-Maffei, ÖBB TS Linz, ÖBB TS Knittelfeld.
Builder – Elec. Parts: Siemens.
One Hour Rating: 6400 kW.
Maximum Tractive Effort: 300 kN.
Wheel Diameter: 1150 mm.
Weight: 85 tonnes.
Length over Buffers: 19.28 m.
Maximum Speed: 230 km/h.
Systems: 15 kV AC 16.7 Hz/25 kV AC 50 Hz.
EVN: 91 81 1116 xxx-c
Non-standard liveries:
A 1116 003 is "RAIL CARGO AUSTRIA".
A 1116 007 is "SOS KINDERDORF".
A 1116 009,010,011,013,015,017,019,020,041,045,048 are "RAIL CARGO HUNGARIA".
A 1116 038 is "SIEMENS".
A 1116 058–061,063–065 are "GYSEV".
A 1116 126 is "LICHT INS DUNKEL".
A 1116 141,142 are "CITY AIRPORT TRAIN".
A 1116 153 is "MUSICAL CATS".
A 1116 250 is "POLIZEI".

* Hungarian ATP (EVM 120) fitted

1116 001		C	*	RCH
1116 002		C	*	RCH
1116 003	**A**	C	*	RCH
1116 004		C	*	RCH
1116 005		C	*	RCH
1116 006		C	*	RCH
1116 007	**A**	C	*	RCH
1116 008		C	*	RCH
1116 009	**A**	C	*	RCH
1116 010	**A**	C	*	RCH
1116 011	**A**	C	*	RCH
1116 012		C	*	RCH
1116 013	**A**	C	*	WW
1116 014		C	*	WW
1116 015	**A**	C	*	WW
1116 016		C	*	WW
1116 017	**A**	C	*	WW
1116 018		C	*	WW
1116 019	**A**	C	*	WW
1116 020	**A**	C	*	WW
1116 021		C	*	WW
1116 022		C	*	WW
1116 023		C	*	WW
1116 024		C	*	WW
1116 025		C	*	WW
1116 026		C		WW
1116 027		C		WW
1116 028		C		SB
1116 029		C		SB
1116 030		C		SB
1116 031		C		SB
1116 032		C		SB
1116 033		C		SB
1116 034		C		SB
1116 035		C		SB
1116 036		C		SB
1116 037		C		SB
1116 038	**A**	C		SB
1116 039		C		SB
1116 040		C		WM
1116 041	**A**	C	*	RCH
1116 042		P	*	WM
1116 043		P	*	WM
1116 044		P	*	WM
1116 045	**A**	C	*	RCH

1116 046		C	*	RCH
1116 047		C	*	RCH
1116 048	**A**	C	*	RCH
1116 049		C	*	RCH
1116 050		P		WM
1116 051		P		WM
1116 052		P		WM
1116 053		P		WM
1116 054		P		WM
1116 055		P		WM
1116 056		P		WM
1116 057		P		WM
1116 058	**A**	C	*	GySEV
1116 059	**A**	C	*	GySEV
1116 060	**A**	C	*	GySEV
1116 061	**A**	C	*	GySEV
1116 062		P	*	WW
1116 063	**A**	P	*	GySEV
1116 064	**A**	P	*	GySEV
1116 065	**A**	P	*	GySEV
1116 066		C		VH
1116 067		C		VH
1116 068		C		VH
1116 069		C		VH
1116 070		C		VH
1116 071		C		VH
1116 072		C		VH
1116 073		C		VH
1116 074		C		VH
1116 075		C		VH
1116 076		C		VH
1116 077		C		VH
1116 078		C		VH
1116 079		C		VH
1116 080		C		VH
1116 081		C		VH
1116 082		C		VH
1116 083		C		VH
1116 084		C		VH
1116 085		C		VH
1116 086		C		IN
1116 087		C		IN
1116 088		C		IN
1116 089		C		IN
1116 090		C		IN
1116 091		C		IN
1116 092		C		IN
1116 093		C		IN
1116 094		C		IN
1116 095		C		IN
1116 096		C		IN
1116 097		C		IN
1116 098		C		IN
1116 099		C		IN
1116 100		C		IN
1116 101		C		IN
1116 102		C		IN
1116 103		C		IN
1116 104		C		IN
1116 105		C		IN
1116 106		C		IN
1116 107		C		IN
1116 108		C		IN
1116 109		C		IN
1116 110		C		IN
1116 111		C		SB
1116 112		C		SB
1116 113		C		SB
1116 114		C		SB
1116 115		C		SB
1116 116		C		SB
1116 117		C		SB
1116 118		C		SB
1116 119		C		SB
1116 120		C		SB
1116 121		C		SB
1116 122		C		SB
1116 123		C		SB
1116 124		C		SB
1116 125		C		SB
1116 126	**A**	C		SB
1116 127		C		SB
1116 128		C		SB
1116 129		C		SB
1116 130		C		SB
1116 131		C		SB
1116 132		C		SB
1116 133		C		SB
1116 134		C		SB
1116 135		C		SB
1116 136		C		SB
1116 137		C		SB
1116 138		C		SB
1116 139		C		SB
1116 140		C		SB
1116 141	**A**	C		WM
1116 142	**A**	C		WM
1116 143		C		WM
1116 144		C		WM
1116 145		C		WM
1116 146		C		WM
1116 147		C		WM
1116 148		C		WM
1116 149		C		WM
1116 150		C		WM
1116 151		C		VH
1116 152		C		VH
1116 153	**A**	C		VH
1116 154		C		VH
1116 155		C		VH
1116 156		C		VH
1116 157		C		VH
1116 158		C		VH
1116 159		C		VH
1116 160		C		VH
1116 161		C		VH
1116 162		C		VH
1116 163		C		VH
1116 164		C		VH
1116 165		C		VH
1116 166		C		VH
1116 167		C		VH
1116 168		C		VH
1116 169		C		VH
1116 170		C		VH
1116 171		C		VH
1116 172		C		VH
1116 173		C		VH
1116 174		C		VH
1116 175		C		VH
1116 176		C		IN
1116 177		C		IN
1116 178		C		IN
1116 179		C		IN
1116 180		C		IN
1116 181		C		IN
1116 182		C		IN
1116 183		C		IN
1116 184		C		IN
1116 185		C		IN
1116 186		C		SB
1116 187		C		SB
1116 188		P		SB
1116 189		P		SB
1116 190		P		SB
1116 191		P		SB
1116 192		P		SB
1116 193		P		SB
1116 194		P		SB
1116 195		P		SB
1116 196		P		SB
1116 197		P		SB
1116 198		P		SB
1116 199		P		SB
1116 200	**J**	P	*	WW
1116 201	**J**	P	*	WW
1116 202	**J**	P	*	WW
1116 203	**J**	P	*	WW
1116 204	**J**	P	*	WW
1116 205	**J**	P	*	WW
1116 206	**J**	P	*	WW
1116 207	**J**	P	*	WW
1116 208	**J**	P	*	WW
1116 209	**J**	P	*	WW
1116 210	**J**	P	*	WW
1116 211	**J**	P	*	WW
1116 212	**J**	P	*	WW
1116 213	**J**	P	*	WW
1116 214	**J**	P	*	WW
1116 215	**J**	P	*	WW
1116 216	**J**	P	*	WW
1116 217	**J**	P	*	WW
1116 218	**J**	P	*	WW
1116 219	**J**	P	*	WW
1116 220	**J**	P	*	WW
1116 221	**J**	P	*	WW
1116 222	**J**	P	*	WW
1116 223	**J**	P	*	WW
1116 224	**J**	P		WW
1116 225	**J**	P		WW
1116 226	**J**	P		WW
1116 227	**J**	P		WW
1116 228	**J**	P		WW
1116 229	**J**	P		WW
1116 230	**J**	P		WW
1116 231	**J**	P		WW
1116 232	**J**	P		WW
1116 233	**J**	P		WW
1116 234	**J**	P		WW
1116 235	**J**	P		WW
1116 236	**J**	P		WW
1116 237	**J**	P		WW

▲ The three remaining ÖBB Class 1822 are now in store at Bludenz. 1822 003 is pictured stored at Innsbruck on 12 March 2010.

▼ ÖBB Class 1142 are now used mostly on passenger trains in push-pull mode. 1142 575 heads a short rake of double-deck stock through a wintry landscape near Eichgraben on 04 February 2011.

1116 238	**J**	P	WW
1116 239	**J**	P	WW
1116 240	**J**	P	WW
1116 241	**J**	P	WW
1116 242	**J**	P	WW
1116 243	**J**	P	WW
1116 244	**J**	P	WW
1116 245	**J**	P	WW
1116 246	**J**	P	WW
1116 247	**J**	P	WW
1116 248	**J**	P	WW
1116 249	**J**	P	WW
1116 250	**A**	P	WW
1116 251		P	WW
1116 252		P	WW
1116 253		P	WW
1116 254		C	WW
1116 255		C	WW
1116 256		C	WW
1116 257		C	WW
1116 258		C	WW
1116 259		C	WW
1116 260		C	WW
1116 261		C	WW
1116 262		C	WW
1116 263		C	VH
1116 264		P	VH
1116 265		P	VH
1116 266		P	VH
1116 267		P	VH
1116 268		P	VH
1116 269		P	VH
1116 270		P	VH
1116 271		P	VH
1116 272		P	VH
1116 273		P	VH
1116 274		P	VH
1116 275		P	VH
1116 276		P	VH
1116 277		P	VH
1116 278		P	VH
1116 279		P	VH
1116 280		P	VH
1116 281		P	VH
1116 282		P	VH

CLASS 1216 TAURUS Bo-Bo

Siemens has classified these locomotives as ES64U4 although this ÖBB version only has three voltages, the additional voltage being 3000 V DC for working into neighbouring countries. The 50 locomotives ordered by ÖBB were originally supplied in three different versions. Version A (1216.0) comprised 25 locomotives to work in Austria, Germany, Italy and Slovenia; Version B (1216.1) comprised 10 locomotives for Austria, Germany and Slovenia, whilst Version C (1216.2) comprised 15 locomotives for Austria, Germany, the Czech Republic and Slovakia. However, some locos have subsequently been retrofitted from one version to another. It must be remembered that not only does an international locomotive need to have the capacity to operate off different voltages but it must also be fitted with the various safety systems used in the respective countries. The 1216 has undergone a slight redesign with the top headlight being repositioned above the cab and each cab being fitted with two doors rather than a central door in the body side giving access to the cab via the equipment room. The prototypes were built in München but the series locomotives have been assembled in Linz.

Built: 2005–08.
Builder – Mech. Parts: Siemens-Krauss-Maffei, ÖBB TS Linz, ÖBB TS Knittelfeld.
Builder – Elec. Parts: Siemens.
One Hour Rating: 6400 kW. **Weight:** 87 tonnes.
Maximum Tractive Effort: 300 kN. **Length over Buffers:** 19.28 m.
Wheel Diameter: 1150 mm. **Maximum Speed:** 230 km/h.
Systems: 15 kV AC 16.7 Hz/25 kV AC 50 Hz/3000 V DC.
EVN: 91 81 1216 xxx-c
Non-standard liveries:
A 1216 011–018 are "ÖBB ITALIA".
A 1216 025 is "WORLD RECORD LOCO".
A 1216 210 is "KAPSCH".

1216 001		C	VH
1216 002		C	VH
1216 003		C	VH
1216 004		C	VH
1216 005		P	VH
1216 006		P	IN
1216 007		P	IN
1216 008		P	IN
1216 009		P	IN
1216 011	**A**	P	IN
1216 012	**A**	P	IN
1216 013	**A**	P	IN
1216 014	**A**	P	IN
1216 015	**A**	P	IN
1216 016	**A**	P	IN
1216 017	**A**	P	IN
1216 018	**A**	P	IN
1216 019		P	IN
1216 020		C	IN
1216 021		C	IN
1216 022		C	IN
1216 023		C	IN
1216 024		C	IN
1216 025	**A**	C	VH
1216 032		C	VH
1216 128		C	VH
1216 129		C	VH
1216 130		C	VH
1216 131		C	VH
1216 141		C	VH
1216 142		C	VH
1216 143		C	VH
1216 144		C	VH
1216 145		C	VH
1216 146		C	VH
1216 147		C	VH
1216 148		P	VH
1216 149		P	VH
1216 150		P	VH
1216 210	**A**	P	WW
1216 226		P	WW
1216 227		P	WW
1216 233		P	WW
1216 234		P	WW
1216 235		P	WW
1216 236		P	WW
1216 237		P	WW
1216 238		C	WW
1216 239		C	WW
1216 240		C	WW

CLASS 1822 Bo-Bo

These dual-voltage locomotives were intended to be the first of 50–75 locos for through workings into Italy. However there were many problems with the class and series production was abandoned. Of the five locos built, two have already been sold to Poland whilst the remaining three are stored at Bludenz shed.

Built: 1991–92.
Builder – Mech. Parts: SGP.
Builder – Elec. Parts: ABB (001/3/5), Siemens (002/4).
One Hour Rating: 4300 kW.
Maximum Tractive Effort: 280 kN.
Wheel Diameter: 1100 mm.
Systems: 15 kV AC 16.7 Hz/3000 V DC.
EVN: 93 81 1822 xxx-c
Weight: 84 tonnes.
Length over Buffers: 19.30 m.
Maximum Speed: 140 km/h.
Non-standard livery: N Red with white lower bodysides, colours reversed on cab.

1822 001 **N** P IN (Z)
1822 003 **N** P IN (Z)
1822 004 **N** P IN (Z)

CLASS 1042 Bo-Bo

These were the standard mixed traffic locomotives dating from the 1960s, starting off with the 1042.0 series and then evolving into the 1042.5. The latter have all either been rebuilt into Class 1142 or withdrawn, whilst a few Class 1042 are still operational but have no fixed diagrams.

Built: 1963–68.
Builder – Mech. Parts: Simmering-Graz-Pauker.
Builder – Elec. Parts: Elin/Siemens/Brown-Boveri.
One Hour Rating: 3560 kW.
Maximum Tractive Effort: 255 kN.
Wheel Diameter: 1250 mm.
EVN: 93 81 1042 xxx-c
Weight: 83.8 tonnes.
Length over Buffers: 16.22 m.
Maximum Speed: 130 km/h.

1042 007 **0** C WW
1042 013 **0** C WW (Z)
1042 018 **V** C WW (Z)
1042 020 **0** C WW
1042 032 **0** C WW
1042 033 **0** C WW
1042 034 **0** C WW (Z)
1042 036 **V** C WW
1042 041 **0** C WW

CLASS 1142 Bo-Bo

These locomotives are Class 1042.5 locos fitted for push-pull working. They were converted from 1042s in the 1995–2004 period as ÖBB changed many regional train services to push-pull operation. Today the 1142s are concentrated in the east and south of the country but they still work through to Salzburg on local trains.

Built: 1969–77.
Builder – Mech. Parts: Simmering-Graz-Pauker.
Builder – Elec. Parts: Elin/Siemens/Brown-Boveri.
One Hour Rating: 4000 kW.
Maximum Tractive Effort: 255 kN.
Wheel Diameter: 1250 mm.
Electric Brake: Rheostatic.
EVN: 93 81 1142 xxx-c
Weight: 83.8 tonnes.
Length over Buffers: 16.22 m.
Maximum Speed: 150 km/h.

1142 542 **0** C GZ
1142 550 **V** P GZ (Z)
1142 554 **V** C GZ
1142 564 **0** P GZ
1142 566 **0** C GZ
1142 567 **0** C GZ
1142 572 **0** P GZ (Z)
1142 575 **0** P GZ
1142 578 **V** P GZ (Z)
1142 586 **V** C GZ
1142 587 **V** C GZ
1142 589 **V** C GZ
1142 593 **V** C GZ
1142 595 **V** C GZ
1142 596 **V** C GZ
1142 598 **V** C GZ
1142 600 **V** P GZ
1142 601 **V** C GZ
1142 606 **V** P GZ
1142 607 **V** C GZ
1142 608 **V** C GZ
1142 609 **V** C GZ
1142 610 **V** C GZ
1142 611 **V** C GZ

1142 612	**V**	P	GZ
1142 613	**V**	P	GZ
1142 614	**V**	P	GZ
1142 615	**V**	C	GZ
1142 616	**V**	C	GZ
1142 617	**V**	C	GZ
1142 618	**V**	C	GZ
1142 619	**V**	C	GZ
1142 620	**V**	C	GZ
1142 621	**V**	C	GZ
1142 623	**0**	C	GZ
1142 624	**V**	C	GZ
1142 625	**V**	C	GZ
1142 626	**V**	C	GZ
1142 627	**V**	P	GZ
1142 628	**V**	P	GZ
1142 630	**V**	P	GZ
1142 631	**V**	P	GZ
1142 632	**V**	P	GZ
1142 633	**V**	C	GZ
1142 634	**V**	P	GZ
1142 636	**V**	P	GZ
1142 637	**V**	C	GZ
1142 638	**V**	P	GZ
1142 639	**V**	C	GZ
1142 640	**V**	P	GZ
1142 642	**V**	P	GZ
1142 643	**V**	P	GZ
1142 644	**V**	P	GZ
1142 646	**V**	C	GZ
1142 647	**V**	C	GZ
1142 648	**V**	C	GZ
1142 649	**V**	P	GZ
1142 651	**V**	C	GZ
1142 653	**V**	P	GZ
1142 654	**V**	C	GZ
1142 655	**V**	P	GZ
1142 656	**V**	P	GZ
1142 658	**V**	P	GZ
1142 659	**V**	P	WM (Z)
1142 662	**V**	P	WM
1142 663	**V**	P	WM
1142 664	**V**	C	WM
1142 665	**V**	P	WM
1142 667	**V**	P	WM
1142 668	**V**	P	WM
1142 669	**V**	P	WM
1142 671	**V**	P	WM
1142 672	**V**	P	WM
1142 673	**V**	P	WM
1142 677	**V**	P	WM
1142 678	**0**	P	WM (Z)
1142 679	**V**	C	WM (Z)
1142 680	**V**	P	WM
1142 682	**0**	P	WM
1142 683	**V**	P	WM
1142 684	**V**	P	WM
1142 685	**V**	P	WM
1142 688	**V**	P	WM
1142 689	**V**	P	WM
1142 691	**V**	C	WM
1142 693	**V**	P	WM
1142 694	**V**	C	WM
1142 696	**V**	P	WM
1142 698	**V**	P	WM
1142 700	**V**	P	WM
1142 703	**V**	C	WM (Z)
1142 704	**V**	P	WM
1142 705	**V**	P	WM
1142 707	**V**	C	WM

▲ ÖBB continues to retrofit their Class 1044 with multiple control, renumbering them into Class 1144. On 19 August 2009 1144 272 passes Purkersdorf-Gablitz with a local train to St.Pölten.

CLASS 1044 Bo-Bo

These thyristor locos are a development of Class 1043 which was in effect the Swedish Rc2 type. The 1044s are the standard locomotives of the 1970/80s (1044.0) and 1980/90s (1044.2). They are mixed traffic locomotives and can be found working mostly freight trains all over Austria. All Class 1044.2 have been rebuilt into Class 1144.2 and Class 1044.0 is now being retrofitted for push-pull working as well.

Built: 1974–95.
Builder – Mech. Parts: Simmering-Graz-Pauker.
Builder – Elec. Parts: Brown-Boveri/Elin/Siemens.
One Hour Rating: 5300 kW.
Maximum Tractive Effort: 314 kN.
Wheel Diameter: 1300 mm.
Weight: 83 tonnes.
Length over Buffers: 16.00 m.
Maximum Speed: 160 km/h.
EVN: 91 81 1044 xxx-c
Non-standard livery: **N** Cream and orange sides, colours reversed on cab.

1044 009	**V**	C	LZ
1044 014	**V**	C	LZ
1044 015	**V**	C	LZ
1044 025	**V**	C	LZ
1044 034	**V**	C	LZ
1044 041	**V**	C	VH
1044 043	**V**	C	VH
1044 046	**V**	C	VH
1044 049	**V**	C	VH
1044 053	**V**	C	VH
1044 055	**V**	C	VH
1044 058	**V**	C	VH
1044 068	**V**	C	VH
1044 071	**V**	C	VH
1044 084	**V**	C	VH
1044 085	**V**	C	VH
1044 086	**V**	C	VH
1044 089	**V**	C	VH
1044 096	**V**	C	BL
1044 108	**V**	C	BL
1044 110	**V**	C	BL
1044 112	**V**	C	BL
1044 116	**V**	C	BL
1044 117	**N**	C	BL

CLASS 1144 Bo-Bo

Class 1044 locomotives fitted for push-pull working. 1144 200–219 are additionally fitted with remote radio control for banking duties on the Brenner line and potentially elsewhere. The rebuilt locomotives can also work in multiple with Classes 1142, 1016/1116/1216, 1014, 2016, and DB 182 and can be controlled from ÖBB driving trailers of Classes 8033 and 8073.

Details as Class 1044.

EVN: 91 81 1144 xxx-c
Non-standard livery: **N** Cream and orange sides, colours reversed on cab.

1144 003	**V**	C	LZ
1144 004	**V**	P	LZ
1144 005	**V**	P	LZ
1144 006	**V**	P	LZ
1144 007	**V**	P	LZ
1144 008	**V**	C	LZ
1144 010	**V**	P	LZ
1144 011	**V**	P	LZ
1144 012	**V**	P	LZ
1144 013	**V**	P	LZ
1144 016	**V**	P	LZ
1144 017	**V**	P	LZ
1144 018	**V**	P	LZ
1144 019	**V**	P	LZ
1144 020	**V**	P	LZ
1144 021	**V**	P	LZ
1144 023	**V**	P	LZ
1144 024	**V**	P	LZ
1144 026	**V**	P	LZ
1144 027	**V**	P	LZ
1144 028	**V**	C	LZ
1144 029	**V**	P	LZ
1144 030	**V**	P	LZ
1144 031	**V**	P	LZ
1144 032	**V**	P	LZ
1144 033	**V**	P	LZ
1144 035	**V**	C	LZ
1144 036	**V**	P	LZ
1144 037	**V**	P	LZ
1144 039	**V**	P	LZ
1144 040	**O**	P	VH
1144 042	**V**	C	VH
1144 044	**V**	P	VH
1144 045	**V**	C	VH
1144 048	**V**	P	VH
1144 050	**V**	C	VH
1144 052	**V**	C	VH
1144 054	**V**	C	VH
1144 056	**V**	C	VH
1144 057	**V**	C	VH
1144 059	**V**	C	VH
1144 060	**V**	C	VH
1144 061	**V**	C	VH
1144 062	**V**	C	VH
1144 063	**V**	C	VH
1144 064	**V**	C	VH
1144 065	**V**	C	VH
1144 066	**V**	C	VH
1144 067	**V**	C	VH
1144 069	**V**	C	VH
1144 070	**V**	C	VH
1144 072	**V**	P	VH
1144 073	**V**	P	VH
1144 074	**V**	P	VH
1144 075	**V**	P	VH
1144 077	**V**	C	VH
1144 078	**V**	P	VH
1144 079	**V**	P	VH
1144 080	**V**	P	VH
1144 081	**V**	C	VH
1144 082	**V**	C	VH
1144 083	**V**	C	VH
1144 087	**V**	C	VH
1144 088	**V**	C	VH
1144 090	**V**	C	VH
1144 091	**V**	C	VH
1144 092	**N**	C	VH
1144 093	**V**	C	BL
1144 094	**V**	C	BL
1144 095	**V**	C	BL
1144 097	**V**	C	BL
1144 098	**V**	P	BL

1144 099	**V**	C	BL
1144 100	**V**	C	BL
1144 101	**V**	C	BL
1144 102	**V**	C	BL
1144 103	**V**	C	BL
1144 104	**V**	C	BL
1144 105	**V**	C	BL
1144 106	**V**	C	BL
1144 107	**V**	C	BL
1144 109	**V**	C	BL
1144 111	**V**	C	BL
1144 113	**V**	C	BL
1144 114	**V**	C	BL
1144 115	**V**	C	BL
1144 118	**V**	C	BL
1144 119	**V**	P	BL
1144 120	**V**	P	BL
1144 121	**V**	C	BL
1144 122	**V**	C	VH
1144 123	**V**	C	VH
1144 124	**V**	C	VH
1144 125	**V**	C	VH
1144 126	**V**	C	VH
1144 200	**V**	C	IN
1144 201	**V**	C	IN
1144 202	**V**	C	IN
1144 203	**V**	C	IN
1144 204	**V**	C	IN
1144 205	**V**	C	IN
1144 206	**V**	C	IN
1144 207	**V**	C	IN
1144 208	**V**	C	IN
1144 209	**V**	C	IN
1144 210	**V**	C	IN
1144 211	**V**	C	IN
1144 212	**V**	C	IN
1144 213	**V**	C	IN
1144 214	**V**	C	IN
1144 215	**V**	C	IN
1144 216	**V**	C	IN
1144 217	**V**	C	IN
1144 218	**V**	C	IN
1144 219	**V**	C	IN
1144 220	**V**	C	BL
1144 221	**V**	C	BL
1144 222	**V**	C	BL
1144 223	**V**	C	BL
1144 224	**V**	C	BL
1144 225	**V**	C	BL
1144 226	**V**	C	BL
1144 227	**V**	C	BL
1144 228	**V**	C	BL
1144 229	**V**	C	BL
1144 230	**V**	C	BL
1144 231	**V**	C	BL
1144 232	**V**	C	IN
1144 233	**V**	C	IN
1144 234	**V**	C	IN
1144 235	**V**	C	IN
1144 236	**V**	C	IN
1144 237	**V**	C	IN
1144 238	**V**	C	IN
1144 239	**V**	C	IN
1144 240	**V**	C	IN
1144 241	**V**	C	IN
1144 242	**V**	C	IN
1144 243	**V**	C	IN
1144 244	**V**	C	IN
1144 245	**V**	C	IN
1144 246	**V**	C	IN
1144 247	**V**	C	IN
1144 248	**V**	C	WW
1144 249	**V**	C	IN
1144 250	**V**	C	IN
1144 251	**V**	C	IN
1144 252	**V**	C	IN
1144 253	**V**	C	IN
1144 254	**V**	C	IN
1144 255	**V**	C	IN
1144 256	**V**	C	IN
1144 257	**V**	C	IN
1144 258	**V**	C	IN
1144 259	**V**	C	IN
1144 260	**V**	C	IN
1144 261	**V**	C	IN
1144 262	**V**	C	IN
1144 263	**V**	C	IN
1144 264	**V**	C	IN
1144 265	**V**	C	WW
1144 266	**V**	P	WW
1144 267	**V**	P	WW
1144 268	**V**	P	WW
1144 269	**V**	P	WW
1144 270	**V**	P	WW
1144 271	**V**	P	WW
1144 272	**V**	P	WW
1144 273	**V**	P	WW
1144 274	**V**	P	WW
1144 275	**V**	P	WW
1144 276	**V**	P	WW
1144 277	**V**	P	WW
1144 278	**V**	P	WW
1144 279	**V**	P	WW
1144 280	**V**	P	WW
1144 281	**V**	P	WW
1144 282	**V**	P	WW
1144 283	**V**	P	WW
1144 284	**V**	P	WW
1144 285	**V**	P	WW
1144 286	**V**	P	WW
1144 287	**V**	P	WW
1144 288	**V**	P	WW
1144 289	**V**	P	WW
1144 290	**V**	P	WW

CLASS 1063 — Bo-Bo

This class of three-phase motored centre-cab shunting locomotives helped to replace many older classes including 1040, 1245, 1061, 1161, 1062 and 1067. The first 37 locomotives are dual-voltage. The locos are used as yard and station pilots and trip locos all over Austria.

Built: 1982–91.
Builder – Mech. Parts: Simmering-Graz-Pauker.
Builder – Elec. Parts: Brown Boveri/Siemens/Elin.
Continuous Rating: 2000 kW.
Maximum Tractive Effort: 260 kN.
Wheel Diameter: 1145 mm.
Systems: 15 kV AC 16.7 Hz/25 kV AC 50 Hz.
EVN: 93 81 1063 xxx-c
Weight: 75.5 tonnes.
Length over Buffers: 15.56 m.
Maximum Speed: 100 km/h.

1063 001	C	LZ
1063 002	C	LZ
1063 003	C	LZ
1063 004	C	LZ
1063 007	C	LZ
1063 008	C	LZ
1063 009	C	LZ
1063 010	C	LZ
1063 011	C	LZ
1063 012	C	LZ
1063 013	C	GZ
1063 014	C	GZ
1063 015	C	GZ
1063 016	C	GZ
1063 017	C	GZ
1063 018	C	GZ
1063 019	C	GZ
1063 020	C	GZ
1063 021	C	GZ
1063 022	C	GZ
1063 023	P	WM
1063 024	P	WM
1063 025	P	WM
1063 026	C	WM
1063 027	C	WM
1063 028	C	WM
1063 029	C	WM

▲ ÖBB electric shunting locomotive 1063 028 is seen at Wien West on 17 July 2007.

▼ Class 1163 is ÖBB's most recent electric shunting locomotive. 1163 012 is seen at Gmunden on 26 September 2008.

1063 030	C	WM	1063 037	C	IN	1063 044	C	IN
1063 031	C	WM	1063 038	C	IN	1063 045	C	IN
1063 032	C	WM	1063 039	C	IN	1063 046	C	IN
1063 033	C	WM	1063 040	C	IN	1063 047	P	BL
1063 034	C	WM	1063 041	C	IN	1063 048	C	BL
1063 035	C	WM	1063 042	C	IN	1063 049	C	BL
1063 036	C	WM	1063 043	C	IN	1063 050	C	BL

CLASS 1163 Bo-Bo

This is an updated and restyled version of 1063 but only single voltage. The locomotives shunt and trip in the Salzburg and Villach areas.

Built: 1994–95.
Builder – Mech. Parts: Simmering-Graz-Pauker.
Builder – Elec. Parts: Brown Boveri/Siemens/Elin.
Continuous Rating: 2000 kW.
Maximum Tractive Effort: 260 kN.
Wheel Diameter: 1145 mm.
Weight: 80.0 tonnes.
Length over Buffers: 15.56 m.
Maximum Speed: 100 km/h.
EVN: 93 81 1163 xxx-c
Non-standard livery: N White & red.

1163 001	**N**	P	SB	1163 008	**N**	C	SB	1163 015	**N**	C	VH
1163 002	**N**	C	SB	1163 009	**N**	C	SB	1163 016	**N**	C	VH
1163 003	**N**	C	SB	1163 010	**N**	C	SB	1163 017	**N**	C	VH
1163 004	**N**	C	SB	1163 011	**N**	C	SB	1163 018	**N**	C	VH
1163 005	**N**	C	SB	1163 012	**N**	C	SB	1163 019	**N**	C	VH
1163 006	**N**	C	SB	1163 013	**N**	C	VH	1163 020	**N**	P	VH
1163 007	**N**	C	SB	1163 014	**N**	C	VH				

CLASS 1064 Co-Co

For the major new marshalling yards at Wien (Kledering) and Villach Süd (Fürnitz) a new heavy duty hump shunter was needed and these yards are where this class can be found.

Built: 1984–90.
Builder – Mech. Parts: Simmering-Graz-Pauker.
Builder – Elec. Parts: Elin/Siemens.
One Hour Rating: 2340 kW.
Maximum Tractive Effort: 370 kN.
Wheel Diameter: 1145 mm.
Weight: 112.2 tonnes.
Length over Buffers: 18.50 m.
Maximum Speed: 80 km/h.
EVN: 93 81 1064 xxx-c

1064 001	C	VH	1064 005	C	WM	1064 008	C	WM
1064 002	C	VH	1064 006	C	WM	1064 009	C	WM
1064 003	C	VH	1064 007	C	WM	1064 010	C	WM
1064 004	C	VH						

1.2. DIESEL LOCOMOTIVES

CLASS 2016 HERCULES Bo-Bo

These locomotives are amongst the quietest diesel locomotives ever produced. They are in effect a diesel version of the Taurus with which they share some common parts. All were built at the Siemens–Krauss Maffei works in München but as with the 1116s there is some Austrian input (Bogies from Siemens SGP, Graz). The locomotives feature three-phase motors and can work in multiple with Classes 1016/1116/1216, 1014, 1142, 1144 and can be controlled from driving trailers. The class has replaced most Class 2043s and 2143s but not all of them. The NS locomotives work all over the north east of Austria and as far south as Graz via the Wechsel route; WE locomotives are used on the lines radiating from Ried im Innkreis; VH locomotives work Knittelfeld–Klagenfurt–Villach–Kötschach-Mauthen and can even be found on freight trains to Koper (Slovenia); GZ locomotives work to Wiener Neustadt and Szombathely in Hungary.

Built: 2002–04.
Builder – Mech Parts: Siemens-Krauss-Maffei.
Builder – Elec Parts: Siemens Erlangen.
Engine: MTU 16V4000 R41 of 2000kW.
Transmission: Electric.
Maximum Tractive Effort: 235 kN.
Wheel Diameter: 1100 mm.
Train Heating: Electric.
Weight: 80 tonnes.
Length over Buffers: 19.275 m.
Maximum Speed: 140 km/h.
Multiple Working: Up to six members of this class can work in multiple.
EVN: 92 81 2016 xxx-c

2016 001	C	NS
2016 002	C	NS
2016 003	C	NS
2016 004	C	NS
2016 005	C	NS
2016 006	C	NS
2016 007	P	NS
2016 008	P	NS
2016 009	P	NS
2016 010	P	NS
2016 011	P	NS
2016 012	P	NS
2016 013	P	NS
2016 014	P	NS
2016 015	P	NS
2016 016	P	NS
2016 017	P	NS
2016 018	P	NS
2016 019	P	NS
2016 020	P	NS
2016 021	P	NS
2016 022	P	NS
2016 023	P	NS
2016 024	P	NS
2016 025	P	NS
2016 026	C	NS
2016 027	P	NS
2016 028	P	NS
2016 029	P	NS
2016 030	P	NS
2016 031	P	NS
2016 032	P	NS
2016 033	P	NS
2016 034	P	NS
2016 035	P	NS
2016 036	C	NS
2016 037	C	NS
2016 038	C	NS
2016 039	C	NS
2016 040	C	NS
2016 041	C	NS
2016 042	C	NS
2016 043	C	NS
2016 044	C	VH
2016 045	C	VH
2016 046	C	VH
2016 047	C	VH
2016 048	C	VH
2016 049	C	VH
2016 050	C	VH
2016 051	C	VH
2016 052	C	VH
2016 053	C	VH
2016 054	C	VH
2016 055	C	VH
2016 056	C	VH
2016 057	C	VH
2016 058	C	VH
2016 059	C	VH
2016 060	C	VH
2016 061	C	NS
2016 062	C	GZ
2016 063	C	WE
2016 064	C	WE
2016 065	C	WE
2016 066	C	WE
2016 067	C	WE
2016 068	C	WE
2016 069	C	WE
2016 070	C	WE
2016 071	P	WE
2016 072	P	WE
2016 073	P	WE
2016 074	P	WE
2016 075	P	WE
2016 076	P	WE
2016 077	P	WE
2016 078	P	WE
2016 079	C	GZ
2016 080	C	GZ
2016 081	C	GZ
2016 082	C	VH
2016 083	C	VH
2016 084	C	GZ
2016 085	C	GZ
2016 086	C	GZ
2016 087	C	GZ
2016 088	C	GZ
2016 089	C	GZ
2016 090	C	GZ
2016 091	C	GZ
2016 092	P	GZ
2016 093	P	GZ
2016 094	P	GZ
2016 095	P	GZ
2016 096	P	GZ
2016 097	P	GZ
2016 098	P	NS
2016 099	P	NS
2016 100	P	NS

▲ ÖBB Hercules Class 2016 can be found on most diesel operated lines. 2016 004 passes Oberweiden on 13 August 2010.

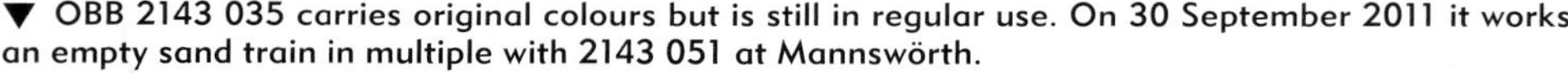

▼ ÖBB 2143 035 carries original colours but is still in regular use. On 30 September 2011 it works an empty sand train in multiple with 2143 051 at Mannswörth.

CLASS 2043 B-B

This class is in the process of being withdrawn with all regular duties already taken over by the new Classes 2016 and 2070 or even new DMUs. ÖBB is keeping a few examples in working order for engineering trains or extra traffic, but most are now in store. 2043 555 is still fitted with additional braking going back to the time when it worked iron ore trains on the Eisenerz–Vordernberg route.

Built: 1964–74.
Builder – Mech Parts: Jenbach.
Engine: Jenbach LM1500 of 1100 kW (1475 h.p.) plus 224 kW (300 h.p.) for train heating.
Transmission: Hydraulic. Voith L830 rU2.
Maximum Tractive Effort: 196 kN.
Wheel Diameter: 950 mm.
Train Heating: Electric.
EVN: 93 81 2043 xxx-c
Weight: 68 tonnes.
Length over Buffers: 14.76 m.
Maximum Speed: 110 km/h.

Note: 2043 062 has a Caterpillar engine of type 3516 STD for traction and a type 3408 DI-TR engine for heating.

2043 005 **O** C LZ
2043 006 **V** C VH (Z)
2043 008 **V** C VH (Z)
2043 009 **V** C KD (Z)
2043 010 **V** C LZ
2043 011 **V** C KD (Z)
2043 012 **V** C WE (Z)
2043 013 **V** C IN (Z)
2043 014 **V** C GM (Z)
2043 016 **V** C LZ
2043 017 **V** C GM (Z)
2043 020 **V** C WE
2043 021 **V** C WE
2043 022 **V** C WE
2043 023 **V** C IN (Z)
2043 025 **V** C WE
2043 026 **V** C WE (Z)
2043 028 **V** C IN (Z)
2043 029 **V** C WE
2043 032 **V** C WE
2043 034 **V** C LZ
2043 035 **V** C KR (Z)
2043 037 **V** C VH (Z)
2043 038 **V** C VH (Z)
2043 039 **V** C VH (Z)
2043 041 **V** C WE (Z)
2043 042 **V** C WE (Z)
2043 043 **V** C VH (Z)
2043 044 **V** C VH (Z)
2043 045 **V** C LZ (Z)
2043 046 **V** C LZ (Z)
2043 047 **V** C LZ (Z)
2043 048 **V** C LZ (Z)
2043 049 **V** C VH
2043 050 **V** C IN
2043 051 **V** C LZ (Z)
2043 052 **V** C IN (Z)
2043 053 **V** C VH (Z)
2043 056 **V** C VH
2043 057 **V** C IN (Z)
2043 058 **V** C VH
2043 059 **V** C IN (Z)
2043 060 **V** C WE
2043 061 **V** C KR (Z)
2043 062 **V** C WE
2043 063 **V** C LZ (Z)
2043 064 **V** C VH (Z)
2043 066 **V** C IN (Z)
2043 067 **V** C LZ (Z)
2043 068 **V** C VH (Z)
2043 069 **V** C VH (Z)
2043 070 **V** C VH (Z)
2043 071 **V** C GM (Z)
2043 073 **V** C IN (Z)
2043 074 **V** C VH (Z)
2043 075 **V** C VH (Z)
2043 076 **V** C VH
2043 077 **V** C KR (Z)
2043 555 **V** C LZ

CLASS 2143 B-B

As with Class 2043 this class is also being phased out. Several locomotives have already been withdrawn or sold and more are to follow. The remaining examples work diagrams around Gmünd and Krems.

Built: 1965–77.
Builder – Mech Parts: SGP.
Engine: SGP T12c of 1100 kW (1475 h.p.) plus 224 kW (300 h.p.) for train heating.
Transmission: Hydraulic. Voith L830 rU2.
Maximum Tractive Effort: 197 kN.
Wheel Diameter: 950 mm.
Train Heating: Electric.
EVN: 93 81 2143 xxx-c
Weight: 67 tonnes.
Length over Buffers: 15.76 m.
Maximum Speed: 100 km/h.

Notes: 2143 034–075 are fitted for multiple working. 2143 035 and 2143 040 have been restored to blood orange and green liveries respectively as "nostalgic" locomotives.

2143 009 **V** C NS
2143 011 **V** C NS
2143 013 **V** C NS
2143 015 **V** C NS (Z)
2143 016 **V** C NS
2143 022 **V** C WM
2143 024 **V** C GZ (Z)
2143 027 **V** C KR (Z)
2143 028 **V** C KR (Z)
2143 029 **V** C IN
2143 030 **V** C KR
2143 033 **V** C KD
2143 034 **V** C KR
2143 035 **O** C IN
2143 036 **V** C WM (Z)
2143 037 **V** P WM
2143 038 **V** P WM
2143 039 **V** C KR (Z)

2143 040	**G**	C	NS
2143 042	**V**	C	GM (Z)
2143 043	**V**	C	KR (Z)
2143 044	**V**	C	GZ
2143 045	**V**	C	GZ
2143 046	**V**	C	KR
2143 048	**V**	C	KR
2143 049	**V**	C	KR
2143 050	**V**	C	GM
2143 051	**V**	C	WM
2143 052	**V**	C	WM
2143 053	**V**	C	NS
2143 055	**V**	C	KR
2143 056	**V**	C	WM
2143 057	**V**	C	WM (Z)
2143 058	**V**	C	GM
2143 062	**V**	C	KD
2143 064	**V**	C	IN
2143 066	**V**	C	IN
2143 067	**V**	C	IN
2143 068	**V**	C	IN
2143 069	**V**	C	GM
2143 070	**V**	C	NS
2143 071	**V**	C	WM (Z)
2143 072	**V**	C	GM
2143 073	**V**	C	WM
2143 075	**V**	C	GM

CLASS 2067 C

Whilst all members of Classes 2060 and 2062 have been withdrawn or transferred into departmental use, the arrival of 100 Class 2016s and 90 Class 2070s has only partially affected the 2067s. However many locomotives have already been withdrawn or stored and others will follow. Since they have not been fitted with PZB cab signalling they are no longer allowed to work on the main line.

Built: 1959–77.
Builder – Mech Parts: SGP.
Engine: SGP S12a of 450 kW (603 h.p.).
Transmission: Hydraulic. Voith L28.
Maximum Tractive Effort: 147 kN.
Wheel Diameter: 1140 mm.
Train Heating: None.
EVN: 93 81 2067 xxx-c
Weight: 48.3 tonnes.
Length over Buffers: 10.34 m.
Maximum Speed: 65 km/h.

Note: 2067 042–045 and 2067 101–108 are fitted for multiple working.

2067 001	P	GZ
2067 003	P	SB
2067 006	C	GZ
2067 008	P	VH
2067 009	P	VH
2067 011	P	GZ (Z)
2067 018	P	GZ (Z)
2067 024	P	LZ
2067 026	C	LZ
2067 028	C	WE
2067 037	C	WE
2067 038	C	LZ
2067 041	P	KD
2067 042	C	KD
2067 044	C	GZ
2067 045	C	KD
2067 050	P	WM
2067 052	C	LZ
2067 054	C	NS
2067 055	C	GZ (Z)
2067 057	C	BL
2067 058	P	BL
2067 061	C	SP
2067 063	C	NS
2067 065	C	LZ
2067 068	C	GZ
2067 070	P	SB
2067 071	C	GM (Z)
2067 073	C	NS (Z)
2067 074	C	WM
2067 075	C	NS
2067 077	C	GM
2067 078	C	NS (Z)
2067 079	C	GZ
2067 080	C	KD
2067 081	P	WM
2067 084	P	WM
2067 085	C	KD
2067 086	C	SP
2067 087	C	KD (Z)
2067 088	C	GZ
2067 089	C	WM
2067 090	C	WM
2067 094	C	BL
2067 095	C	IN
2067 096	C	VH
2067 097	C	SP
2067 098	C	WM
2067 099	C	IN
2067 100	C	GZ
2067 101	C	SB
2067 102	C	GZ
2067 103	P	GZ
2067 104	C	VH
2067 105	C	IN
2067 106	C	KD
2067 107	C	LZ
2067 108	C	IN

CLASS 2068 B-B

These shunting locomotives have been concentrated in the western part of Austria now that the Class 2070s have settled in.

Built: 1989.
Builder – Mech. Parts: Jenbacher Werke.
Engine: JW 608DS (480 D*) of 820 kW (1100 h.p.) at 1500 rpm.
Transmission: Hydraulic. Voith L4r4zsU2.
Maximum Tractive Effort: 176 (147*) kN.
Wheel Diameter: 950 mm.
Train Heating: None.
Multiple Working: With one other member of the same class.
EVN: 93 81 2068 xxx-c
Weight: 75.5 tonnes.
Length over Buffers: 13.30 m.
Maximum Speed: 100 km/h.

▲ On 20 April 2008 ÖBB 2067 105 + 094 coupled back-to-back work light engine in multiple at Kledering yard.

▼ ÖBB 2068 012 arrives at Jenbach with a trip freight from Hall in Tirol on 24 July 2008.

2068 001	C	*	VH
2068 002	C	*	VH
2068 003	C	*	BL
2068 004	C	*	BL
2068 005	C	*	BL
2068 006	C		VH
2068 007	P		IN
2068 008	C		IN
2068 009	C		IN
2068 010	C		IN
2068 011	C		IN
2068 012	C		IN
2068 013	C		KD
2068 014	C		IN
2068 015	C		VH
2068 016	C		VH
2068 017	C		VH
2068 018	C		VH
2068 019	P		GZ
2068 020	C		BL
2068 021	C		SB
2068 022	C		SB
2068 023	C		SB
2068 024	C		SB
2068 025	C		BL
2068 026	C		BL
2068 027	C		IN
2068 028	C		SB
2068 029	C		SB
2068 030	C		VH
2068 031	C		VH
2068 032	C		SB
2068 033	C		VH
2068 034	C		IN
2068 035	C		VH
2068 036	C		SB
2068 037	C		VH
2068 038	C		BL
2068 039	P		VH
2068 040	C		SB
2068 041	C		KD
2068 042	C		KD
2068 043	C		GZ
2068 044	C		KD
2068 045	C		KD
2068 046	C		KD
2068 047	C		KD
2068 048	C		KD
2068 049	C		GZ
2068 050	C		GZ
2068 051	C		GZ
2068 052	C		GZ
2068 053	C		GZ
2068 054	C		GZ
2068 055	C		GZ
2068 056	C		IN
2068 057	C		GZ
2068 058	C		SB
2068 059	C		GZ
2068 060	C		GZ

▲ The introduction of ÖBB Class 2070 has led to the withdrawal of some older diesel shunters. 2070.073 is seen in use as pilot locomotive at Wien Westbahnhof on 04 March 2011.

CLASS 2070 HECTOR B-B

This is a standard Vossloh/MaK single cab locomotive adapted to ÖBB requirements and nicknamed "HECTOR". Extras include remote radio control and automatic shunting couplers. An auxiliary engine of 21kW powers pre-heating equipment and cab air conditioning. The arrival of these new shunting and trip locomotives has allowed all Class 2048 to be withdrawn and Classes 2060 and 2062 to be withdrawn or cascaded into departmental use.

Built: 2001–04.
Builder – Mech Parts: VSFT Kiel.
Engine: Caterpillar 3412E01-TTA JW 12 cyl of 738 kN.
Transmission: Hydraulic. Voith L3t4zseU2. **Weight**: 72 tonnes.
Maximum Tractive Effort: 151/233 kN at 100/45 km/h.
Wheel Diameter: 1000 mm. **Length over Buffers**: 14.13 m.
Train Heating: None. **Maximum Speed**: 100 km/h.
EVN: 93 81 2070 xxx-c

2070 001	C	WE	2070 031	C	WE	2070 061	C	WM
2070 002	C	WE	2070 032	C	WE	2070 062	C	WM
2070 003	C	WE	2070 033	P	WE	2070 063	C	WM
2070 004	C	WE	2070 034	P	WE	2070 064	C	WM
2070 005	C	WE	2070 035	P	WE	2070 065	C	WM
2070 006	C	WE	2070 036	P	WE	2070 066	C	WM
2070 007	C	WE	2070 037	P	SP	2070 067	C	WM
2070 008	C	WE	2070 038	C	SP	2070 068	C	WM
2070 009	C	WE	2070 039	C	SP	2070 069	C	WM
2070 010	C	WE	2070 040	C	SP	2070 070	C	WM
2070 011	C	WE	2070 041	C	SP	2070 071	C	WM
2070 012	C	WE	2070 042	C	SP	2070 072	C	WM
2070 013	C	WE	2070 043	C	SP	2070 073	C	WM
2070 014	C	WE	2070 044	C	SP	2070 074	C	WM
2070 015	C	WE	2070 045	P	WM	2070 075	C	WM
2070 016	C	WE	2070 046	P	WM	2070 076	C	WM
2070 017	C	WE	2070 047	P	WM	2070 077	C	WM
2070 018	C	WE	2070 048	P	WM	2070 078	C	WM
2070 019	C	WE	2070 049	P	WM	2070 079	C	WM
2070 020	C	WE	2070 050	C	WM	2070 080	C	WM
2070 021	C	WE	2070 051	C	WM	2070 081	C	WM
2070 022	C	WE	2070 052	C	WM	2070 082	C	WM
2070 023	C	WE	2070 053	C	WM	2070 083	C	WM
2070 024	C	WE	2070 054	C	WM	2070 084	C	WM
2070 025	C	WE	2070 055	C	WM	2070 085	C	WM
2070 026	C	WE	2070 056	C	WE	2070 086	C	WM
2070 027	C	WE	2070 057	C	WM	2070 087	C	WM
2070 028	C	WE	2070 058	C	SP	2070 088	C	WM
2070 029	C	WE	2070 059	C	SP	2070 089	C	WM
2070 030	C	WE	2070 060	C	WM	2070 090	C	WM

1.3. ELECTRIC MULTIPLE UNITS

CLASS 4011 — 7-CAR INTER-CITY UNITS

These EMUs are former DB Class 411 units and have been bought for the joint Wien-Frankfurt ICE service. Class 4011 is being maintained by DB in München and therefore the units have no depot allocation in Austria. Class 4011 is equipped with tilt mechanism but this is not used on the Austrian rail network.

(DTFO–MCO–MURB–TSO–MSO–MSO–DTSO).

Built: 1999–2000
Builder–Mech. Parts: Bombardier/DWA (Ammendorf and Görlitz) (trailers), Siemens (Power cars).
Builder–Elec. Parts: Siemens.
Traction Motors: 8 x 500 kW.
Accommodation: 48/– + 12/47 2T + –/30 + –/64(3) 2T + –/62 2T + –/62 1W 1TD 1T + –/62.
Wheel Arrangement: 2-2 + 1A-A1 + 1A-A1 + 2-2 + 1A-A1 + 1A-A1 + 2-2.
Weight: 56 + 53 + 53 + 47 + 53 +52 + 56 tonnes.
Length over Couplers: 27.45 + 25.90 + 25.90 + 25.90 + 25.90 + 25.90 + 27.45m.
Maximum Speed: 230 km/h.
EVN: 93 81 4011 xxx-c

Note: Formerly DB Class 411 sets, 411 014–016.

4011 090	4011 190	4011 290	4011 890	4011 790	4011 690	4011 590	**N**	MH1	Wien
4011 091	4011 191	4011 291	4011 891	4011 791	4011 691	4011 591	**N**	MH1	Salzburg
4011 092	4011 192	4011 292	4011 892	4011 792	4011 692	4011 592	**N**	MH1	Linz

CLASS 4020 — 3-CAR UNITS

This suburban EMU covers most of the Wien area as far as Amstetten and Krems. The sets have been fitted with an emergency alarm brake override so that the driver can avoid the train stopping in tunnels etc when an emergency arises; 200 has been added to the original running number when this modification was carried out. Some of these units have lost their traditional blue and cream S-Bahn livery for the new red, grey and white but this has now been discontinued.

B4hET + B4hTI + B4hES (DMSO–TSO–DTSO).

Built: 1978–87.
Builder-Mech Parts: SGP.
Builders-Elec.Parts: BBC/Elin/Siemens.
Traction Motors: 4 x 300 kW.
Accommodation: –/56 + –/64 2T + –/64.
Wheel Arrangement: Bo-Bo + 2-2 + 2-2.
Length over Buffers: 23.30 + 22.80 + 23.30 m.
Maximum Speed: 120 km/h.
EVN: 93 81 4020 xxx-c

4020 201	7020 201	6020 201	**S**	FD
4020 202	7020 202	6020 202	**S**	FD
4020 203	7020 203	6020 203	**S**	FD
4020 204	7020 204	6020 204	**S**	FD
4020 205	7020 205	6020 205	**S**	FD
4020 206	7020 206	6020 206	**S**	FD
4020 207	7020 207	6020 207	**S**	FD
4020 208	7020 208	6020 208	**S**	FD
4020 209	7020 209	6020 209	**S**	FD
4020 210	7020 210	6020 210	**S**	FD
4020 211	7020 211	6020 211	**S**	FD
4020 212	7020 212	6020 212	**S**	FD
4020 213	7020 213	6020 213	**S**	FD
4020 214	7020 214	6020 214	**S**	FD
4020 215	7020 215	6020 215	**S**	FD
4020 216	7020 216	6020 216	**S**	FD
4020 217	7020 217	6020 217	**S**	FD
4020 218	7020 218	6020 218	**S**	FD
4020 219	7020 219	6020 219	**S**	FD
4020 220	7020 220	6020 220	**S**	FD
4020 221	7020 221	6020 221	**S**	FD
4020 222	7020 222	6020 222	**S**	FD
4020 223	7020 223	6020 223	**S**	FD
4020 224	7020 224	6020 224	**S**	FD
4020 225	7020 225	6020 225	**S**	FD
4020 226	7020 226	6020 226	**S**	FD
4020 227	7020 227	6020 227	**S**	FD
4020 228	7020 228	6020 228	**S**	FD

▲ ÖBB Class 4020 is still the staple motive power on the Wien S-Bahn system. 4020 221 is seen near Südtirolerplatz on 16 October 2011.

▼ Only eleven of the shorter 3-section Talent EMUs of Class 4023 were ordered by ÖBB. Most of them are used around Salzburg. 4023 003 stands at Taxham on 10 May 2007.

4020 229	7020 229	6020 229	**S**	FD
4020 230	7020 230	6020 230	**S**	FD
4020 231	7020 231	6020 231	**S**	FD
4020 232	7020 232	6020 232	**S**	FD
4020 233	7020 233	6020 233	**S**	FD
4020 234	7020 234	6020 234	**S**	FD
4020 235	7020 235	6020 235	**S**	FD
4020 236	7020 236	6020 236	**S**	FD
4020 237	7020 237	6020 237	**S**	FD
4020 238	7020 238	6020 238	**S**	FD
4020 239	7020 239	6020 239	**S**	FD
4020 240	7020 240	6020 240	**S**	FD
4020 241	7020 241	6020 241	**S**	FD
4020 242	7020 242	6020 242	**S**	FD
4020 243	7020 243	6020 243	**S**	FD
4020 244	7020 244	6020 244	**S**	FD
4020 245	7020 245	6020 245	**S**	FD
4020 246	7020 246	6020 246	**S**	FD
4020 247	7020 247	6020 247	**S**	FD
4020 248	7020 248	6020 248	**S**	FD
4020 249	7020 249	6020 249	**S**	FD
4020 250	7020 250	6020 250	**S**	FD
4020 251	7020 251	6020 251	**S**	FD
4020 252	7020 252	6020 252	**S**	FD
4020 253	7020 253	6020 253	**S**	FD
4020 254	7020 254	6020 254	**S**	FD
4020 255	7020 255	6020 255	**S**	FD
4020 256	7020 256	6020 256	**S**	FD
4020 257	7020 257	6020 257	**S**	FD
4020 258	7020 258	6020 258	**S**	FD
4020 259	7020 259	6020 259	**S**	FD
4020 260	7020 260	6020 260	**S**	FD
4020 261	7020 261	6020 261	**S**	FD
4020 262	7020 262	6020 262	**S**	FD
4020 263	7020 263	6020 263	**S**	FD
4020 264	7020 264	6020 264	**S**	FD
4020 266	7020 266	6020 266	**S**	FD
4020 267	7020 267	6020 267	**S**	FD
4020 268	7020 268	6020 268	**S**	FD
4020 269	7020 269	6020 269	**S**	FD
4020 270	7020 270	6020 270	**S**	FD
4020 271	7020 271	6020 271	**S**	FD
4020 272	7020 272	6020 272	**S**	FD
4020 273	7020 273	6020 273	**S**	FD
4020 274	7020 274	6020 274	**S**	FD
4020 275	7020 275	6020 275	**S**	FD
4020 276	7020 276	6020 276	**S**	FD
4020 277	7020 277	6020 277	**S**	FD
4020 278	7020 278	6020 278	**S**	FD
4020 279	7020 279	6020 279	**S**	FD
4020 280	7020 280	6020 280	**S**	FD
4020 281	7020 281	6020 281	**R**	FD
4020 282	7020 282	6020 282	**S**	FD
4020 283	7020 283	6020 283	**R**	FD
4020 284	7020 284	6020 284	**S**	FD
4020 285	7020 285	6020 285	**S**	FD
4020 286	7020 286	6020 286	**S**	FD
4020 287	7020 287	6020 287	**S**	FD
4020 288	7020 288	6020 288	**S**	FD
4020 289	7020 289	6020 289	**S**	FD
4020 290	7020 290	6020 290	**S**	FD
4020 291	7020 291	6020 291	**S**	FD
4020 292	7020 292	6020 292	**S**	FD
4020 293	7020 293	6020 293	**S**	FD
4020 294	7020 294	6020 294	**R**	FD
4020 295	7020 295	6020 295	**S**	FD
4020 296	7020 296	6020 296	**R**	FD
4020 297	7020 297	6020 297	**R**	FD
4020 298	7020 298	6020 298	**S**	FD
4020 299	7020 299	6020 299	**R**	FD
4020 300	7020 300	6020 300	**R**	FD
4020 301	7020 301	6020 301	**S**	FD
4020 302	7020 302	6020 302	**S**	FD
4020 303	7020 303	6020 303	**S**	FD
4020 304	7020 304	6020 304	**S**	FD
4020 305	7020 305	6020 305	**S**	FD
4020 306	7020 306	6020 306	**S**	FD
4020 307	7020 307	6020 307	**S**	FD
4020 308	7020 308	6020 308	**R**	FD
4020 309	7020 309	6020 309	**S**	FD
4020 310	7020 310	6020 310	**R**	FD
4020 311	7020 311	6020 311	**R**	FD
4020 312	7020 312	6020 312	**R**	FD
4020 313	7020 313	6020 313	**R**	FD
4020 314	7020 314	6020 314	**R**	FD
4020 315	7020 315	6020 315	**R**	FD
4020 316	7020 316	6020 316	**R**	FD
4020 317	7020 317	6020 317	**R**	FD
4020 318	7020 318	6020 318	**R**	FD
4020 319	7020 319	6020 319	**R**	FD
4020 320	7020 320	6020 320	**R**	FD

CLASS 4023 TALENT 3-SECTION UNITS

These new articulated EMUs are electric versions of the Bombardier (Talbot) Talent DMUs. They have been obtained to modernise the local services around Salzburg which are now classed as S-Bahn services. When first delivered the three sections were numbered as 4023/7023/6023 just as a classic three-car set but those involved in this did not take into account that both driving cars are power cars. ÖBB then changed their minds and the whole set is referred to as 4023 001 etc. (With some internal number or letter to denote in which actual part of a set a defect is located!). Besides covering the S-Bahn services some trains work through to such places as Schwarzach St. Veit and even Saalfelden. Some have now moved on to Graz and Villach.

BDhET (DMSO–TSO–DMSO).

Built: 2004.
Builder – Mech Parts: Bombardier.
Builder – Elec. Parts: Elin.
Traction Motors: 4 x 250 kW.
Accommodation: –/38 (16) + –/48 + –/40 (9) 1W 1TD.
Wheel Arrangement: Bo-2-2-Bo.
Weight: 93.2 tonnes.
Length over Couplers: 52.12 m.
Maximum Speed: 140 km/h.
EVN: 93 81 4023 xxx-c

4023 001	**R**	SB	Marktgemeinde Schwarzach i. Pg. / Tauernbahngemeinde
4023 002	**R**	SB	Marktgemeinde Strasswalchen
4023 003	**R**	SB	Stadt Freilassing
4023 004	**R**	SB	Marktgemeinde Kuchl
4023 005	**R**	SB	Oberalm
4023 006	**R**	SB	Stadt Salzburg
4023 007	**R**	SB	Stadt Seekirchen a.W.
4023 008	**R**	IN	Stadt Hallein
4023 009	**R**	VH	
4023 010	**R**	VH	Golling an der Salzach
4023 011	**R**	GZ	

CLASS 4024 TALENT 4-SECTION UNITS

This new EMU is a four-car version of Class 4023 from the same manufacturer. The units are employed on suburban duties around Wien and other areas. As with Class 4023, the first Class 4024 units were found to be lacking in braking power and had their speed restricted to 120 km/h for a while. These problems have now been resolved and all units are now commissioned for 140 km/h. Like the 4023s each set just has one number.

BDhET (DMSO–TSO–TSO–DMSO).

Built: 2005–2008.
Builder – Mech Parts: Bombardier, Aachen.
Builder – Elec. Parts: Elin.
Traction Motors: 4 x 250 kW.
Accommodation: –/38 (16) + –/48 + –/48 + –/40 (9) 1W 1TD.
Wheel Arrangement: Bo-2-2-2-Bo.
Weight: 112.4 tonnes.
Length over Couplers: 66.87 m.
Maximum Speed: 140 km/h.
EVN: 93 81 4024 xxx-c
Non-standard livery: A 4024 120 is in blue and grey livery "S-BAHN STEIERMARK".

4024 001	**R**	BL	Leiblachtal
4024 002	**R**	GZ	
4024 003	**R**	BL	Klostertal
4024 004	**R**	BL	Bludenz
4024 005	**R**	GZ	
4024 006	**R**	SB	
4024 007	**R**	SB	
4024 008	**R**	LZ	Wien Josefstadt
4024 009	**R**	LZ	Alsergrund
4024 010	**R**	LZ	
4024 011	**R**	LZ	Innviertel
4024 012	**R**	LZ	Hausruckviertel
4024 013	**R**	LZ	Hietzing
4024 014	**R**	LZ	Wien Penzing
4024 015	**R**	LZ	
4024 016	**R**	LZ	Ottakring
4024 017	**R**	LZ	
4024 018	**R**	SB	
4024 019	**R**	BL	
4024 020	**R**	SB	
4024 021	**R**	LZ	
4024 022	**R**	LZ	
4024 023	**R**	BL	
4024 024	**R**	BL	
4024 025	**R**	BL	
4024 026	**R**	BL	
4024 027	**R**	BL	
4024 028	**R**	BL	
4024 029	**R**	BL	
4024 030	**R**	BL	
4024 031	**R**	BL	
4024 032	**R**	BL	
4024 033	**R**	BL	
4024 034	**R**	BL	
4024 035	**R**	BL	
4024 036	**R**	BL	
4024 037	**R**	GZ	
4024 038	**R**	GZ	
4024 039	**R**	GZ	
4024 040	**R**	GZ	
4024 041	**R**	GZ	
4024 042	**R**	GZ	
4024 043	**R**	GZ	Einkaufsstadt Liezen
4024 044	**R**	GZ	S-Bahn Steiermark

4024 045	**R**	GZ	
4024 046	**R**	GZ	
4024 047	**R**	GZ	Hernals
4024 048	**R**	LZ	Währing
4024 049	**R**	LZ	Döbling
4024 050	**R**	LZ	Mühlviertel
4024 051	**R**	LZ	
4024 052	**R**	LZ	Traunviertel
4024 053	**R**	LZ	Wien Landstrasse
4024 054	**R**	LZ	
4024 055	**R**	LZ	Margareten
4024 056	**R**	LZ	Wien Mariahilf
4024 057	**R**	IN	Wien Neubau
4024 058	**R**	IN	
4024 059	**R**	IN	
4024 060	**R**	IN	
4024 061	**R**	IN	
4024 062	**R**	LZ	
4024 063	**R**	LZ	
4024 064	**R**	LZ	
4024 065	**R**	LZ	
4024 066	**R**	IN	
4024 067	**R**	IN	
4024 068	**R**	IN	
4024 069	**R**	IN	
4024 070	**R**	IN	
4024 071	**R**	IN	
4024 072	**R**	IN	
4024 073	**R**	IN	
4024 074	**R**	IN	
4024 075	**R**	IN	
4024 076	**R**	IN	
4024 077	**R**	IN	
4024 078	**R**	IN	
4024 079	**R**	IN	
4024 080	**R**	IN	
4024 081	**R**	IN	
4024 082	**R**	IN	
4024 083	**R**	IN	
4024 084	**R**	IN	
4024 085	**R**	IN	
4024 086	**R**	IN	
4024 087	**R**	IN	
4024 088	**R**	IN	
4024 089	**R**	IN	
4024 090	**R**	IN	
4024 091	**R**	IN	
4024 092	**R**	IN	
4024 093	**R**	IN	
4024 094	**R**	IN	
4024 095	**R**	IN	
4024 096	**R**	SB	
4024 097	**R**	VH	
4024 098	**R**	BL	
4024 099	**R**	IN	
4024 100	**R**	WW	Wien Favoriten

▲ ÖBB 4124 026 leaves Wulkaprodersdorf with a passenger train to Deutschkreutz via Sopron on 22 September 2009. The green poles indicate that this line is owned by GySEV.

4024 101	**R**	WW	Simmering
4024 102	**R**	WW	Brigittenau
4024 103	**R**	WW	Donaustadt
4024 104	**R**	VH	
4024 105	**R**	GZ	
4024 106	**R**	SB	
4024 107	**R**	SB	
4024 108	**R**	SB	
4024 109	**R**	SB	Schwarzach-St. Veit - Goldegg
4024 110	**R**	SB	
4024 111	**R**	VH	Einkaufsstadt Feldkirchen
4024 112	**R**	VH	
4024 113	**R**	VH	
4024 114	**R**	VH	Klagenfurt am Wörthersee
4024 115	**R**	VH	
4024 116	**R**	VH	
4024 117	**R**	VH	
4024 118	**R**	VH	Burgenstadt Friesach
4024 119	**R**	GZ	
4024 120	**N**	GZ	
4024 121	**R**	GZ	
4024 122	**R**	VH	
4024 123	**R**	VH	Spittal an der Drau-Schloss Porcia
4024 124	**R**	VH	Nationalpark Hohe Tauern
4024 125	**R**	VH	Kärnten läuft
4024 126	**R**	SB	
4024 127	**R**	WW	
4024 128	**R**	WW	
4024 129	**R**	WW	
4024 130	**R**	WW	
4024 131	**R**	WW	
4024 132	**R**	WW	Leopoldstadt
4024 133	**R**	WW	
4024 134	**R**	WW	
4024 135	**R**	WW	
4024 136	**R**	WW	
4024 137	**R**	WW	
4024 138	**R**	IN	
4024 139	**R**	GZ	Kulturstadt Leoben
4024 140	**R**	WW	

CLASS 4124 TALENT 4-SECTION UNITS

These are dual-voltage Class 4024s for use in the Wien area on services that run over the frontier into Hungary and Slovakia and on the GySEV network where the lines are electrified at 25 kV AC.

BDhET (DMSO–TSO–TSO–DMSO).

Built: 2006–2009.
Builder – Mech Parts: Bombardier, Aachen.
Builder – Elec. Parts: Elin.
Traction Motors: 4 x 250 kW.
Accommodation: –/38 (16) + –/48 + –/48 + –/40 (9) 1W 1TD.
Wheel Arrangement: Bo-2-2-2-Bo.
Weight: 112.4 tonnes.
Length over Couplers: 66.87 m.
Maximum Speed: 140 km/h.
Systems: 15 kV AC 16.7 Hz/25 kV AC 50 Hz.
EVN: 93 81 4124 xxx-c

4124 001	**R**	WW	
4124 002	**R**	WW	
4124 003	**R**	FD	
4124 004	**R**	FD	VOR
4124 005	**R**	FD	
4124 006	**R**	FD	
4124 007	**R**	FD	
4124 008	**R**	FD	VOR
4124 009	**R**	FD	UITP 2009
4124 010	**R**	FD	
4124 011	**R**	FD	
4124 012	**R**	FD	
4124 013	**R**	FD	
4124 014	**R**	FD	50 Jahre ÖBB-S-Bahn in Wien
4124 015	**R**	FD	
4124 016	**R**	FD	
4124 017	**R**	FD	
4124 018	**R**	FD	
4124 019	**R**	FD	Hollabrunn
4124 020	**R**	FD	
4124 021	**R**	FD	
4124 022	**R**	FD	PannoniaBahn
4124 023	**R**	FD	
4124 024	**R**	FD	
4124 025	**R**	FD	Mistelbach
4124 026	**R**	FD	
4124 027	**R**	FD	
4124 028	**R**	FD	
4124 029	**R**	FD	
4124 030	**R**	WW	
4124 031	**R**	WW	
4124 032	**R**	FD	
4124 033	**R**	FD	
4124 034	**R**	FD	
4124 035	**R**	FD	
4124 036	**R**	FD	
4124 037	**R**	FD	Chris Lohner

1.4. DIESEL RAILCARS

CLASS 5022 DESIRO 2-SECTION UNITS

Whilst Bombardier has been the supplier of new EMUs it is the Siemens "Desiro" articulated DMU that has been purchased for non-electrified lines. A total of 60 sets have been built in two batches which are allocated to Linz, Graz, Villach and Wiener Neustadt.

BDVT (DMSO–DMSO).

Built: 2005–2008.
Builder: Siemens, Krefeld.
Wheel Arrangement: B-(2)-B.
Engine: Two MTU engines of 315 kW.
Transmission: Mechanical.
Weight: 70.7 tonnes.
Length over Couplers: 20.85 + 20.85 m.
Maximum Speed: 120 km/h.
Floor height: 575/1250 mm.
Accommodation: –/41 (10) 1W 1TD + –/66.
EVN: 93 81 5022 xxx-c (5022.001-020), 95 81 5022 xxx-c (5022 021-060)
Non-standard livery: **A** 5022 045 is in blue and grey livery "S-BAHN STEIERMARK".

5022 001	**R**	GZ	Luftkurort Lassnitzhöhe
5022 002	**R**	GZ	
5022 003	**R**	NS	
5022 004	**R**	NS	
5022 005	**R**	LZ	Hans
5022 006	**R**	LZ	Machland
5022 007	**R**	LZ	Strudengau
5022 008	**R**	LZ	Niederwaldkirchen, St.Martin im Mühlkreis
5022 009	**R**	LZ	Stadt Perg
5022 010	**R**	LZ	Böhmerwald
5022 011	**R**	LZ	Aigen im Mühlkreis, Schlägl
5022 012	**R**	LZ	
5022 013	**R**	LZ	
5022 014	**R**	LZ	
5022 015	**R**	LZ	Neufelden
5022 016	**R**	LZ	Stadt Rohrbach, Berg bei Rohrbach
5022 017	**R**	LZ	

▲ ÖBB operates a fleet of 60 Siemens Desiro DMUs on many of its branch lines. 5022 058 leaves Graz Hbf on 20 October 2008 with a train bound for Fehring.

5022 018	**R**	LZ	Neufelden
5022 019	**R**	LZ	
5022 020	**R**	LZ	
5022 021	**R**	VH	Stadt Wolfsberg
5022 022	**R**	VH	Söchau
5022 023	**R**	VH	Hermagor-Presseggersee
5022 024	**R**	VH	Arnoldstein-Drei-Länder-Eck
5022 025	**R**	VH	St.Paul/Lavanttal
5022 026	**R**	VH	
5022 027	**R**	VH	
5022 028	**R**	VH	
5022 029	**R**	VH	
5022 030	**R**	VH	Kötschach-Mauthen-Plöckenpass
5022 031	**R**	VH	
5022 032	**R**	VH	
5022 033	**R**	GZ	Gutenstein
5022 034	**R**	GZ	
5022 035	**R**	GZ	Region Bad Radkersburg
5022 036	**R**	GZ	Stadtgemeinde Mureck
5022 037	**R**	GZ	
5022 038	**R**	GZ	
5022 039	**R**	GZ	Kräuterdorf Söchau, Hartberg
5022 040	**R**	GZ	
5022 041	**R**	GZ	
5022 042	**R**	GZ	
5022 043	**R**	GZ	
5022 044	**R**	GZ	
5022 045	**N**	GZ	
5022 046	**R**	GZ	
5022 047	**R**	GZ	
5022 048	**R**	GZ	
5022 049	**R**	GZ	
5022 050	**R**	GZ	
5022 051	**R**	GZ	
5022 052	**R**	NS	
5022 053	**R**	NS	
5022 054	**R**	NS	
5022 055	**R**	NS	
5022 056	**R**	NS	
5022 057	**R**	NS	
5022 058	**R**	NS	
5022 059	**R**	NS	
5022 060	**R**	NS	

CLASS 5047 SINGLE UNITS

Branch line closures and the delivery of Class 5022 have seen these single unit DMUs redistributed in recent years. Some of them have already been withdrawn and sold to GySEV.

BD4VT (DMBSO).

Built: 1987–95.
Builder: JW.
Wheel Arrangement: B-2.
Engine: Daimler Benz OM444LA 419 kW.
Transmission: Hydraulic.
Accommodation: –/62 (6) 1T.
EVN: 93 81 5047 xxx-c
Weight: 43.7 tonnes.
Length over Buffers: 25.42 m.
Maximum Speed: 120 km/h.

5047 002	**C**	KR
5047 003	**R**	KR
5047 004	**R**	KR
5047 005	**R**	KR
5047 006	**R**	KR
5047 007	**R**	KR
5047 009	**R**	KR
5047 010	**C**	KR
5047 011	**R**	KR
5047 012	**R**	KR
5047 013	**C**	KR
5047 014	**R**	KR
5047 015	**C**	KR
5047 016	**C**	KR
5047 017	**C**	KR
5047 018	**R**	KR
5047 019	**R**	KR
5047 021	**C**	KR
5047 022	**C**	KR
5047 023	**C**	KR
5047 024	**C**	KR
5047 025	**C**	KR
5047 026	**C**	KR
5047 027	**C**	NS
5047 028	**C**	KR
5047 029	**C**	NS
5047 030	**C**	NS
5047 032	**C**	NS
5047 033	**GR**	NS
5047 034	**GR**	NS
5047 035	**GR**	NS
5047 036	**GR**	NS
5047 037	**GR**	KR
5047 038	**GR**	NS
5047 039	**GR**	KR
5047 040	**GR**	NS
5047 041	**GR**	NS
5047 042	**GR**	NS
5047 043	**GR**	NS
5047 045	**GR**	KR
5047 046	**GR**	KR
5047 047	**GR**	KR
5047 048	**GR**	KR
5047 049	**GR**	NS
5047 050	**GR**	NS
5047 051	**GR**	NS
5047 052	**GR**	NS
5047 053	**GR**	NS
5047 054	**GR**	NS
5047 055	**GR**	NS
5047 056	**GR**	NS
5047 057	**GR**	NS
5047 058	**GR**	NS
5047 059	**GR**	NS
5047 060	**GR**	KR
5047 061	**GR**	WE
5047 063	**GR**	WE
5047 064	**GR**	WE
5047 065	**GR**	WE
5047 066	**GR**	WE
5047 067	**GR**	WE
5047 069	**GR**	WE
5047 070	**GR**	WE
5047 071	**GR**	WE
5047 072	**GR**	WE
5047 073	**GR**	WE
5047 074	**GR**	WE
5047 075	**GR**	WE
5047 076	**GR**	WE
5047 077	**GR**	WE
5047 078	**GR**	WE
5047 079	**GR**	WE

5047 080	**GR**	WE
5047 081	**GR**	WE
5047 082	**GR**	WE
5047 083	**GR**	WE
5047 084	**GR**	WE
5047 085	**GR**	WE
5047 086	**GR**	NS
5047 087	**GR**	WE
5047 088	**GR**	WE
5047 089	**GR**	WE
5047 090	**R**	NS
5047 091	**GR**	NS
5047 092	**GR**	WE
5047 093	**GR**	WE
5047 094	**GR**	NS
5047 095	**GR**	NS
5047 096	**GR**	NS
5047 097	**R**	WE
5047 098	**GR**	WE
5047 099	**R**	WE

Name:

5047 090 Manfred

CLASS 5147 — 2-CAR UNITS

This is a two-car version of Class 5047 for use on local services around Krems. Four units have been sold to GySEV.

BD4VT (DMBSO).

Built: 1992.
Builder: JW.
Wheel Arrangement: B-2.
Engine: Daimler Benz OM444LA 419 kW.
Transmission: Hydraulic.
Accommodation: –/62 (6) 1T.
EVN: 93 81 5147 xxx-c
Weight: 43.7 tonnes.
Length over Buffers: 25.42 m.
Maximum Speed: 120 km/h.

5147 001	**GR**	KR
5147 002	**GR**	KR

▲ Although some ÖBB Class 5047 DMUs have recently been sold to GySEV, ÖBB still relies on the class for many of its branch line services. On 05 November 2011 5047 032 leaves Wien Ost with a passenger train to Marchegg.

1.5. NOSTALGIC FLEET

In the run up to the 150th Anniversary of railways in Austria which took place in 1987, ÖBB restored some of its older locomotives and railcars to original condition. Many of these were then still in capital stock. Since that time ÖBB has recognised the value of its restored stock and these locomotives and railcars having been withdrawn from normal service have been kept at dedicated depots for public excursions under the Nostalgic theme. However, in 2008 a decision was taken to get rid of most of the historical vehicles. Only a few have been scrapped but ownership of most of them has passed on to various preservation societies. Today only a few locomotives, a single railcar and some coaches are still owned by ÖBB. GE Erlebnisbahn is the division within ÖBB Personenverkehr that keeps these vehicles operational. Some excursions use rolling stock from preservation societies which have been certified for main line running.

ELECTRIC LOCOMOTIVES

CLASS 1010 Co-Co

These main line locomotives became surplus to requirements with the arrival of the Taurus fleet. ÖBB has retained some for use on its nostalgic trains whilst others have gone to preservation groups.

Built: 1955–56.
Builder – Mech. Parts: SGP.
Builder – Elec. Parts: BBC/Siemens/Elin.
One Hour Rating: 4000 kW.
Maximum Tractive Effort: 275 kN.
Wheel Diameter: 1300 mm.
Weight: 106 tonnes.
Length over Buffers: 16.92 m.
Maximum Speed: 130 km/h.

1010 003		WF		1010 010	**G**	WF

CLASS 1110 Co-Co

This class was the mountain 1010 with the 1110.5 version having rheostatic braking. All were rendered surplus by the arrival of the Taurus fleet, being withdrawn in 2004.

Built: 1957–60.
Builder – Mech. Parts: SGP.
Builder – Elec. Parts: BBC/Siemens/Elin.
One Hour Rating: 4000 kW.
Maximum Tractive Effort: 275 kN.
Wheel Diameter: 1300 mm.
Weight: 106 tonnes.
Length over Buffers: 17.86 m.
Maximum Speed: 110 km/h.

1110 505	**G**	IN		1110 524		WF

CLASS 1020 Co-Co

These locomotives are former DRB locos left in Austria after World War II or built there later. Towards the end of their lives they were allocated to Innsbruck, Bludenz and Salzburg. Normal operation of this class ceased in 1995 when the last of the 1044s entered service. A few have been retained for special trains with private preservation societies.

Built: 1945.
Builder – Mech Parts: Kraus-Maffei/AEG.
Builder – Elec Parts: Siemens/AEG.
One Hour Rating: 3300 kW.
Maximum Tractive Effort: 314 kN.
Wheel Diameter: 1250 mm.
Weight: 118.5 tonnes.
Length over Buffers: 18.60 m.
Maximum Speed: 90 km/h.

Former DRB numbers in parentheses.

1020.44 (E94.156) **G** IN

CLASS 1042 Bo-Bo

These were the standard mixed traffic locos dating from the 1960s, starting off with the 1042.0 series then evolving into the 1042.5. One loco has been retained in nearly original livery as a museum loco.

Built: 1964.
Builder – Mech. Parts: Simmering-Graz-Pauker.
Builder – Elec. Parts: Elin/Siemens/Brown-Boveri.
One Hour Rating: 3560 kW.
Maximum Tractive Effort: 255 kN.
Wheel Diameter: 1250 mm.
Weight: 83.8 tonnes.
Length over Buffers: 16.22 m.
Maximum Speed: 130 km/h.

1042.23 WF

CLASS 1245 Bo+Bo

A development of Classes 1045 and 1145 latterly used on freight trip workings. This locomotive is still formally owned by ÖBB.

Built: 1935.
Builder – Mech. Parts: Floridsdorf.
Builder – Elec. Parts: BBC/Elin/Siemens Wien/AEG.
One Hour Rating: 1840 kW.
Maximum Tractive Effort: 196 kN.
Wheel Diameter: 1350 mm.
Electric Braking: Rheostatic.
Weight: 83 tonnes.
Length over Buffers: 12.92 m.
Maximum Speed: 80 km/h.

1245.04 **G** Strasshof

DIESEL LOCOMOTIVES

CLASS 2050 Bo-Bo

Locomotives of this class were all taken out of service towards the end of 2004 but the following have been retained for excursion trains.

Built: 1958–59.
Builder – Mech Parts: Henschel.
Engine: GM 567C of 1050 kW (1408 h.p.).
Maximum Tractive Effort: 179 kN.
Driving Wheel Diameter: 1040 mm.
Maximum Speed: 100 km/h.
Transmission: Electric.
Weight: 74.9 tonnes.
Length over Buffers: 17.76 m.
Train Heating: None.

2050.04 **G** WF | 2050.09 **0** WF

DIESEL RAILCARS/MULTIPLE UNITS

CLASS 5042 1A-A1

Introduced in 1935 these units were first used on fast services between Wien and Graz, Villach, etc. After the war some were used on the Villach–Innsbruck corridor trains before all gathered in the Wien area for use on the branch lines to the north of the city. The survivor was restored in time for the 1987 celebrations and is now operational again.

Built: 1937.
Builder: Simmering.
Engine: Two Simmering R8 of 155 kW.
Accommodation: –/78 1T.
Weight: 56.8 tonnes.
Transmisson: Electric.
Length over Buffers: 22.44 m.
Maximum Speed.: 110 km/h.

5042.14 WF

CLASS 5047 B-2

Some of these railcars have already been withdrawn and sold to GySEV, whilst one unit has been transferred to GE Erlebnisbahn

BD4VT (DMBSO).

Built: 1987.
Builder: JW.
Engine: Daimler Benz OM444LA 419 kW.
Accommodation: –/62 (6) 1T.
Weight: 43.7 tonnes.
Transmission: Hydraulic.
Length over Buffers: 25.42 m.
Maximum Speed: 120 km/h.

5047 001 WF

1.6. ÖBB DEPARTMENTAL STOCK

Numbering System

Since the 1950s ÖBB has used a specific numbering system for its departmental stock. The stock is identified by a three digit number preceded by X e.g. X 534. The number breaks down as follows:

The hundred digit indicates:

1 Traction
2 Special Traction
3 Not used (originally rail automobiles)
4 Test vehicles
5 Overhead Line Vehicles (Motor Turm Wagen – MTW)
6 Light vehicles for track staff (Motor Bahn Wagen)
7 Draisines
8 Temporary numbers for vehicles on acceptance
9 Private stock

In the case of the 100 series the ten digit indicates:

1 Mechanical transmission
3 Electric transmission

In the case of the 500 series vehicles (MTW) the last digit also details the engine used as follows:

0 Vomag 113 hp engine
1 Saurer 118-150 hp engine
2 Oberhansli 100 hp engine
3 SGP G6 115 hp engine
4 Jenbach JW100 engine
5 Deutz engine

In the case of the 60x–62x series vehicles the ten digit 1 denotes the vehicle is not fitted with normal buffing gear and other digits indicate that normal buffing gear is fitted. The final digit is also related to engines as follows:

0 Daimler 20 hp engine, light duty
1 Daimler 30 hp engine, heavy duty
2 Daimler 45 hp engine, heavy duty
3 Kromag 60 hp engine, heavy duty
4 JW 35 hp engine, heavy duty
5 JW 70 jp engine heavy duty
6 All others

Private vehicles have also been numbered and carry numbers in the 900 range.

Meanwhile 12 digit EVN have also been introduced for departmental stock. ÖBB departmental vehicles have been renumbered accordingly although in most cases the original X number has been retained as well. The 12 digit EVN reads as follows: 99 81 9xxx yyy-c. When the new numbers were introduced they were applied in sequence to existing vehicles so that there were no gaps due to withdrawals at the beginning.

X 100 SERIES. SMALL SHUNTERS ('KLEINLOKS')

The X 100 series had once been allocated to various types of ex-DRB Kleinloks. These have now all been withdrawn except for Class X 170.

X 170 BATTERY POWERED SHUNTING LOCOS B

1957 No.	*DRB System*	*Location*	*Type*	*Power (kW)*
X 170.01	Ks 4866	TS Jedlersdorf	Bo ae	80
X 170.02	Ks 4818	TS Jedlersdorf	Bo ae	80

X 200 SERIES. SHUNTING LOCOMOTIVES

The following sector codes are used in this section:

F Fahrweg
N Netz
P Produktion
TS Technische Services

X 260/X 631.0 B

These are Class 2060 shunters downgraded for departmental use. Although they have been renumbered into Class X 631.0 only a few actually carry this number. The new EVN is also not carried very often.

Built: 1954–62.
Builder – Mech Parts: JW.
Engine: JW 200 of 150 kW (200 h.p.). * re-engined with a KHD BF6M 1013 CP engine
Transmission: Hydraulic. Voith L33 yUB.
Maximum Tractive Effort: 100 kN.
Wheel Diameter: 950 mm.
Maximum Speed: 60 km/h.
Weight: 27.0 tonnes.
Length over Buffers: 6.68 m.

Number	*New number*	*EVN*		*Sector*	*Location*
X 260 006				*F*	KD stored
X 260 012				*TS*	LZ
X 260 013	X 631 013			*P*	LZ
X 260 015	X 631 015		**0** *	*F*	Linz Wegscheid
X 260 045	X 631 045	9281 001		*TS*	SL
X 260 051	X 631 051	9281 002		*P*	LZ
X 260 056	X 631 056	9481 508	**0** *	*F*	Zeltweg
X 260 079				*TS*	WE
X 260 087				*TS*	WE
X 260 089	X 631 089			*P*	KR
X 260 090	X 631 090			*P*	WM
X 260 096				*TS*	WE
X 260 097				*TS*	LZ
X 260 098				*P*	WE
X 260 100	X 631 100			*P*	LZ

X 262/X 631.5 B

These are Class 2062 shunters downgraded for departmental use. Although they have been renumbered into Class X 631.5 only a few actually carry this number.

Built: 1958–66.
Builder – Mech Parts: JW.
Engine: JW 400 of 300 kW (400 h.p.).
Transmission: Hydraulic. Voith L26 St/A 100 KV.
Maximum Tractive Effort: 120 kN.
Wheel Diameter: 950 mm.
Maximum Speed: 60 km/h.
Weight: 32.3 tonnes.
Length over Buffers: 7.92 m.

Number	New number	EVN	Sector	Location
X 262 005	X 631 505		*P*	WE
X 262 008	X 631 508		*P*	VH
X 262 017	X 631 517		*P*	KD
X 262 031		9481 505	*N*	SP
X 262 056			*TS*	WM
X 262 058	X 631 558		*P*	WE
X 262 064			*TS*	BL

X 400 SERIES. TEST VEHICLES, ROTARY SNOWPLOUGHS

X 401 TUNNEL INSPECTION VEHICLE B-2+2

This vehicle is based on an X552 unit permanently coupled to a driving trailer vehicle. The motorised vehicle also has a cab with observation windows, an equipment room and sleeping space. Mounted between this area and the trailing driving cab is a hydraulic telescopic platform for use not only in tunnels but also for use when inspecting retaining walls as it can extend to 13 m.

Technical details as X 552 except:

Built: 1996.
Builder: Plasser.
Engine: Deutz (V12) BF12L513C of 367 kW.
Transmission: Hydraulic. Voith L26 St/A 100 KV.
Maximim Speed: 120 km/h.
Weight: 74 tonnes.
Length over Buffers: 25.43 m.

X 401 001 9131 501 **V** Spratzern

X 432 LZB MESSWAGEN 2-B

This is a Plasser OBW 100 type vehicle and is used for testing 'LZB' cab signalling over the whole ÖBB network.

Built: 1991.
Builder: Plasser.
Engine: Deutz (V12) BF12L513C of 367 kW.
Transmission: Hydraulic. Voith L26 St/A 100 KV.
Maximum Speed: 140 km/h.
Non-Standard Livery: **N** Red, yellow and blue.
Weight: 43.40 tonnes.
Length over Buffers: 15.85 m.

X 432 001 9165 001 **N** Streckenleitung LZ

CLASS X 491 B

These are self-propelled snow-clearing machines with rotary snowploughs. Formerly designated as Classes 2080 and 2081.

Built: 1975–82.
Builder: Beilhack.
Engine: X 491 001: Deutz BF 12L413 of 260 kW (350 h.p.), X 491 002: 370 kW (496 h.p.).
Transmission: Hydraulic.
Wheel Diameter: 1000 mm.
Snowplough Power: X 491 001: 2 x 310 kW, X 491 002: 2 x 370 kW.
Maximum Speed: 80 km/h.
Weight: 42 tonnes
Length over Buffers: 12.35 m.

X 491 001	(ex 2080.001)	9491 001	IN
X 491 002	(ex 2180.001)	9491 002	Saalfelden

X 500 SERIES. SELF-PROPELLED OVERHEAD LINE INSPECTION UNITS ("MOTOR TOWER WAGONS")

These are overhead line maintenance units belonging to the electrical department and are allocated to various places for repairs or maintenance to the catenary. These depots can be found at substations or in specially constructed sheds near stations and yards. A common feature of all these units is the lifting platform found on top of the unit which can be adjusted in height or even revolved so that it sticks out over adjoining lines.

X 521 B

These four units were prototypes for replacing the X 534. The main frame and running gear is borrowed from X 628 (OBW 10) and thus the X 521 is also referred to as a MTW 10. Fitted with a pantograph, work platform and telescopic crane/grab.

Built: 1990–91.
Builder: Plasser & Theurer.
Engine: KHDF8L513 of 177 kW at 2300 r.p.m.
Transmission: Hydrodynamic.
Driving Wheel Diameter: 730 mm.
Maximum Speed: 80 km/h (100 km/h hauled).
Weight: 42 tonnes.
Length over Buffers: 11.94 m.

X 521 001 9231 501 **YR** Fahrleitungsbau Ost
X 521 002 9231 502 **YR** Fahrleitungsbau Süd
X 521 003 9231 503 **YR** Fahrleitungsbau West
X 521 004 9231 504 **YR** Fahrleitungsbau Süd

▲ ÖBB overhead line inspection unit X 552 104 pauses on the Krauselklause viaduct on 27 January 2012 in order to inspect the catenary on the Semmering line.

X 534 1-A

A total of 82 examples of this class were built between 1963 and 1983, based on the earlier X532 (all now withdrawn). There is a diesel engine in a box at one end and a pantograph above this box.

Built: 1963–78, 1970–83*.
Builders: Bombardier, Tobisch, Knotz.
Engine: JW 200 of 122 kW (MAN D2566MTE of 147 kW*).
Transmission: Electric (BBC, ABB).
Wheel Diameter: 940 mm.
Maximum Speed: 80 km/h.
Weight: 20.5 tonnes.
Length over Buffers: 7.74 m.

X 534.101 is ex X 534.78.

Number	*EVN*			*Area/Use*	*Location*
X 534 054	9231 505	**YR**		Landeck	Landeck
X 534 058	9231 506	**YR**		Hütteldorf	Hütteldorf
X 534 062	9231 507	**YR**		Feldkirch	Feldkirch
X 534 063	9231 508	**YR**		Innsbruck	Innsbruck
X 534 064	9231 509	**YR**		St. Veit a.d. Glan	St. Veit a.d. Glan
X 534 065	9231 510	**YR**		Mallnitz	Mallnitz
X 534 066	9231 511	**YR**		Linz Kleinmünchen	Linz Kleinmünchen
X 534 067	9231 512	**YR**		Wiener Neustadt	Wiener Neustadt
X 534 068	9231 513	**YR**		Villach	Villach
X 534 069	9231 514	**YR**		Tulln	Tulln
X 534 070	9231 515	**YR**	*	St. Pölten	St. Pölten
X 534 071	9231 516	**YR**	*	Selzthal	Selzthal
X 534 072	9231 517	**YR**	*	St. Johann in Pongau	St. Johann in Pongau
X 534 073	9231 518	**YR**	*	Linz Kleinmünchen	Linz Kleinmünchen
X 534 074	9231 519	**YR**	*	Wiener Neustadt	Wiener Neustadt
X 534 075	9231 520	**YR**	*	Wörgl	Wörgl
X 534 076	9231 521	**YR**	*	Graz	Graz
X 534 077	9231 522	**YR**	*	Wörgl	Wörgl
X 534 079	9231 523	**YR**	*	Ost	Bruck a.d. Leitha
X 534 080	9231 524	**YR**	*	Villach	Villach
X 534 081	9231 525	**YR**	*	Ost	Zentralfriedhof
X 534 082	9231 526	**YR**	*	Floridsdorf	Floridsdorf
X 534 083	9231 527	**YR**	*	St. Veit/Glan	St. Veit a.d. Glan
X 534 084	9231 528	**YR**	*	Wien Meidling	Wien Meidling
X 534 101	9231 529	**YR**	*	Fahrleitungsbau Ost	

X 552 2-B

After five prototypes had been built and evaluated ÖBB ordered more of these large overhead units. These are the real main line units and they cover large sections of the main lines which is reflected in their maximum speed. They have a 44 kW motor (KHD BR4L1011R) for the ancillary equipment.

X 552.0

These units feature a large workshop area, pantograph, work platform, telescopic crane/grab, and a mess room.

Built: 1990–98.
Builder: Plasser & Theurer.
Engine: KHD Type BF12L513C of 367 kW at 2300 r.p.m.
Transmission: Hydrodynamic.
Wheel Diameter: 840 mm.
Maximum Speed: 120 km/h.
Weight: 52–61 tonnes.
Length over Buffers: 15.84 m.

Number	EVN		Area/Use	Location
X 552 001	9131 502	**YR**	St. Pölten	St. Pölten
X 552 002	9131 503	**YR**	Landeck	Landeck
X 552 003	9131 504	**YR**	Villach	Villach
X 552 004	9131 505	**YR**	Innsbruck	Innsbruck
X 552 005	9131 506	**YR**	Wiener Neustadt	Wiener Neustadt
X 552 006	9131 507	**YR**	Wörgl	Wörgl
X 552 007	9131 508	**YR**	Linz Kleinmünchen	Linz Kleinmünchen
X 552 008	9131 509	**YR**	Salzburg	Salzburg
X 552 009	9131 510	**YR**	Floridsdorf	Floridsdorf
X 552 010	9131 511	**YR**	Ost	Zentralfriedhof
X 552 011	9131 512	**YR**	Hütteldorf	Hütteldorf
X 552 013	9131 513	**YR**	St. Michael	St. Michael
X 552 014	9131 514	**YR**	Attnang-Puchheim	Attnang-Puchheim
X 552 015	9131 515	**YR**	St. Johann in Pongau	St. Johann in Pongau
X 552 016	9131 516	**YR**	Tulln	Tulln
X 552 017	9131 517	**YR**	Feldkirch	Feldkirch
X 552 018	9131 518	**YR**	St. Veit a.d. Glan	St. Veit a.d. Glan
X 552 019	9131 519	**YR**	Riedau	Riedau
X 552 020	9131 520	**YR**	Wien Meidling	Wien Meidling
X 552 021	9131 521	**YR**	Innsbruck	Innsbruck
X 552 022	9131 522	**YR**	Graz	Graz
X 552 023	9131 523	**YR**	Mallnitz	Mallnitz
X 552 024	9131 524	**YR**	Selzthal	Selzthal
X 552 025	9131 525	**YR**	Linz Kleinmünchen	Linz Kleinmünchen
X 552 026	9131 526	**YR**	St. Pölten	St. Pölten
X 552 027	9131 527	**YR**		Fahrleitungsbau Mitte
X 552 028	9131 528	**YR**		Fahrleitungsbau West
X 552 029	9131 529	**YR**		Fahrleitungsbau Ost
X 552 030	9131 530	**YR**		Fahrleitungsbau Süd
X 552 031	9131 531	**YR**	Graz	Bruck a.d. Mur
X 552 032	9131 532	**YR**	Tulln	Göpfritz

▲ **A new series of overhead catenary maintenance vehicles built by Robel has recently been delivered to ÖBB. On 28 January 2012 X 552 402 is seen at Unterpurkersdorf.**

X 552.1 — 2-B

X 552.1, have two separate cabins each housing a driving cab, with a work platform in the centre. Unlike the X552.0 there is no crane, but instead the work platform can be raised and lowered. Details as for X 552.0 except:

Weight: 61 tonnes. **Length over Buffers:** 15.84 m.

Number	*EVN*		*Area/Use*	*Location*
X 552 101	9131 533	**YR**	Landeck	Landeck
X 552 102	9131 534	**YR**	Mallnitz	Leinz
X 552 103	9131 535	**YR**	St. Michael	St. Michael
X 552 104	9131 536	**YR**	Wiener Neustadt	Semmering
X 552 105	9131 537	**YR**	Selzthal	Kleinreifling
X 552 106	9131 538	**YR**	Attnang-Puchheim	Steeg
X 552 107	9131 539	**YR**	Riedau	Wels
X 552 108	9131 540	**YR**	Floridsdorf	Gänserndorf
X 552 109	9131 541	**YR**	Innsbruck	Innsbruck
X 552 110	9131 542	**YR**	Tulln	Brigittenau
X 552 111	9131 543	**YR**	St. Johann/Pongau	Schladming

X 552.4 — B

This is a new series from the Robel firm of Freilassing in Germany based on the X 630 multipurpose vehicle (see below). It is equipped with workshop area, pantograph, work platform and telescopic crane.

Built: 2011.
Builder: Robel, type 54.22.
Engine: Deutz BF 8M 1015CP of 440 kW.
Transmission: Hydraulic.
Wheel Diameter: 840 mm.
Maximum Speed: 100 km/h.
Weight: 27 tonnes.
Length over buffers: 11.90 m.

Number	*New number*		*Location*
X 552 401	9131 401	**YR**	
X 552 402	9131 402	**YR**	Wien Hütteldorf
X 552 451	9131 451	**YR**	
X 552 452	9131 452	**YR**	Wien Heidling

X 554.3 — MGW — B

This class is built on an MTW/OBW 10 frame. Known as "Motorgerüstwagen" (literally scaffolding wagon), they are a variant of the X 552, with an exposed three-part engine and work cage between the two cabs. All three engines can be connected to electric and pneumatic hand tools. The vehicles work in pairs with their cabs at the outer ends.

Built: 2000–01.
Builder: Plasser & Theurer.
Engine: 195 kW.
Maximum Speed: 90 km/h.
Weight: 32 tonnes.
Length over buffers: 10.74 m.

X 554 301 + X 554 302	9231 013 + 014	**YR**	Fahrleitungsbau Süd
X 554 303 + X 554 304	9231 015 + 016	**YR**	Fahrleitungsbau Ost
X 554 305 + X 554 306	9231 017 + 018	**YR**	Fahrleitungsbau West
X 554 307 + X 554 308	9231 019 + 020	**YR**	Fahrleitungsbau Mitte

X 556 — OVERHEAD REBUILDING TRAINS — FUMA/MAGE

These are two trains which can work anywhere on the network. The first is the *Fahrleitungsumbaumaschine* (FUMA) (Overhead line equipment rebuilding machine) and the other is the *Maststellgerät* (MAGE) (mast-erecting machine).

FUMA-Zug

The FUMA-ZUG is made up of X 556 vehicles into a train which is used for renewing the overhead. One vehicle can wind in the old wires (this is an X 501 unpowered vehicle) whilst another plays out the new wires. Work platforms are provided by X 552 vehicles. Wheel arrangement of X 556 001 is 2-B). The formation of a train at a worksite is likely to be X554.1, X 552, X 501, X556.0, X554.2

X 556 301 9135 301 X 501 001 9135 501 X 501 002 9135 502 X 556 001 9133 501

MAGE-Zug

This train consists of X 556 101 (wheel arrangement 3-C) which is the mast-erecting machine and a non-powered trailer. The train can work on its own or as part of a works train.

X 556 101 9133 502

X 600 SERIES. STAFF TRANSPORTERS FOR TRACK MAINTENANCE

BM SERIES STAFF TRANSPORTERS

The BM series are small staff transporters that can haul two or three lightweight trailers on which sleepers, ballast, gas cylinders etc can be transported. Many are also fitted with normal buffing gear and can be used as on-site shunting locos to move for example a wagon of ballast for unloading. They are now being replaced by X 630.

X 626 TYPE BM100 B

Built: 1957 ff.
Builder: ÖBB Werke Wörth.
Engine: Steyr Diesel WD 610 6-cyl. 4-stroke 74 kW.
Tramission: Mechanical.
Wheel Diameter: 500 mm. **Weight**: 7 tonnes.
Haulage capacity: 115 tonnes. **Length over buffers**: 5.25 m.
Maximum Speed: 50 km/h.

g Fitted with GPS.
h Hire vehicle.

Number	*EVN*			*Area/Use*	*Location*
X 626 103	9485 506	**Y**	h	Werke Wörth	Werke Wörth
X 626 104	9485 507	**Y**		Schwarzach	Hofgastein
X 626 109	9485 511	**Y**	g	St. Pölten	Neulengbach
X 626 110	9485 512	**Y**		Linz Vbf	Rohrbach/Berg
X 626 111	9485 513	**Y**		Villach-Süd	Fürnitz
X 626 116	9485 517	**Y**		Mallnitz	Kolbnitz
X 626 137	9485 533	**Y**		Wiener Neustadt	Wiener Neustadt
X 626 139	9485 534	**Y**	g	Krems/Donau	Krems/Donau
X 626 141	9485 536	**Y**		Bruck/Mur	Bruck a.d. Mur
X 626 142	9485 537	**Y**	g	Wels	Sattledt
X 626 143	9485 538	**Y**		Ried im Innkreis	Ried im Innkreis
X 626 144	9485 539	**Y**	g	Bruck a.d. Leitha	Bruck a.d. Leitha
X 626 147	9485 542	**Y**	g	Villach Hbf	Villach
X 626 148	9485 543	**Y**		Wien West	Wien West
X 626 149	9485 544	**Y**	g	Linz Hbf	Freistadt
X 626 151	9485 546	**Y**		Hartberg	Fürstenfeld
X 626 152	9485 547	**Y**	g	Wien ZVB	Wien ZVB
X 626 154	9485 548	**Y**	g	Gänserndorf	Gänserndorf

X 626 161	9485 555	**Y**		Wien West	Wien West
X 626 163	9485 557	**Y**		St.Veit a.d. Glan	Friesach
X 626 165	9485 558	**Y**	g	Mistelbach	Dobermannsdorf
X 626 167	9485 560	**Y**		Schladming	Schladming
X 626 168	9485 561	**Y**		Bruck/Mur	Bruck a.d. Mur
X 626 171	9485 563	**Y**		Neumarkt Kalham	Schärding
X 626 176	9485 567	**Y**		Graz	Leibnitz
X 626 177	9485 568	**Y**	g	Amstetten	Grein Bad Kreuzen
X 626 182	9485 573	**Y**		Villach	Feldkirchen/Kärnten
X 626 185	9485 575	**Y**		Steyr	St. Valentin
X 626 187	9485 576	**Y**		Judenburg	Judenburg
X 626 192	9485 580	**Y**	g	Mistelbach	Mistelbach
X 626 193	9485 581	**Y**		Bad Ischl	Ebensee
X 626 194	9485 582	**Y**		Hartberg	Feldbach
X 626 195	9485 583	**Y**		Klagenfurt	Bleiburg
X 626 196	9485 584	**Y**		Bad Ischl	Bad Ischl
X 626 197	9485 585	**Y**		Floridsdorf	Floridsdorf
X 626 201	9485 589	**Y**		?	
X 626 207	9485 592	**Y**		?	
X 626 214	9485 592	**Y**		?	
X 626 217	9485 600	**Y**		Kirchdorf/Krems	Kirchdorf/Krems
X 626 218	9485 601	**Y**		Spittal/Drau	Spittal/Drau
X 626 220	9485 602	**Y**	g	Hollabrunn	Hollabrunn
X 626 222	9485 603	**Y**		Wien Meidling	Wien Meidling
X 626 223	9485 604	**Y**		Floridsdorf	Wien Nord
X 626 226	9485 607	**Y**	g	Linz Vbf	Linz Vbf
X 626 228	9485 608	**Y**	h	Werke Wörth	Attnang-Puchheim

▲ Several Class 52 steam locomotives have been converted into snow ploughs. ÖBB 9760 314 is the former 52.3636 and has since been renumbered 99 81 9592 521. It is seen at Villach West shed on 7 May 2007.

TRACK MACHINES (OBERBAUWAGEN OBW)

This is the largest group of departmentals after the X 500 series o.l.e. units. They appear in many guises having various attachments to the main frame such as rotary snowploughs, ordinary snowploughs and are also used as ballast spreaders, hydraulic grabs, cranes, etc. They have normal buffing and coupling gear and can be used to haul wagons to engineering sites.

X 627.0 TYPE OBW10 B

These vehicles have a crane and a ballast plough.

Built: 1981–87.
Builder: Plasser & Theurer.
Engine: Deutz of 146 kW.
Transmission: Hydraulic.
Wheel Diameter: 710 mm.
Maximum Speed: 90 km/h.
Weight: 27 tonnes.
Length over Buffers: 9.70–10.13 m.

b Fitted with ballast plough.
s Fitted with sleeper grab.
t Fitted with turntable.

Number	*EVN*			*Area/Use*	*Location*
X 627 021	9120 501	**Y**	t	Bauzug 103	Amstetten
X 627 023	9120 502	**Y**	t	Bruck a.d. Mur	Bruck a.d. Mur
X 627 031	9120 503	**Y**	bst	Reserve	Knittelfeld
X 627 032	9120 504	**Y**	bst	Wien Meidling	Wien Meidling
X 627 033	9120 505	**Y**	bst	Selzthal	Selzthal
X 627 034	9120 506	**Y**	bst	Graz	Graz
X 627 035	9120 507	**Y**	t	Krems	Krems
X 627 036	9120 508	**Y**	t	Wiener Neustadt	Wiener Neustadt
X 627 051	9120 509	**Y**	s	Landeck	Landeck
X 627 052	9120 510	**Y**	s	Kirchdorf/Krems	Kirchdorf/Krems
X 627 053	9120 511	**Y**	bs	Wels	Wels
X 627 054	9120 512	**Y**	bs	Bauzug 102	Strasshof
X 627 055	9120 513	**Y**	bs	Portalkran	Unter-Purkersdorf

X 627.1 SHUNTER B

No crane. Used for shunting.

Built: 1975.
Builder: Plasser.

Number	*EVN*		*Area/Use*	*Location*
X 627 101	9120 514	**Y**	Linz Wegscheid	Linz Wegscheid

X 627.5 TYPE OBW10 B

These vehicles have a crane and winter fittings. Details as for X 627.0 except:

Built: 1978–84.
Builder: Plasser.

b Fitted with ballast plough.
p Fitted with rotary snowplough.
s Fitted with sleeper grab.
t Fitted with turntable.

Number	*EVN*			*Area/Use*	*Location*
X 627 501	9120 515	**Y**	pt	St. Pölten	St. Pölten
X 627 511	9120 516	**Y**	bpst	Stadlau	Wien ZVB
X 627 512	9120 517	**Y**	st	Villach Hbf	Villach Hbf
X 627 513	9120 518	**Y**	st	Villach Süd	Fürnitz
X 627 514	9120 519	**Y**	st	Spittal-Millstättersee	Spittal-Millstättersee

X 627.7 TUNNEL EMERGENCY VEHICLES B

Type OBW10-S2 vehicle. It is similar in appearance to the rest of the X 627 fleet but has a longer cab and no crane.

Built: 1987–88.
Builder: Plasser & Theurer.
Engine: MWM D232V12 of 165 kW.
Transmission: Hydraulic. Clark 13.7LHR.
Wheel Diameter: 730 mm.
Maximum Speed: 80 km/h.
Weight: 37 tonnes.
Length over Buffers: 10.63 m.

Number	*EVN*		*Area/Use*	*Location*
X 627 701	9120 520	**Y**	Netz Sicherheit	Hall in Tirol
X 627 702	9120 521	**Y**	Netz Sicherheit	Pöchlarn

X 627.8 ULTRASONIC TEST CAR B

This is an ultrasonic rail testing vehicle. It is similar in appearance to the rest of the X 627 fleet but has a longer cab and no crane.

Built: 1985.
Builder: Plasser & Theurer.
Engine: KHD F8L413F of 147 kW at 2500 r.p.m.
Transmission: Hydraulic.
Wheel Diameter: 710 mm.
Maximum Speed: 80 km/h.
Weight: 24 tonnes.
Length over Buffers: 12.64 m.

Number	*EVN*		*Area/Use*	*Location*
X 627 801	9120 522	**V**	Messgruppe	Tulln Hbf

X 628 TYPE OBW10 B

These OBW 10 vehicles are used by the permanent way department as a multipurpose vehicle. Staff transport, shunting engine, trench digger, crane are some of the uses. The crane, indeed the whole vehicle can be remotely controlled by radio!

Built: 1989–96.
Builder: Plasser & Theurer.
Engine: KHD 12 cyl of 268 kW.
Transmission: Hydromechanical.
Wheel Diameter: 730 mm.
Maximum Speed: 90 km/h.
Weight: 42 tonnes.
Length over Buffers: 11.35 m.

t Fitted with turntable.
* Equipped for winter operation.

Number	*EVN*			*Area/Use*	*Location*
X 628 001	9120 524	**Y**	t*	Wörgl	Wörgl
X 628 002	9120 525	**Y**	t*	Spittal-Millstättersee	Lienz
X 628 003	9120 526	**Y**		Wolfurt	Wolfurt
X 628 004	9120 527	**Y**	t*	Leoben	St. Michael
X 628 005	9120 528	**Y**		Schnell Umbau Zug	Unter-Purkersdorf
X 628 006	9120 529	**Y**		Wien Stadlau	Wien Stadlau
X 628 007	9120 530	**Y**		Innsbruck	Innsbruck
X 628 008	9120 531	**Y**		Salzburg	Salzburg
X 628 009	9120 532	**Y**		Amstetten	Amstetten
X 628 010	9120 533	**Y**		Attnang-Puchheim	Attnang-Puchheim
X 628 011	9120 534	**Y**		Floridsdorf	Floridsdorf
X 628 012	9120 535	**Y**		Wien West	Wien West
X 628 013	9120 536	**Y**		Gloggnitz	Gloggnitz
X 628 014	9120 537	**Y**		Bauzug 101	Wiener Neustadt
X 628 015	9120 538	**Y**	*	Bauzug 402	Villach

X 629 TYPE OBW9 B

This is classed as OBW9 and is smaller than the OBW10. It is a development of the X 628 with a more powerful motor. Other new features include an air conditioned cab, low-level loading area, disc brakes and remote-controlled track pliers. An intermediate size of vehicle which replaced some of the X 626 series. Staff compartment and telescopic crane/grab.

Built: 1990 (001–004), 1984 (005).
Builder: Plasser & Theurer.
Engine: KHD 6 cyl of 123 kW at 2500 r.p.m.
Transmission: Hydromechanical.
Wheel Diameter: 730 mm.
Maximum Speed: 90 km/h.
Weight: 18 tonnes.
Length over Buffers: 9.24 m.

Number	*EVN*		*Area/Use*	*Location*
X 629 001	9220 501	**Y**	St. Pölten Hbf	St. Pölten Hbf
X 629 002	9220 502	**Y**	Attnang-Puchheim	Ried im Innkreis
X 629 003	9220 503	**Y**	Steyr	Steyr
X 629 004	9220 504	**Y**	Innsbruck	Innsbruck
X 629 005	9220 505	**Y**	Gänserndorf	Gänserndorf

X 630 MULTIPURPOSE VEHICLES B

This is a new series from the Robel firm of Freilassing in Germany. A large cabin has room not only for the driver but also up to six personnel and gives good all round visibility. Because of this the cabin is air conditioned and darkened glass used. Fitted with ZBF, PZB 90, crane. There are various subtypes on which more details are welcome. These new vehicles will replace the remaining X 626 series.

Built: 2001–11.
Builder: Robel, type 54.22.
Engine: Deutz BF 8M 1015CP of 440 kW.
Transmission: Hydraulic.
Wheel Diameter: 840 mm.
Maximum Speed: 100 km/h.
Weight: 27 tonnes.
Length over buffers: 11.90 m.

Number	*EVN*		*Area/Use*	*Location*
X 630 001	9130 008	**0**	Bauzug 401	Leoben
X 630 002	9130 009	**0**	Schwarzenau	Schwarzenau
X 630 003	9130 010	**0**	Linz Hbf	Linz Hbf
X 630 004	9130 011	**0**	Bludenz	Bludenz
X 630 301	9120 301	**0**		
X 630 302	9120 302	**0**		
X 630 303	9120 303	**0**	Wörgl	Wörgl
X 630 304	9120 304	**0**		
X 630 305	9120 305	**0**	Wiener Neustadt	Wiener Neustadt
X 630 306	9120 306	**0**	Schwarzach-St.Veit	Schwarzach-St.Veit
X 630 307	9120 307	**0**		
X 630 501	9130 001	**0**	Salzburg	Salzburg
X 630 502	9130 002	**0**	Wien West	Wien Hütteldorf
X 630 503	9130 003	**0**	Innsbruck	Innsbruck
X 630 504	9130 004	**0**		
X 630 505	9130 005	**0**	Wels	Attnang-Puchheim
X 630 506	9130 006	**0**	Wien Süd	Wien Meidling
X 630 507	9130 007	**0**		
X 630 551	9150 551	**0**		
X 630 552	9150 552	**0**	St.Michael	St.Michael
X 630 553	9150 553	**0**	Floridsdorf	Floridsdorf
X 630 554	9150 554	**0**		
X 630 555	9150 555	**0**		
X 630 556	9150 556	**0**		
X 630 557	9150 557	**0**		
X 630 558	9150 558	**0**	Wels	Wels

X 631 B

These are former Class 2060/2062 locomotives (later X 260/X 262). Most still carry old X 260/X 262 numbers, for details see above.

X 651 TRACK RECORDING CARS 2-B

These are three track recording coaches also known as EM-SAT 120. They have a laser camera and a detachable battery-operated satellite which beams its lasers onto the camera. The EM vehicle is the main track recording unit which is connected to a "Satellite Trolley", the SAT part of the class description.

Built: 2000.
Builder: Plasser & Theurer.
Engine: Deutz BF8M 1015C of 400 kW.
Transmission: Hydraulic.
Wheel Diameter: 840 mm.
Maximum Speed: 120 km/h.
Weight: 49.6 tonnes.
Length over Buffers: 16.14 m.

X 651 001	9163 501	**V**	Wels
X 651 002	9163 502	**V**	Spratzern
X 651 003	9163 503	**V**	Villach Hbf

X 651 004 VIADUCT INSPECTION UNIT 2-B

This is a bridge examination vehicle with a work platform and crane in the centre and cabins containing driving cabs at either end.

Built: 2000.
Builder: Plasser & Theurer.
Engine: Deutz of 400 kW.
Transmission: Hydraulic.
Wheel Diameter: 840 mm.
Maximum Speed: 100 km/h (120 km/h hauled).
Weight: 89 tonnes.
Length over Buffers: 18.80 m.

X 651 004	9142 501	**YR**	Spratzern

X 690 TUNNEL RESCUE TRAINS B-B

These trains have been converted by ÖBB from DB Cargo Sprinters. One power car is fitted out as a fire fighting vehicle for leading into a tunnel. The rear power car is fitted out as a rescue vehicle the intention being to split the train and the rear part takes people away from an incident.

Built: 1996.
Builder: Windhoff.
Engine: 2x Volvo 6-cyl. of 265 kW.
Transmission: Mechanical.
Wheel Diameter: 920 mm.
Maximum Speed: 100 km/h.
Weight: 43.7 tonnes.
Length over Buffers: 20.19 m.

X 690 002	9173 001; ex DB 690.002	Spittal-Millstättersee
X 690 003	9173 003; ex DB 690.003	Mallnitz
X 690 004	9173 005; ex DB 690.004	Böckstein
X 690 502	9173 002; ex DB 690.502	Spittal-Millstättersee
X 690 503	9173 004; ex DB 690.503	Mallnitz
X 690 504	9173 006; ex DB 690.504	Böckstein

OTHER DEPARTMENTALS

SNOWPLOUGHS

The snowploughs detailed here have been generally built on the frames of old locomotives. Snowploughs have now been renumbered in the departmental series.

EVN	*Old No.*		*Converted*	*Frame of*	*Allocation*
99 81 9592 501	985.200	**R**	1954	52.765	Saalfelden
99 81 9592 502	985.201	**R**	1955	52.458	VH
99 81 9592 503	985.202	**R**	1955	52.1448	SP (Weinfeld)
99 81 9592 504	985.203	**R**	1955	52.357	Bischofshofen
99 81 9592 505	985.204	**N**	1956	52.401	SB
99 81 9592 506	985.207	**R**	1959	52.433	Wörgl
99 81 9592 507	985.209	**R**	1960	52.3602	SP
99 81 9592 508	985.213	**R**	1962	52.6940	SL
99 81 9592 509	985.219	**G**	1970	52.6969	Bruck a.d. Leitha
99 81 9592 510	985.220	**R**	1971	52.7052	Spittal-Millstättersee
99 81 9592 511	985.222	**R**	1974	52.3553	LZ
99 81 9592 512	985.227	**G**	1979	52.2374	VH
99 81 9592 513	985.229	**R**	1981	52.2428	BL
99 81 9592 514	985.230	**R**	1984	52.7100	IN
99 81 9592 515	985.231	**R**		52.7595	Reutte in Tirol
99 81 9592 516	-	**R**		52.1442	Landeck
99 81 9592 517	-	**R**		52.7053	Wien ZVBf.
99 81 9592 518	-	**R**		52.6428	Attnang-Puchheim
99 81 9592 519	985.211	**G**	1961	52.6649	BL
99 81 9592 520	985.212	**R**	1961	52.4943	GZ
99 81 9592 521	985.214	**O**	1966	52.3636	VH
99 81 9592 522	985.217	**R**	1968	52.1719	NS
99 81 9592 523	985.223	**G**	1975	52.6312	SL
99 81 9592 524	985.224	**G**	1976	52.478	Schwarzenau
99 81 9592 525	985.225	**G**	1977	52.3615	LZ
99 81 9592 526	985.226	**G**	1978	52.3520	Saalfelden
99 81 9592 527	985.228	**G**	1980	52.7213	Klagenfurt

HEATING UNITS

These are former locomotives used as stationary heating units. They cannot be used for traction.

Number	*Formerly*		*Location*
01117	1670 021	**G**	KD
01137	1146 002	**N**	Wulkaprodersdorf
01138	1042 512		Wörgl RoLa terminal
01139	1042 014		SB
01140	4010 019		Jedlersdorf works
01141	1042 059		Wien Ost
01142	1042 054		Wien Ost
01143	1042 050		Wien Ost
-	1141 019		Bischofshofen

Non-standard livery: N Yellow and green (GySEV colours)

Being transformers for carriage heating, the units are found in yards or stations where carriages stable.

2. INDEPENDENT RAILWAYS

Austria has two types of independent railways. Firstly there is the group of integrated railway undertakings which own their infrastructure and operate trains on it. These railways usually have a long and rich history. In 2001 open access started in Austria. Some of the traditional independent railways were the first to receive open access licenses but these were soon joined by new companies, some of these being (part) owned by existing independent railways. The only foreign operator was Lokomotion who started open access trains over the Brenner route. Today this is still the busiest route for open access in Austria, but Passau-Wien-Hegyeshalom also has a lot of trains operated by new entrants.

CODES

Austria still has many private railways offering feeder services into the ÖBB network or simply providing local transport often in quite delightful backwaters. Most of these lines have retained the old style classifications which have a prefix letter to explain the type of traction:

E	(Elektrolokomotive)	Electric locomotive.
ET	(Elektrotriebewagen)	Electric railcar.
V	(Verbrennungsmotoren)	Diesel locomotive.
VT	(Verbrennungstriebwagen)	Diesel railcar.
X		Departmental.

On the Steiermarkische Landesbahnen some additional classifications exist whilst GySEV uses the MAV (Hungarian State Railways) classification. Lines are standard gauge except where otherwise shown.

2.1. ACHENSEEBAHN AB

Gauge: 1000 mm.
Route: Jenbach–Achensee.
Timetable: 311.
System: Riggenbach rack and adhesion.
Depot: Jenbach.
Website: www.achenseebahn.at

This line is only open in the summer months. The locomotives propel their trains on the rack from Jenbach to Eben and then run round to haul their trains back to the terminus.

STEAM LOCOMOTIVES

1–4 0-4-0RT

In recent years the Achenseebahn has been quite thriving and in 2005 had a surprise for visitors when locomotive No. 4 was added to stock. See section 5 for more details.

Built: 1889/2004*.
Builder: Floridsdorf.
Wheel Diameter: 898 mm.
Length over Buffers: 5.60 m.
Boiler pressure: 0.95 MN/sq m. (135 lbf/sq in).
Weight: 18.3 tonnes.
Cylinders: 330 x 500 mm.
Maximum Speed: 20 km/h.

1	Eben am Achensee
2	Jenbach
3	Achenkirch
4*	Hannah

DIESEL LOCOMOTIVE

D1 B

The Achenseebahn decided it needed a diesel shunting locomotive for shunting at the depot. The loo has no rack gear and thus cannot be used for line work. The locomotive it acquired is interesting in that it is former Inselbahn Langeoog No.3 which was taken into stock in July 1995.

Built: 1949.
Builder: Schöma.
Engine: Deutz F4L514 of 59 kW.
Transmission: Hydraulic.
Wheel Diameter: 580 mm.
Weight: 7.5 tonnes.
Length: 5.00 m.
Maximum Speed:

D1

2.2. GRAZ KÖFLACHER BAHN GKB

Routes: Graz–Wies-Eibiswald/Köflach.
Depots: Graz GKB (Main Depot/Works). Wies-Eibiswald, Köflach (Subsheds).
Timetable: 550.
Website: www.gkb.at

The staple traffic of the GKB used to be coal but this has long since gone. Today the line is a busy commuter route using DMUs and push-pull double-decker trains. Gone are the days of just a few passenger trains a day! Some freight traffic has been retained. For open access GKB is a shareholder of LTE (q.v.) and also has shares in Slovenian open access operator Adria Transport. The latter owns three electrics and one diesel locomotive, which are all registered in Austria under GKB but are operated by LTE. These locomotives are listed under LTE (q.v.). In recent years GKB has been adding a full UIC style number to its locomotives but the old number is still displayed on some of them. GKB now also operates passenger trains under open access on the ÖBB line from Graz to Wettmannstätten via Werndorf and onwards to Wies-Eibiswald.

▲ The Achenseebahn still operates its original rack locomotives. Whilst trains are propelled uphill on the gradient section, on the flat section the loco is in front as could be seen on 24 July 2008 with locomotive 4 at Maurach.

STEAM LOCOMOTIVES

671 0-6-0

This loco is a grand old lady of the former Südbahn which ran on the GKB between 1878 and 1924 and stayed on when it became a private company once again. It was stored in the 1970s but has recently been fitted with a new boiler and is set to steam on for many more years. This locomotive is the oldest locomotive in service on a main line and has never been withdrawn from traffic in its long lifetime!

Built: 1860.
Builder: StEG.
Wheel Diameter: 1285 mm.
Length over Buffers: 14.25 m.
Power: 420 kW.
Boiler Pressure: 0.68 MN/sq m. (110 lbf/sq in).
Weight: 65.6 tonnes.
Cylinders: 460 x 632 mm.
Maximum Speed: 45 km/h.

671 98 45 0029 671-5

CLASS 56 2-8-0

GKB once had 16 of these two-cylinder compound 2-8-0s which were all obtained from ÖBB after WW2 to strengthen its loco fleet as traffic picked up after the war. Being a major coal haulier at that time meant it had priority traffic. This locomotive is now retired from service and has been placed in a new museum at Lieboch station whilst funds are gathered for an overhaul.

Built: 1914.
Builder: Floridsdorf.
Driving Wheel Diameter: 1258 mm.
Length over Buffers: 17.70 m.
Power: 840 kW.
Boiler Pressure: 1.00 MN/sq m. (140 lbf/sq in).
Weight: 68.1 tonnes.
Cylinders: 540/800 x 632 mm.
Maximum Speed: 60 km/h.

56.3115 98 45 0563 115-5

DIESEL LOCOMOTIVES

CLASS DH 80 B

The GKB has had this diesel in stock since 1968 but for many years it never appeared in the inventory. It is a typical German Köf that was used in industry before the GKB acquired it.

Built: 1938.
Builder: BMAG.
Engine: 85 kW.
Transmission: Hydraulic.
Wheel Diameter: 850 mm.
Weight: 16 tonnes.
Length over Buffers: 6.45 m.
Maximum Speed: 45 km/h.

DH 80.1

CLASS DM 100 A-1

These two "locomotives" are in fact track maintenance vehicles something akin to an OBW 10 but converted by GKB from two track machines; V100.1 was a former tamping machine whilst V100.2 was a lining machine.

Built: 19xx; Rebuilt 1978, 1980.
Builder: GKB.
Engine: 76 kW.
Transmission: Mechanical.
Wheel Diameter:
Weight:
Length over Buffers:
Maximum Speed: 25 km/h

V100.1 | V100.2

CLASS DH 600 C

Typical Jenbach shunters but of a type not found on ÖBB.

Built: 1973.
Builder: JW.
Engine: Caterpillar CAT 3412C-DITA of 445 kW.
Length over Buffers: 10.50 m.
Transmission: Hydraulic.
EVN: 92 81 2600 xxx-c
Wheel Diameter: 950 mm.
Weight: 48 tonnes.
Maximum Speed: 60 km/h.

DH 600.1 | DH 600.2 | DH 600.3

CLASS DH 700 C

A one-off shunter built new for GKB.

Built: 1977.
Builder: MaK.
Engine: 6M282A of 515 kW.
Transmission: Hydraulic.
Wheel Diameter: 1000 mm.
Weight: 60 tonnes.
Length over Buffers: 9.86 m.
Maximum Speed: 60 km/h.

DH 700.01 98 45 0700 001-1

CLASS DH 1100 B-B

These are former DB Class 211s rebuilt with Caterpillar engines.

Built: 1961–62.
Builder: Henschel.
Engine: Caterpillar 3512D1 of 840 kW at 1500 rpm.
Length over Buffers: 12.10 m.
Transmission: Hydraulic.
EVN: 92 81 2011 xxx-c
Wheel Diameter: 950 mm.
Weight: 64 tonnes.
Maximum Speed: 110 km/h.

DH 1100.01 (ex DB 211 170-6) | DH 1100.02 (ex DB 211 182-1)

CLASS DH 1500 B-B

These locomotives were the first big diesel locos to be built for the line and brought about the demise of steam in the 1970s. After years of freight-only use they now appear with the modern double-deck passenger stock for which purpose they have been equipped for push-pull working.

Built: 1975–78.
Builder: JW.
Engine: MTU 12V396TC14 of 1200 kW at 1700 rpm.
Length over Buffers: 12.00 m.
Transmission: Hydraulic.
EVN: 92 81 2015 xxx-c
Wheel Diameter: 1000 mm.
Weight: 64 tonnes.
Maximum Speed: 100 km/h.

DH 1500.01 | DH 1500.02 | DH 1500.03 | DH 1500.04 | DH 1500.05 | DH 1500.06

CLASS DH 1700 B-B

With open access giving more opportunities for traffic and heavier trains, GKB acquired a new locomotive from Vossloh in 2003.

Built: 2002.
Builder: Vossloh.
Engine: CAT 3512B-HD of 1700 kW.
Transmission: Hydraulic, Voith L620reU2.
Wheel Diameter: 1000 mm.
Weight: 80 tonnes.
Length over Buffers: 15.20 m.
Maximum Speed: 100 km/h.

DH 1700.1 98 45 0017 001-9

DIESEL RAILCARS

CLASS VT 10 A-A

GKB eliminated steam from its main passenger trains at quite an early date when it obtained these railbuses in the mid 1950s. The arrival of double-deck sets has meant that these vehicles are now spare and are used for occasional excursions only.

Built: 1955/58.
Builder: Uerdingen WMD.
Engine: Büssing U10 of 110 kW.
Transmission: Mechanical.
Weight: 24 tonnes.
Length over Couplers: 13.30 m.
Maximum Speed: 90 km/h.
Accommodation: –/61.

VT10.03 99 45 9001 003-3
VT10.09 99 45 9001 009-0

CLASS VT 70 Bo-2-Bo

An articulated railcar built just a stone's throw from Graz GKB station! These DMUs started the turnaround in GKB passenger operations. Following the arrival of GTW Class 5063 the older type is now used on peak-hours services only.

Built: 1980–85.
Builder: SGP Graz.
Engines: Two MAN D3256 BTYOE of 225 kW.
Transmission: Electric (BBC).
EVN: 95 81 5070 xxx-c
Weight: 54 tonnes.
Length over Couplers: 30.19 m.
Maximum Speed: 90 km/h.
Accommodation: –/50 1T + –/54 (2).

VT 70.01
VT 70.02
VT 70.03
VT 70.04
VT 70.05
VT 70.06
VT 70.07
VT 70.08
VT 70.09
VT 70.10
VT 70.11
VT 70.12
VT 70.13

▲ Both LTE and GKB own a Vossloh type G1700. On 6 July 2006 GKB DH 1700.1 works a LTE cement train at Liesing.

CLASS 5063 2-Bo-2-2

These Stadler GTW 2/8 have been obtained to replace Class VT 70 and to cope with extra traffic via the new (ÖBB owned) Werndorf-Wettmannstätten link. They can work in multiple of up to 3 units.

Built: 2010–11.
Builder: Stadler.
Engines: MAN 640 kW.
Transmission: Electric (ABB).
EVN: 95 81 5063 xxx-c
Weight: 93 tonnes.
Length over Couplers: 55.94 m.
Maximum Speed: 140 km/h.
Accommodation: –/151.

5063 001	5063 004	5063 006	5063 008	5063 010	5063 012
5063 002	5063 005	5063 007	5063 009	5063 011	5063 013
5063 003					

2.3. GYÖR–SOPRON–EBENFURTI VASÚT GySEV RAAB–ÖDENBURG–EBENFURTHER EISENBAHN

Routes: Györ–Sopron–Ebenfurth; Neusiedl–Fertöszentmiklós; Sopron–Szombathely–Szentgotthárd; Rajka–Hegyeshalom–Szombathely; Szombathely–Zalaszentivan; Szombathely–Köszeg.
Depots: Sopron (Main Depot/Works). Györ, Sombathely (Subsheds).
Timetable: 512, 731. **Website**: www.gysev.hu
Liveries: All GySEV stock now carries a green and yellow livery.

This is an international railway jointly owned by Austria and Hungary – a survivor of the old empire! It uses the Hungarian style of classification. In recent years GySEV has been trading locos with MAV and lost its M43, M47 and M62 but gained more V43, M44 some M40s and the solitary M42. It has also obtained new Taurus locomotives. Further Taurus locos are leased from ÖBB (q.v.). Recently GySEV acquired some ÖBB Class 5047 and 5147 DMUs for their lines around Szombathely which have been taken over from MÁV. The old class numbers are now disappearing and the new Hungarian class numbers are starting to appear.

DIESEL LOCOMOTIVES

CLASS 408 (M40) Bo-Bo

Both these locomotives were acquired from MAV in 2001 when the Sopron–Szombathely line was taken over from MAV. The locos were previously M40 208/222.

Built: 1968/69.
Builder: Ganz Mavag.
Engine: Ganz 16VFE17/24 of 735 kW.
Transmission: Electric.
EVN: 92 43 0408 xxx-c
Wheel Diameter: 1040 mm.
Weight: 76 tonnes.
Length: 14.25 m.
Maximum Speed: 100 km/h.

408 401	408 402

CLASS 428 (M42) Bo-Bo

This locomotive was acquired from MAV where it had the same number. It is a one-off being a prototype for a new series which never went into production as MAV decided to modernise its diesel locomotives rather than have new locomotives built.

Built: 1994.
Builder: Ganz Hunslet.
Engine: Deutz MWM TBD604BV12 of 640 kW.
Transmission: Electric.
Wheel Diameter: 1040 mm.
Weight: 66 tonnes.
Length: 14.64 m.
Maximum Speed: 80 km/h.

428 401 98 43 0428 001-4

CLASS 448 (M44) Bo-Bo

These are standard MAV-type shunters some of which were obtained from MAV, some built for GySEV and the last four acquired from Hungarian industry. The type also exists in several former eastern-bloc countries.

Built: 1957–77.
Builder: Ganz Mavag.
Engine: Ganz 16JV 17/24 of 450 kW.
Transmission: Electric.
EVN: 98 43 0448 xxx-c

Wheel Diameter: 1040 mm.
Weight: 62 tonnes.
Length: 11.24 m.
Maximum speed: 80 km/h.

448 301/02/05/08/09/10/11 were formerly MAV M44 001/025/525/008/018/073/122.
448 312/13/14/15 were formerly Hungarian industrial locomotives A25-070/080/038/095.

448 301
448 302
448 303
448 304
448 305
448 306
448 307
448 308
448 309
448 310
448 311
448 312
448 313
448 314
448 315

ELECTRIC LOCOMOTIVES

CLASS 430 (V43) Bo-Bo

These are standard 25 kV electric locos obtained from MAV when GySEV electrified in 1984. In turn GySEV sold its M41 diesels to MAV, none of which now remain on the line. The former MAV numbers are in parentheses.

Built: 1970–80.
Builder-Mech. Parts: Ganz-Mavag.
Builder-Elec. Parts: Ganz.
One hour rating: 4300 kW.
EVN: 91 43 0430 xxx-c

Wheel Diameter: 1180 mm.
Weight: 80 tonnes.
Length over Buffers: 15.70 m.
Maximum Speed: 130 km/h.

430 320 (V43.1320)
430 321 (V43.1321)
430 322 (V43.1322)
430 323 (V43.1323)
430 324 (V43.1324)
430 325 (V43.1325)
430 326 (V43.1326)
430 327 (V43.1327)
430 328 (V43.1328)
430 329 (V43.1329)
430 330 (430 1330)
430 332 (430 1164)
430 333 (430 1130)
430 334 (430 1267)
430 335 (430 1155)

CLASS 470 (1047) Bo-Bo

GySEV and MAV joined forces to order a batch of Taurus electric locomotives which on MAV are Class 470.0 whilst on GySEV they are Class 470.5. GySEV locomotives work Sopron and Szombathely to Budapest but also into Austria on freight trains to Wien and recently on LTE open access trains from Ebenfurth to Gratwein.

Technical details as ÖBB Class 1116.
EVN: 91 43 0470 xxx-c

470 501 ("Sisi"), 470 503 ("Liszt") and 470 505 ("Széchenyi") carry special liveries.

470 501
470 502
470 503
470 504
470 505

DIESEL RAILCARS

CLASS Bamot 1A-A1

This unit was built new for MAV and obtained and rebuilt in 1970. It is now kept at the Budapest Railway Park but is still in GySEV stock.

Built: 1962.
Builder: Györ.
Engine: Two Ganz JH13 5-17 of 110 kW.
Transmission: Hydraulic.
Weight: 37 tonnes.
Length over Buffers: 22.70 m.
Maximum speed: 90 km/h.
Accommodation: –/64.

Bamot 702

CLASS 5047/247

This class is the same as ÖBB Class 5047 but built in 1995. See ÖBB Class 5047 for technical details. 247 503–509 have been obtained second hand from ÖBB.

EVN: 90 43 5047 xxx-c, 95 55 0247 xxx-c

5047 501 | 5047 502

247 503 (5047 008)
247 504 (5047 020)
247 505 (5047 031)
247 506 (5047 044)
247 507 (5047 062)
247 508 (5047 068)
247 509 (5047 100)

▲ GySEV Class V43 has now become rare in Austria. On 21 January 2006 V43 328 hauls a short passenger train near Neufeld. Class V43 has since been reclassified as Class 430.

CLASS 5147/446

This class is the same as ÖBB Class 5147 but built in 1996. See ÖBB Class 5147 for technical details. 446 513–516 have been obtained second hand from ÖBB. Whilst 5147 511–512 have separate numbers for each car, the recent Class 446 additions have one running number per unit and only the long EVR distinguishes the two cars.

EVN: 90 43 5147 xxx-c, 95 55 1446 xxx-c + 95 55 2446 xxx-c

5147 511 | 5147 512

446 513 (5147 003 + 004)
446 514 (5147 005 + 006)
446 515 (5147 007 + 008)
446 516 (5147 009 + 010)

DEPARTMENTAL STOCK

Number	*Built*	*Notes*
APRÓKA	Ruhrtaler 1948	Small shunter at Sopron shed (B-dm).
FJ-001	1987	Overhead line unit with crane.
FJ-205	1987	Overhead line unit with crane.
VF 100	1966	Heating unit, Sopron station. Ex-MAV V42 529.
VF 101	1966	Heating unit, Sopron station. Ex-MAV V42 531.

2.4. HÖHENBAHN REISSECK

Gauge: 600 mm.
Route: Schoberboden–Reisseck.
Timetable:
Website: www.verbund.com/tm/de/reisseck

This is a difficult line for most people to visit being high in the mountains above Kolbnitz from where the access is by funicular. Originally the line's two locomotives were both standard Jenbach types. In 1984 the line received a new Jenbach locomotive which is coupled to two driving trailers and sits in the middle of the train. This is now the regular motive power, the two older locos are in reserve and used on engineering trains.

Number	*Type*	*Built*	*Power*	*Type*
D 1	B dm	Jenbach 2240/1960	15 kW	JW20
D 2	B dm	Jenbach 2406/1963	15 kW	JW20
D 3	B dh	Jenbach 3.274-04/1983	30 kW	DH 40 B6

2.5. LAVAMÜNDER BAHN BETRIEBS GmbH LBB

This new company has taken over a closed ÖBB line. Local saw mills, the GKB, Lavamünd council and Nostalgie Bahnen im Kärnten are partners in moving timber traffic using one of the NBiK preserved diesel locomotives. There have also been diesel hauled excursion trains. GKB provides its license as railway undertaking. Since 2010 the line has been closed and is in need of repairs.

CLASS 383 C

This diesel locomotive was built for the VOEST steel works in Linz but in 1983 was sold to a power station at Jenbach and later came into the hands of ÖDK Zeltweg. It was acquired by NBiK for preservation in 1995.

Built: 1957.
Builder: Mavag/VOEST.
Engine: Deutz F4L514 of 510 kW.
Transmission: Hydraulic.
Wheel Diameter:
Weight: 45 tonnes.
Length: 10.10 m.
Maximum Speed: 30 km/h.

383.10 92 81 2875 000-9

2.6. LOGSERV LOGS

LogServ is an open access operator and a subsidiary of VOEST Alpine Stahl, Linz GmbH. Apart from managing the internal traffic of Linz steelworks it operates open access trains under the brand CargoServ. Under open access the steel works has taken over the movement of raw materials to the works in Linz (Iron ore from Eisenerz, limestone from Steyrling and coal from the Czech Republic) as well as delivering steel coils to various destinations. It also has contracts for freight movements of third parties.

DIESEL LOCOMOTIVES

CLASS V 1504 B-B

These locomotives are former Deutsche Reichsbahn V100s rebuilt by Adtranz in Kassel. Regretfully the original identities have not yet come to light. These locos usually perform trip work around Linz steelworks.

Built: 19xx.
Builder: LEW, Rebuilt 2001 by Adtranz, Kassel.
Engine: CAT 3512 DITA of 1060 kW.
Transmission: Hydraulic.
EVN: 93 81 1504 xxx-c
Wheel Diameter:
Weight: 72 tonnes.
Length: 14.24 m.
Maximum Speed: 80 km/h.

V1504.01 | V1504.02 | V1504.03

▲ Both Logserv and WLC operate three refurbished former DB Class V100 diesel locomotives. Logserv V1504.02 in Cargoserv livery provides the power for an engineering train at Wien Matzleinsdorf on 19 May 2009.

ELECTRIC LOCOMOTIVES

CLASS ES64U2 Bo-Bo

LogServ has three Taurus locomotives leased from MRCE for use on their open access trains. ES64U2 080/081/082 have remote radio control for shunting operations. Otherwise technical details are as ÖBB Class 1116. For full details of MRCE please refer to the Platform 5 European Handbook on German Railways – Part 2 Private Operators, a new edition of which is in preparation.

EVN: 91 80 6182 5xx-c

ES64U2 080 | ES64U2 081 | ES64U2 082

CLASS 1216 Bo-Bo

LogServ also owns three multisystem Class 1216 locomotives for use on its open access trains. These are of subtype B and are identical to ÖBB Class 1216.

EVN: 91 81 1216 xxx-c

1216 930 | 1216 931 | 1216 932

2.7. LTE LOGISTIK und TRANSPORT GmbH LTE

LTE is an open access operator and a subsidiary of the Graz Köflacher Bahn. LTE has also set up its own subsidiary companies in Slovakia, Hungary and Czech Republic to permit through workings to these countries. LTE hauls mostly block trains on the Passau–Wien–Hegyeshalom line as well as from Breclav to Gratwein via Semmering.

DIESEL LOCOMOTIVES

CLASS 2016 Bo-Bo

These locomotives were built by Siemens (type ER 20). In contrast to ÖBB Class 2016 they have no electric train supply but the space is used for greater fuel tank capacity. 2016 920 is in advertising livery for sister company Adria Transport (Slovenia).

See ÖBB 2016 for technical details.

EVN: 92 81 2016 xxx-c

2016 903 Maria
2016 904
| 2016 909
| 2016 920

CLASS 2170 B-B

This is a Vossloh/Mak product and is in fact the prototype locomotive that was exhibited at Innotrans in 2002.

Built: 2002
Builder: VSFT (1001159).
Engine: Caterpillar 3512 B-HD of 1700 kW.
Power: 1700 kW.
Transmission: Hydraulic, Voith L620reU2.
EVN: 92 81 2170 xxx-c
Wheel Diameter: 1000 mm.
Weight: 80 tonnes.
Length: 15.20 m.
Maximum Speed: 100 km/h.

2170 001 Johanna

ELECTRIC LOCOMOTIVES

CLASS 185 Bo-Bo

These locomotives are Bombardier Traxx F140 AC (DB Class 185) hired from Alpha Trains and from RBSAF. They are certified for operation in Germany, Austria and Hungary.

(Technical details as per DB Class 185 – see German Railways Part 1)

EVN: 91 80 6185 xxx-c

185 528	Hermine	185 608	185 609
185 529	Michaela		

CLASS 1216 Bo-Bo

LTE owns one multisystem Class 1216 locomotive and also uses three of the type built for sister company Adria Transport (Slovenia) but registered in Austria. They are of subtype B and are identical to ÖBB Class 1216.

EVN: 91 81 1216 xxx-c

1216 910	(LTE)	1216 921	(Adria)	1216 922	Adria)
1216 920	(Adria)				

2.8. MONTAFONERBAHN AG MBS

Route: Bludenz–Schruns.
Timetable: 420.
Depot: Schruns.
Website: www.montafonerbahn.at

This 12.8 km line runs from the ÖBB junction at Bludenz to a terminal at Schruns, hence the abbreviation MBS. There are through passenger workings onto the ÖBB.

ELECTRIC RAILCARS

ET 10.103/04 Bo-Bo

These two units are former DB diesel railcars (VT 63) acquired in 1961 and rebuilt to Electric. Both these units were made spare in 2001 after the arrival of the new units from Stadler. ET 10.103 is now stored to provide spares for ET 10.104 which is used occasionally on excursion trains. They are still owned by MBS but kept on an industrial line near Dornbirn.

Built: 1935, Rebuilt 1965/74.
Builder – Mech. Parts: Lindner.
Builder – Elec. Parts: AEG Berlin.
Motors: Two of 370 kW.
Weight: 40 tonnes.
Length over Buffers: 22.08 m.
Maximum Speed: 100 km/h.
Accommodation: 8/56.

ET 10.103	(VT 63 905)	ET 10.104	94 81 4142 104-0	(VT 63 907)

ET 10.107/08 Bo-Bo+2-2

These are Swiss built NPZ units.

Built: 1990/94.
Builder – Mech. Parts: SIG/SWP.
Builder – Elec. Parts: ABB.
One Hour Rating: 1650 kW.
EVN: 97 39 9010 xxx-c
Weight: 70 tonnes.
Length over Buffers: 25.00 m.
Maximum Speed: 140 km/h.
Accommodation: –/65 1T.

ET 10.107	ET 10.108

ET10.109/10 Bo-Bo

These new units have allowed older stock to be stored.

Built: 2000.
Builder – Mech. Parts: Stadler.
Builder – Elec. Parts: Adtranz.
One Hour Rating: 800 kW.
EVN: 97 39 9010 xxx-c
Length: 23.514 m.
Weight: 46 tonnes.
Maximum Speed: 140 km/h.
Accommodation: –/56 1T.

ET 10.109 Ernest Hemingway
ET 10.110 Anita Wachter

ET 10.121/22 Bo-Bo+2-2

These are prototypes of the Swiss NPZ units which have been obtained second hand from SBB.

Built: 1984.
Builder – Mech. Parts: FFA.
Builder – Elec. Parts: BBC.
One Hour Rating: 1650 kW.
EVN: 94 81 4480 xxx-c
Weight: 70 tonnes.
Length over Buffers: 25.00 m.
Maximum Speed: 140 km/h.
Accommodation: –/65 1T.

ET 10.121 (RBDe 560 003)
ET 10.122 (RBDe 560 001)

DIESEL LOCOMOTIVES

CLASS V 10.015 D

This is former KFBE V 51.

Built: 1956.
Builder: KHD.
Engine: Deutz T12M625 of 59 kW.
Transmission: Hydraulic.
Wheel Diameter: 1120 mm.
Weight: 60 tonnes.
Length over Buffers:
Maximum Speed: 64km/h.

V 10.016 93 81 2010 016-3

CLASS V10.016 B-B

This locomotive is a former Deutsche Reichsbahn V100 rebuilt by Alstom in Stendal.

Built: 1972.
Builder: LEW, Rebuilt 2009 by Alstom, Stendal.
Engine: CAT 3512 DITA of 1305 kW.
Transmission: Hydraulic.
Wheel Diameter:
Weight: 68 tonnes.
Length: 14.24 m.
Maximum Speed: 100 km/h.

V 10.017 92 80 1203 159-9

DEPARTMENTAL STOCK

CLASS X10 A-1

A former ÖBB Class 5081 converted into an overhead line maintenance unit.

Built: 1965.
Builder: JW.
Engine: Büssing U10.
Transmission: Mechanical.
Length over Buffers: 13.95 m.
Maximum Speed: 90 km/h.

X 10.903 (5081.12)

▲ LTE 185 608 + 529 haul a train of slag from Linz to Miskolc, Hungary near the former Wien Süd station on 14 August 2011.

▼ NÖVOG continues to use 100 year old ex-ÖBB Class 1099 electric locomotives on the Mariazellerbahn, although many of these locos are due to be displaced in 2013 by the arrival of new Stadler EMUs. NÖVOG 1099 011 is seen at Klangen on 26 August 2011.

2.9. NIEDERÖSTERREICHISCHE SCHNEEBERGBAHN GmbH — NÖSBB

Route: Puchberg-Hochschneeberg (9.8 km).
Timetable: 523.
Gauge: 1000 mm.
Website: www.schneebergbahn.at

The ÖBB line from Puchberg to Hochschneeberg was privatised on 01/01/1997. The new company was initially owned 50% by ÖBB and 50% by NÖVOG but is now 100% NÖVOG; since 2010 the infrastructure has been the property of NÖVOG. The biggest change has been the acquisition of some rack fitted push-pull diesel trains.

RACK STEAM LOCOMOTIVES

CLASS 999.0 — 0-4-2RT

Class 999.0 were built for and continue to operate this line. Only two are kept operational at a time and are used on special trains only for which an extra fare applies.

Built: 1893–94.
Builder: Krauss, Linz.
Boiler Pressure: 1.40 MN/sq m. (200 lbf/sq in).
Driving Wheel Diameter: 706 mm.
Rack Wheel Diameter: 575 mm.
Trailing Wheel Diameter: 520 mm.
Max. Speed: 12 km/h.
Gauge: 1000 mm.
System: Abt rack.
Cylinders (2): 320 x 600 mm.
Weight: 18 tonnes.
Length: 5.55 m.
Tractive Effort – Adhesion: 89.2 kN (20070 lbf).
Tractive Effort – Rack: 110.6 kN (24700 lbf).

999 001 | 999 002 | 999 003 | 999 004 | 999 005

RACK DIESEL LOCOMOTIVES

11-13 — B

These new trains were ordered in 1997 and delivered in 1999. The locomotives have a single cab and form a set with a trailer and a driving trailer. The overall length of loco and carriages is 30.416 m whilst seating capacity is 119. The trailers are numbered 21–23 whilst the driving trailers are 31–33. The builders of the carriages are Waagner-Biró and Swoboda. These trains have a bizarre yellow and black colour scheme, hence their nickname of "Salamanders".

Built: 1999.
Builder: Hunslet Barclay.
Engine: Caterpillar 3412E DITTA JW 12 cyl.
Power: 544 kW at 1800 rpm.
Tractive Effort: 100 kN.
Wheel Diameter:
Weight: 15.25 tonnes.
Length:
Maximum Speed: 15 km/h.
Transmission: Hydraulic.

11 FRANZ JOSEF | 12 SISSI | 13 LEO ARNOLDI

14-15 — B

In 2010 two rack and adhesion diesel locomotives were delivered from Stadler. Whilst number 15 immediately passed on to SKGB where it is on long term hire the other is used at the Schneeberg for works trains. On summer weekends it may also appear on passenger trains using a spare set of coaches originally built for steam traction.

Built: 2010.
Builder: Stadler.
Engine: MTU 12V183TB32
Power: 550 kW.
Tractive Effort: 140 kN.
Wheel Diameter: 780 mm.
Weight: 18.3 tonnes.
Length: 8.15 m.
Maximum Speed: 250 km/h.
Transmission: Electric.

14 | 15 (on hire to SKGB)

2.10. NIEDERÖSTERREICHISCHE VERKEHRS-ORGANISATIONSGESELLSCHAFT mbH NÖVOG

Website: www.noevog.at

NÖVOG took over several ÖBB branch lines in Niederösterreich. Whilst most of these were formally closed before the handover as they had not seen any trains for years some have regular services. These are the narrow gauge lines St.Pölten–Mariazell and Waidhofen/Ybbs–Gstadt. The narrow gauge lines from Gmünd to Groß Gerungs and Litschau are tourist operations as are the standard gauge lines Krems–Emmersdorf and Retz–Drosendorf. Trains on the latter are operated by ÖBB whilst Krems–Emmersdorf trains use NÖVOG rolling stock.

2.10.1. ST. PÖLTEN–MARIAZELL

84.2 km. Electrified in 1911.

Gauge: 760 mm.
System: 6.5 kV 25 Hz AC.
Depots: St.Pölten Alpenbahnhof, Obergrafendorf (subshed). A new shed is being built at Laubenbachmühle.
Timetable: 115.

STEAM LOCOMOTIVES

CLASS 298.2 0-6-2T

This two cylinder compound locomotive is the last of a class of three built for the Niederösterreichischen Landesbahnen (NÖLB) for use on the line from St. Pölten to Mariazell. It was based at Gmünd for many years for use on the narrow gauge network there, but has now returned to home territory and is currently under overhaul.

Built: 1905.
Builder: Krauss, Linz.
Tractive Effort: 76.5 kN (17200 lbf).
Driving Wheel Diameter: 800 mm.
Length over Couplings: 7.804 m.
Boiler Pressure: 1.28 MN/sq m. (185 lbf/sq in).
Weight: 27.5 tonnes.
Cylinders: (2) 320 x 400 mm, 500 x 400 mm.
Maximum Speed: 35 km/h.

298.207

CLASS 399 0-8+4

Four Class 399 have been taken over from ÖBB, of which 399.006 is operational on the Mariazellerbahn.

Built: 1908.
Builder: Krauss, Linz.
Tractive Effort: 80.4 kN (18080 lbf).
Driving Wheel Diameter: 900 mm.
Length Over Couplings: 11.665 m.
Boiler Pressure: 1.28 MN/sq m. (185 lbf/sq in).
Weight: 45.1 tonnes.
Cylinders: 410 x 450 mm.
Maximum Speed: 40 km/h.

399.06 (as "Mh.6")

ELECTRIC LOCOMOTIVES

CLASS 1099 C-C

These old locomotives are still struggling on, not helped by the poor availability of the two EMU sets of Class 4090. Most services to Laubenbachmühle are now worked by DMUs! At the end of 2012 the first new EMUs will arrive from Stadler. Only a few Class 1099 will then be kept for excursion trains. Go now while the old locos are still in regular use! 1099 003/005/006/009/012 are stored.

Built: 1909–14.
Builder – Mech.Parts: Krauss, Linz.
Builder – Elec.Parts: Siemens Wien.
One Hour Rating: 420 kW.
Maximum Tractive Effort: 102 kN.
Wheel Diameter: 800 mm.
Weight: 49.8 tonnes.
Length over Buffers: 11.02 m.
Maximum Speed: 50 km/h.

1099 001	1099 004	1099 007	1099 010	1099 012	1099 014
1099 002	1099 005	1099 008	1099 011	1099 013	1099 016
1099 003	1099 006	1099 009			

DIESEL LOCOMOTIVES

CLASS 2092 C

Previously a station shunter, this loco was kept at Obergrafendorf and was taken over by NÖVOG.

Built: 1943.
Builder: Windhoff.
Engine: Deutz 6 M517 of 100 kW (134 h.p.).
Gauge: 760 mm.
Maximum Tractive Effort: 49 kN.
Driving Wheel Diameter: 700 mm.
Transmission: Hydraulic.
Weight: 16.5 tonnes.
Length over Buffers: 5.325 m.
Maximum Speed: 25 km/h.

2092.04 OG

CLASS 2095 B-B

The standard ex-ÖBB locomotive for the narrow gauge.

Built: 1961–62.
Builders: SGP Floridsdorf.
Engine: SGP 12a of 440 kW (590 hp).
Maximum Tractive Effort: 98 kN.
Driving Wheel Diameter: 900 mm.
Maximum Speed: 60 km/h.
Transmission: Hydraulic.
Weight: 30 tonnes.
Length over Buffers: 10.40 m.

2095 007	2095 008	2095 009	2095 010	2095 011	2095 015

ELECTRIC MULTIPLE UNITS

CLASS 4090 — 3/4-CAR UNITS

Two new units were built in 1994.

4090 001 + 7090.001 + 7090.002 + 4090.002: B4hET + B4hTI + B4hTI + B4hET (DMBSO–TSO–TSO–DMBSO).
4090 003 + 7090.003 + 6090.001: B4hET + B4hTI + B4hES (DMBSO–TSO–DTSO).

Built: 1994.
Builder – Mech Parts: SGP.
Builder – Elec. Parts: Elin.
Traction Motors: 4 x 330 kW three phase.
Accommodation: –/40 1T + –/56 (+ –/56) + –/40 1T.
Wheel Arrangement: Bo-Bo + 2-2 (+ 2-2) + 2-2.
Weight: 36 + 28 (+28) + 36 or 23 tonnes.
Length over Couplers: 17.30 + 16.30 (+ 16.30) + 17.30 m.
Maximum Speed: 70 km/h.

4090 001 | 4090 002 | 4090 003

▲ 4090 002 was still owned by ÖBB when it approached Kirchberg an der Pielach on 09 July 2010. The EMU is now owned by NÖVOG.

DIESEL MULTIPLE UNITS

CLASS 5090 SINGLE UNITS

Single cars based on the VT30 design of the Steiermärkische Landesbahnen.

B4VT (DMSO).

Built: 1991–95.
Builder: Bombardier Wien.
Engine: 188 kW.
Accommodation: –/62.
Weight: 31.50 tonnes.
Wheel Arrangement: Bo-Bo.
Transmission: Electric.
Length over Couplings: 18.30 m.
Max. Speed: 70 km/h.

5090 007 is on hire to SLB.

5090 007 | 5090 011 | 5090 012 | 5090 014 | 5090 015 | 5090 016

2.10.2. WAIDHOFEN/YBBS–GSTADT

5.5 km. Rest of the system is now closed. The former Ybbstalbahn is now called Citybahn.

Gauge: 760 mm.
Depot: Waidhofen/Ybbs.
Timetable: 132.

DIESEL LOCOMOTIVES

CLASS 2095 B-B

See section 2.10.1 for technical details.

2095 013 | 2095 014

DIESEL MULTIPLE UNITS

CLASS 5090 SINGLE UNITS

See section 2.10.1 for technical details.

5090 009 | 5090 010 | 5090 017

2.10.3. GMÜND–GROSS GERUNGS, GMÜND–LITSCHAU

68.4 km. This is a summer-only tourist operation.

Gauge: 760 mm.
Depot: Gmünd.
Timetables: 801,802.

STEAM LOCOMOTIVES

CLASS 399 0-8+4

Three Class 399 are kept at Gmünd, of which only 399.01 is operational. See section 2.10.1 for technical details.

399.01 | 399.03 | 399.04

DIESEL LOCOMOTIVES

CLASS 2091 1-Bo-1

These two locomotives had been part of the ÖBB nostalgic fleet. Other examples have been preserved by preservation groups.

Built: 1937.
Builder: Simmering.
Engine: Simmering R8 of 155 kW (208 hp).
Maximum Tractive Effort: 34 kN.
Driving Wheel Diameter: 820 mm.
Maximum Speed: 50 km/h.
Transmission: Electric. Siemens.
Weight: 23.2 tonnes.
Length over Buffers: 10.80 m.

2091.07 | 2091.09

CLASS 2095 B-B

See section 2.10.1 for technical details.

2095 005 | 2095 012

DIESEL MULTIPLE UNITS

CLASS 5090 SINGLE UNITS

See section 2.10.1 for technical details.

5090 008 | 5090 013

2.10.4. KREMS–EMMERSDORF

34.1 km. This is a summer-only tourist operation. The section between Emmersdorf and Sarmingstein is now closed.

Depot: Etsdorf-Straß.
Timetable: 811.

DIESEL LOCOMOTIVES

CLASS 2043 B-B

Three of these have been bought from Österreichischer Club für Diesellokomotivgeschichte who had obtained them from ÖBB. 2043.015 is used for spares only. 2043.024 is in fact former ÖBB 2043.065.

See ÖBB Class 2043 for technical details.

2043.015 | 2043.024 | 2043.027

2.11. RAIL PROFESSIONALS STÜTZ GmbH RPS

This privately owned new entrant has been active since the end of 2010. RPS works spot trains on the Passau–Hegyeshalom route in co-operation with various German operators. Locos used are mostly from partners but the ex-ÖBB electrics are being used as well as pilots or on trains with less weight.

ELECTRIC LOCOMOTIVES

CLASS 1041 Bo-Bo

This 1950s design was the follow-on from Class 1040 and has now been withdrawn by ÖBB. RPS obtained its locomotive second hand from the ÖBB nostalgic fleet. Locos are formally based at Amstetten but may be stabled at Wien Penzing or Gramatneusiedl as well.

Built: 1952–54.
Builder – Mech. Parts: SGP.
Builder– Elec. Parts: Siemens/BBC/AEG.
One Hour Rating: 2360 kW.
Maximum Tractive Effort: 196 kN.
Wheel Diameter: 1350 mm.
Weight: 83.8 tonnes.
Length over Buffers: 15.32 m.
Maximum Speed: 80 km/h.

1041.202 93 81 1041 202-1 Amstetten

▲ In 2011 NÖVOG started to operate the Krems-Emmersdorf branch line. The excursion trains were hauled by ex-ÖBB 2043.024 in a rather strange livery. The train waits at Spitz station on 29 May 2011.

CLASS 1141 Bo-Bo

A development of Class 1041 with similar duties.

Built: 1955–57.
Builder – Mech. Parts: Floridsdorf.
Builder – Elec. Parts: Siemens/AEG/Elin.
One Hour Rating: 2480 kW.
Maximum Tractive Effort: 196 kN.
Wheel Diameter: 1300 mm.
Weight: 83 tonnes.
Length over Buffers: 15.26 m.
Maximum Speed: 110 km/h.

1141 024 93 81 1141 024-8 Amstetten

DIESEL LOCOMOTIVE

CLASS 2060 B

Obtained second hand from ÖBB and is used on shunting duties and occasional engineering trains. For technical details see ÖBB Class X 260 (Departmental Stock).

2060 082 93 81 2060 082-1 Amstetten

2.12. RAIL TRANSPORT SERVICE GmbH RTS

RTS is 100% owned by constructor Swietelsky who is active in the field of track works. RTS has been active since 2005 and moves track machines and other equipment to construction sites as well as hauling ballast trains. RTS has a sister company in Hungary (MÁV Épcell) and a subsidiary in Germany (RTS Germany). In addition to engineering trains RTS is also active in the spot market, mostly on the Passau–Hegyeshalom route. RTS has a huge depot for its diesel locos and for all kinds of track machines at Fischamend on the Fischamend–Götzendorf branch line.

ELECTRIC LOCOMOTIVES

CLASS 1216 Bo-Bo

RTS owns three multisystem Class 1216 locomotives for use on their open access trains. These are of subtype C and are identical to ÖBB Class 1216. They are commissioned to work in Austria, Germany, Hungary and Slovakia. Electric locos are usually stabled at Gramatneusiedl. See ÖBB Class 1216 for technical details.

EVN: 91 81 1216 xxx-c

1216 901 | 1216 902 | 1216 903

DIESEL LOCOMOTIVES

CLASS 2016 Bo-Bo

These locomotive were built by Siemens (type ER 20) In contrast to ÖBB Class 2016 they have no electric train supply but the space is used for greater fuel tank capacity. Diesel locos are either kept at the RTS depot at Fischamend or stabled at Gramatneusiedl. See ÖBB Class 2016 for technical details.

EVN: 92 81 2016 xxx-c

2016 905 | 2016 906 | 2016 907 | 2016 908

▲ Open access operator RPS uses former ÖBB Classes 1041 and 1141 on some of their freight trains. On 29 September 2011 1141 024 (carrying the pre-computer number 1141.24) waits to take over a freight train at Jedlersdorf.

▼ RTS operates a fleet of refurbished former ÖBB Class 2143 diesels mostly on engineering trains. 2143.032 performs such a duty at Klosterneuburg-Weidling on 16 July 2011.

CLASS 2143 B-B

These locomotives have been obtained second hand from ÖBB via various locomotive dealers. Some have been modernised with rebuilt cab interiors and new engines. For more technical details see ÖBB Class 2143.

Engine: SGP T12c of 1100 kW (1475 hp); Caterpillar of 1385 kW *.
Weight: 67 (* 70) tonnes. **Train Heating**: None.
EVN: 92 81 2143 xxx-c

2143 004	2143 007 *	2143 012 *	2143 025 *	2143 032 *
2143 005 *	2143 010	2143 014 *	2143 026 *	2143 077 *

CLASS 2062 B

This locomotive was obtained second hand from ÖBB and is used on shunting duties at Fischamend depot. For technical details see ÖBB Class X262 (Departmental Stock).

2062 031

CLASS 2067 C

Like Class 2143 these locos have been obtained second hand from ÖBB and have been re-engined. For more technical details see ÖBB Class 2067.

Engine: Caterpillar of 440 kW.
EVN: 93 81 2067 xxx-c

2067 017	2067 023	2067 091

CLASS 9485 TYPE BM100 B

Obtained second hand from ÖBB. For technical details see ÖBB Class X626 (Departmental Stock).

99 81 9485 541-2 (ex ÖBB X626 146)

2.13. SALZBURGER LOKALBAHN SLB

2.13.1. STANDARD GAUGE LINES

Routes: Salzburg–Lamprechtshausen, Bürmoos–Trimmelkam (35.3 km).
System: 1000 V DC. **Depot/Works**: Salzburg Itzling.
Timetable: 210. **Website**: www.slb.at

This line is the remnant of a former light railway, the Salzburger Eisenbahn & Tramway Gesellschaft (SETG) which was formed in 1888. This ran from Berchtesgaden (with a branch to Königsee) in Germany. The line was taken over by the city in 1947 and was known as the Salzburger Stadtwerke Verkehrsbetriebe (SVB). Only the line from Salzburg to Lamprechtshausen remains plus the branch from Bürmoos to Trimmelkam which was taken over from Stern & Hafferl on 1st January 1994. Major alterations have taken place at the Salzburg end where the terminal station has been put underground. The line is now known as the Salzburger Lokalbahn, but is still owned by the city. SLB is also licensed as an open access operator and carries block trains from Salzburg Liefering to Hüttau as well as shunting at Salzburg and Hallein. SLB also provides pilot locos for the Logserv steel train to Tarvisio.

ELECTRIC LOCOMOTIVES

E 11 Bo

This small electric locomotive was obtained second hand in 1982 from Bahnen der Stadt Monheim in Germany, where it was No.14.

Built: 1913.
Builder – Mech. Parts: AEG.
Builder – Elec. Parts: AEG.
Power: 150 kW.
Wheel Diameter: 900 mm.
Weight: 48 tonnes.
Length over Buffers: 6.25 m.
Maximum Speed: 30 km/h.

E 11

E 60 Bo-Bo

The first two locos were built new for the line and the last two were obtained from SAKOG in 1974 and 1994 respectively.

Built: 1952.
Builder – Mech. Parts: SGP Graz.
Builder – Elec. Parts: BBC (Elin§).
Power: 380 kW (270 kW*, 292 kW§).
Wheel Diameter: 900 mm.
Weight: 46 (* 44.8) tonnes.
Length over Buffers: 11.90 m.
Maximum Speed: 60 km/h (*§ 50 km/h).

E 61
E 62
E 63 (E 27 002)*
E64 (E 27 001)§

▲ SLB keeps an interesting collection of vintage rolling stock. On 11 October 2009 E 11 and ET 1 stand in front of Itzling shed.

E 71 Bo-Bo

Built new for the line to handle increasing freight tonnage that was getting too much for the older locos.

Built: 1986.
Builder – Mech. Parts: Knotz.
Builder – Elec. Parts: AEG.
Power: 600 kW.
Wheel Diameter: 1000 mm.
Weight: 73 tonnes.
Length over Buffers: 12.96 m.
Maximum Speed: 60 km/h.

E 71

E 91(1216)/183 Bo-Bo

Built new for open access freight traffic. This is a Siemens locomotive of the same type as ÖBB Class 1216. It is of subtype C. For technical details see ÖBB Class 1216. 183 701 hired from Siemens is of the same type but registered in Germany.

EVN: 91 81 1216 xxx-c 91 80 6183 xxx-c

E 91 (1216 940) | 183 701

DIESEL LOCOMOTIVES

SLB has obtained some diesel shunters in recent years which are involved in the open access arrangements. SLB uses the diesels for shunting and trip working from Salzburg to final destinations such as Hallein, Schwanenstadt and Hüttau as well as on RCA trip freights from Golling to Werfen.

V 82 C

The SLB has obtained this diesel from the Wiener Lokalbahn, the former WLB V 80.

Built: 1962.
Builder: JW.
Engine: JW 600 of 445 kW.
Transmission: Hydraulic.
Wheel Diameter: 950 mm.
Weight: 48 tonnes.
Length over Buffers: 10.50 m.
Maximum Speed: 60 km/h.

V 82 (92 81 2000 082-5)

V 83–87 B-B

The search for new locomotives coincided with ÖBB receiving its new Class 2070s and disposing of Class 2048s. SLB has bought some 2048s and had them overhauled at St.Pölten works. The locomotives are DB Class 211s that were re-engined by Layritz and became ÖBB Class 2048.

Built: 1962.
Wheel Diameter: 950 mm.
Builder: Krauss Maffei, MaK, KHD (rebuilt by Layritz).
Engine: Caterpillar type 351281 of 810 kW (1085 hp) at 1500 rpm.
Transmission: Hydraulic, Voith.
Length over Buffers: 12.10 m.
Maximum Speed: 100 km/h.
Weight: 64 tonnes.
EVN: 92 81 2000 08x-c

V 83 (ex MWB V 1101, ex ÖBB 2048 001-8 ex DB 211 297-7)
V 84 (ex ÖBB 2048 002-6 ex DB 211 084-9)
V 85 (ex ÖBB 2048 003-4 ex DB 211 099-7)
V 86 (ex ÖBB 2048 004-2 ex DB 211 100-3)
V 87 (ex ÖBB 2048 018-2 ex DB 211 119-3)

ELECTRIC RAILCARS

ET 1 — Bo

Built for the Salzburger Lokalbahn then to Stern & Hafferl in 1954. Used on various lines but ended up at Bürmoos and passed back to SVB in 1994 when SVB took over the Bürmoos-Trimmelkam line. It has since regained its original number. Departmental car.

Built: 1908.
Builder – Mech. Parts: MAN.
Builder – Elec. Parts: SSW.
Power: 138 kW.
Weight: 18 tonnes.
Length over Buffers: 9.31 m.
Maximum Speed: 50 km/h.
Accommodation: –/32.

ET 1 (StH 20.105)

MBC 3 — Bo

This old railcar is now in "Nostalgic" service.

Built: 1908.
Builder – Mech. Parts: MAN.
Builder – Elec. Parts: SSW.
Power: 126 kW.
Weight: 17.8 tonnes.
Length over Buffers: 9.37 m.
Maximum Speed: 40 km/h.
Accommodation: 8/24.

MBC 3 (ET 3)

ET 6–7 — Bo

No. 6 is an original unit built for the line but 7 was originally Konigl. Bayr. Staatsbahn No. 101 becoming DRB ET 184 01. In 1943 it became SETG MC 16 then MC 27 and ET 27 until 1981 when it became ET 7. Both in "Nostalgic" service.

Built: 1908, 1907.
Builder – Mech. Parts: MAN.
Builder – Elec. Parts: SSW.
Power: 306 kW.
Weight: 18 tonnes.
Length over Buffers: 9.37 m.
Maximum Speed: 60 km/h.
Accommodation: –/32.

ET6 Georg Rendl | ET7

ET 10 — Bo

Another original Salzburg unit built as SETG MG1 later becoming ET 11 and from 1981 it was ET 1 but in 1994 the original ET 1 returned so it has now been renumbered yet again to ET 10! Latterly used as a breakdown vehicle; in 2011 it was restored to original condition and is now considered part of the "Nostalgic" fleet.

Built: 1919.
Builder – Mech. Parts: MAN.
Builder – Elec. Parts: SSW.
Power: 126 kW.
Weight: 16.6 tonnes.
Length over Buffers: 9.70 m.
Maximum Speed: 40 km/h.

ET 10

ET 32–33 — Bo-Bo

Built for SVB (ET 33) and StH (ET 32). Now in "Nostalgic" service and as reserve.

Built: 1951.
Builder – Mech. Parts: SGPG.
Builder – Elec. Parts: SSW.
Power: 612 kW.
Weight: 37.5 tonnes.
Length over Buffers: 16.90 m.
Maximum Speed: 60 km/h.
Accommodation: –/48.

ET 32 (StH 20.108) | ET 33

ET 41–54 Bo-2-Bo

These new articulated light rail-style vehicles were built over a period of 9 years and have transformed the line. ET 49–54 are to have low floor sections added during 2012/13.

Built: 1983 (41–45), 1988 (46–50), 1992 (51–54).
Builder – Mech. Parts: SGP Graz.
Builder – Elec. Parts: AEG.
Power: 600 kW.
Weight: 50.0 tonnes.
Length over Couplers: 28.40 m.
Maximum Speed: 80 km/h.
Accommodation: 32 (8) + 32 (8). 100 standees.

ET 41 Stadt Salzburg
ET 42 Bergheim
ET 43 Oberndorf
ET 44 Bürmoos
ET 45 Lamprechtshausen
ET 46 Anthering
ET 47 Nußdorf
ET 48 Göming
ET 49 St. Georgen
ET 50 Freilassing
ET 51 Berchtesgaden
ET 52 Dorfbeuern
ET 53 St. Pantaleon
ET 54 Laufen

ET 55–58 Bo-2-Bo

A development of ET 41–54 with swing-plug doors and a GPS-based information system. They will have low floor sections added during 2012/13.

Built: 2001–2002.
Builder – Mech. Parts: Siemens SGP.
Builder – Elec. Parts: Bombardier
Power: 600 kW.
Weight: 49.4 tonnes.
Length over Couplers: 28.40 m.
Maximum Speed: 80 km/h.
Accommodation: 32 (8) + 32 (8). 100 standees.

ET 55 Land Salzburg
ET 56 Land Oberösterreich
ET 57 Ober Innviertel
ET 58 Partnerstadt Dresden

▲ Some SLB standard EMUs are now being rebuilt by adding a low floor section in the middle. SLB ET48 is seen in original condition on 11 May 2007 passing Muntigl.

2.13.2. PINZGAUER LOKALBAHN (NARROW GAUGE)

Route: Zell am See–Krimml (52.7 km).
Gauge: 760 mm.
Timetable: 230.
Depot/Works: Tischlerhäusl.
Website: www.pinzgauerlokalbahn.at

In 2008 SLB took over the narrow gauge line from Zell am See to Krimml. Since then the closed Mittersill–Krimml section has been rebuilt and new rolling stock introduced.

STEAM LOCOMOTIVES

Ds 03 — 0-8+4

This former ÖBB Class 399 locomotive is in regular use on the summer only steam excursions. For technical details see NÖVOG Class 399 (section 2.10.1).

Ds 03 (ex 399.03)

Ds 07 — 0-6-2T

This former ÖBB Class 498 locomotive had been plinthed at Obergrafendorf for many years. It has been bought by Pinzgauer Lokalbahn with a view to restoring it into working order sometime in the future.

Built: 1931.
Builder: Krauss Linz.
Driving Wheel Diameter: 800 mm.
Length over Buffers: 8.02 m.
Maximum Speed: 40 km/h.
Boiler Pressure: 1.25 MN/sq m. (180 lbf/sq in).
Weight: 28.1 tonnes.
Power: 250 kW.
Cylinders: 350 x 400 mm.

Ds 07 (ex 498.07)

DIESEL LOCOMOTIVES

Vs 51 — C

Used as station shunters (ÖBB Class 2092) they had all been withdrawn by their previous owner. One locomotive was acquired by Pinzgauer Lokalbahn and has been restored into working order for shunting at Tischlerhäusl depot.

Built: 1943–44.
Builder: Windhoff.
Gauge: 760 mm.
Maximum Tractive Effort: 49 kN.
Driving Wheel Diameter: 700 mm.
Engine: Deutz 6 M517 of 100 kW (134 hp).
Transmission: Hydraulic.
Weight: 16.5 tonnes.
Length over Buffers: 5.325 m.
Maximum Speed: 25 km/h.

Vs 51 (ex 2092.02)

Vs 71–73 — B-B

Three ÖBB Class 2095 locomotives have been taken over by Pinzgauer Lokalbahn, of which Vs 71 is in its original livery from 1958. The locos are used on occasional freight trains and on the summer only "vintage diesel" train. See section 2.10.1 for technical details.

Vs 71		(ex 2095 001)
Vs 73		(ex 2095 006)
Vs 72	"Wald im Pinzgau"	(ex 2095 004)

▲ SLB uses some former ÖBB Class 2095 locomotives on the narrow gauge Pinzgauer Lokalbahn mostly on freight and engineering trains. On 13 July 2010 Vs 73 works an engineering train near Neukirchen.

▼ After taking over the Pinzgauer Lokalbahn SLB quickly repainted the ex-ÖBB Class 5090 DMUs. VTs 15 leaves Pirtendorf with a service bound for Zell am See on 13 July 2010.

Vs 81–83 B-B

These new diesel locomotives were based on a successful design built for the Zillertalbahn. The first of these new locomotives was obtained by ÖBB and received the number 2096 001 but has never been in regular use. It was only after privatisation that the loco was quickly put into service. Two more have been added later. Together with push pull sets they can be found on passenger trains.

Built: 2007–2012.
Builder: Gmeinder (Type D75 BB-SE).
Engine: Caterpillar 3412 E DI-TTA of 746 kW at 2100 rpm.
Transmission: Hydraulic, Voith L3r4zseU2.
Maximum speed: 70 km/h.
Wheel Diameter: 920 mm.
Weight: 50 tonnes.
Length: 14.53 m.

Vs 81 "Land Salzburg" (ex 2096 001)
Vs 83
Vs 82 "Pinzgau"

DIESEL MULTIPLE UNITS

VTs 11–16 SINGLE UNITS

These are former ÖBB Class 5090 DMUs. For technical details see section 2.10.1.

VTs 11 "Hollersbach" (ex 5090.001)
VTs 12 "Niedernsill" (ex 5090.002)
VTs 13 "Smaragddorf Bramberg" (ex 5090.003)
VTs 14 "Piesendorf" (ex 5090.004)
VTs 15 "Uttendorf/Weißsee" (ex 5090.005)
VTs 16 "Stuhlfelden" (ex 5090.006)
VTs 17 hired from NÖVOG (ex 5090.007)

2.14. SALZKAMMERGUTBAHN GmbH SKGB

Route: St. Wolfgang–Schafbergspitze (5.9 km).
Timetable: 173.
Gauge: 1000 mm.
Website: www.schafbergbahn.at

In 2006 ÖBB privatised their rack railway on the Schafberg. The new company is majority owned by Salzburg AG, the parent company of Salzburger Lokalbahn (SLB).

STEAM LOCOMOTIVES

Z 1–6 0-4-2RT

This class was originally built for the Schafbergbahn and taken over by SKGB including the sole loco which had worked on the Schneebergbahn for several years. 999 105 is now owned by the Technical Museum and is plinthed at St.Wolfgang. Only two locos are kept operational at a time and are used on special trains only for which an extra fare applies.

Built: 1896–1900.
Builder: Krauss, Linz.
Boiler Pressure: 1.38 MN/sq m. (200 lbf/sq.in).
Driving Wheel Diameter: 706 mm.
Rack Wheel Diameter: 575 mm.
Trailing Wheel Diameter: 520 mm.
Max. Speed: 12 km/h.
System: Abt rack.
Cylinders (2): 320 x 600 mm.
Weight: 17.4 tonnes.
Length: 5.50 m.
Tractive Effort – Adhesion: 89.2 kN (20070 lbf).
Tractive Effort – Rack: 110.6 kN (24700 lbf).

Z 1 (999 101)
Z 2 (999 102
Z 3 (999 103)
Z 4 (999 104)
Z 6 (999 106)

Z 11–14 — 0-4-2RT

These relatively new locomotives are oil fired and designed for one-man operation and were introduced by ÖBB as Class 999.2. This is the regular motive power of most passenger trains.

Built: 1991, 1996.
Builder: SLM Winterthur.
Boiler Pressure: 1.6 MN/sq m.
Driving Wheel Diameter: 705 mm.
Trailing Wheel Diameter: 493 mm.
Max. Speed: 12 km/h.
System: Abt rack.
Cylinders (2): 280 x 400 mm.
Rack Wheel Diameter: 573 mm.
Weight: 15.5 tonnes.
Length: 6.26 m.

Z 11 (999 201)
Z 12 (999 202)
Z 13 (999 203)
Z 14 (999 204

DIESEL LOCOMOTIVE

VZ 31 — B

This is one of the two new diesel locomotives built for NÖSBB. For technical details see section 2.9. The loco is on hire to SKGB.

VZ 31 (NÖSBB 15)

▲ One of the two new Stadler rack diesel locomotives delivered to NÖSBB has been leased to SKGB where it has been allocated number VZ 31. On 14 July 2010 the loco passes Aschinger on an engineering train.

DIESEL RAILCARS

VTZ 21–22 2-B

These railcars had been ordered by ÖBB to work exclusively on the Schafbergbahn. They passed to SKGB and are used during peak hours on summer weekends.

Built: 1964.
Builder: SGP.
Engine: SGP S8 of 330 kW.
Transmisson: Hydraulic.
Maximum Speed: 12 km/h (rack), 20 km/h (adhesion).
Accommodation: –/78.
System: Abt rack.
Weight: 32.9 tonnes.
Length over couplings: 14.89 m.

VTZ 21 | VTZ 22

2.15. STEIERMARKBAHN STB

This new entrant is the open access subsidiary of Steiermärkische Landesbahnen (StLB). STB operates automotive trains from Gleisdorf to Wiener Neustadt as well as engineering trains in Steiermark. Recently STB has also operated a lot of spot traffic with block trains between Passau and Hegyesahlom with various partners from Germany. The latter trains use electric locos from partners whilst the automotive trains have two Class 2016 from StLB. STB now has a locomotive of its own which can usually be found shunting at Kalsdorf container terminal.

DIESEL LOCOMOTIVE

CLASS 212 B-B

This loco has been obtained second hand from Germany and is a former DB Class 212.

Built: 1965.
Builder: KHD.
Engine: Mercedes Benz 835 Ab of 993 kW.
Maximum Speed: 100 km/h.
Wheel Diameter: 950 mm.
Weight: 63 tonnes.
Transmission: Hydraulic, Voith.
Length over Buffers: 12.30 m.

212 381   92 80 1212 381-8

2.16. STEIERMÄRKISCHE LANDESBAHNEN StLB

The Austrian province of Steiermark has many standard and narrow gauge lines grouped together and run by the local government. There are some 47 km of standard gauge and 120 km of narrow gauge lines. StLB also operates the container terminal at Kalsdorf. Although managed by a central office, stock rarely changes from one line to another. For open access trains StLB has a subsidiary called Steiermarkbahn (see above).

Website: www.stlb.at

2.16.1. FELDBACH–BAD GLEICHENBERG

21.2 km. Electrified at opening in 1931.

System: 800 V DC.
Depot: Feldbach.
Timetable: 532.

ELECTRIC LOCOMOTIVE

E 41 Bo-Bo

Built: 1930.
Builder – Mech. Parts: Graz.
Builder – Elec. Parts: AEG.
Power: 400 kW.
Wheel Diameter: 1000 mm.
Weight: 38.3 tonnes.
Length: 9.78 m.
Maximum Speed: 50 km/h.

E 41

ELECTRIC RAILCARS

ET 1/2 Bo-Bo

These two units also appear to be from the opening period but within the last 25 years both have been rebodied and rebuilt internally. (1978, 1990).

Built: 1930, Rebuilt 1978/90.
Builder – Mech. Parts: Graz.
Builder – Elec. Parts: Elin.
Power: 295 kW.
Weight: 35.3 tonnes.
Length over Buffers: 16.24 m.
Maximum Speed: 50 km/h.
Accommodation: –/45.

ET 1 | ET 2

DEPARTMENTAL STOCK

This is a track maintenance vehicle kept at Feldbach.

X 51

2.16.2 GLEISDORF–WEIZ

In addition to locomotives for the Weiz–Gleisdorf line, Weiz shed also maintains locos for open access trains of subsidiary STB. For this purpose extra locomotives have been acquired. StLB also won the contract for shunting duties at the new container and freight terminal at Graz Süd (Kalsdorf) where some locomotives are being employed. These are frequently being exchanged with Weiz depot.

Depots: Weiz, Kalsdorf terminal
Timetable: 531.

DIESEL LOCOMOTIVES

DE 1/2 Co

DE 1 usually shunts at Weiz whilst DE 2 is spare at Kalsdorf container terminal.

Built: 1964–65.
Builder – Mech. Parts: ÖAM.
Builder – Elec. Parts: BBC.
Engine: MTU 8V396TC II of 550 kW.
Transmission: Electric.
Wheel Diameter: 1000 mm.
Weight: 48 tonnes.
Length over Buffers: 9.50 m.
Maximum Speed: 60 km/h.

DE 1 | DE 2

D 3 B-B

StLB surprised everyone in 1993 by acquiring a new locomotive from Germany and not from a local manufacturer. Like all modern shunting locos it is capable of remote radio control.

Built: 1993.
Builder : Gmeinder.
Engine: 1100 kW.
Transmission: Hydraulic.
Wheel Diameter: 1000 mm.
Weight: 72 tonnes.
Length over Buffers: 12.90 m.
Maximum Speed: 100 km/h.

D 3 90 34 0020 003-1

D 4–6 B-B

These modern locomotives were obtained for open access trains. They are capable of remote control by radio and are fitted with automatic shunting couplers. Like some other lines UIC style numbers are starting to appear. D 4 and D 6 work trips between Weiz and Gleisdorf whilst D 5 shunts at the Graz Süd Freight Terminal (Kalsdorf).

Built: 1999 (D 4), 2002.
Builder: Gmeinder.
Engine: MTU V12 4000 R20 of 1500 kW.
Transmission: Hydraulic, Voith L5r4zseU2.
Wheel Diameter: 1000 mm.
Weight: 72 tonnes.
Length over Buffers: 13.93 m.
Maximum Speed: 60/120 km/h.

D 4 92 81 2020 004-5
D 5 90 34 0020 005-6
D 6 90 34 0020 006-4

▲ StLB owns several Gmeinder diesel locomotives. D5 works an engineering train near Mödling on 19 July 2009.

V61 D

This locomotive is a second hand acquisition from the now closed Hohenau sugar factory. The loco was repaired by using spares from a sister locomotive obtained from the ELIN factory in Weiz. It is a standard DR V60D, later DB Class 346. (Technical details as DB Class 346 – see German Railways Part 1.)

V 61

CLASS 2016 Bo-Bo

The need for more locomotives intensified as ÖBB was receiving the last of its 2016s. The loco intended to be 2016 090 was diverted to StLB becoming 2016 901! Both locos are normally used in multiple on an overnight freight from Weiz to Wiener Neustadt and return. For technical details see ÖBB Class 2016.

EVN: 93 81 2016 xxx-c

2016 901 | 2016 902

CLASS 2048 B-B

StLB followed the example of SLB and acquired a second hand Class 2048 which had once been owned by ÖBB (and before by DB). This was followed by another one bought directly from Germany. The locos can usually be found at Kalsdorf Terminal and on various engineering trains. For technical details see SLB V83–87.

2048 024	90 34 2048 024-1	(ex ÖBB 2048 024, DB 211 146)
2048 035	92 81 2048 035-7	(ex DB 211 124)

SHUNTING ROBOTS

StLB needed some more shunting engines so that main line locomotives could be used elsewhere. This was at the time when ÖBB was disposing of surplus Class 2060 diesel shunting locomotives. They have had their diesel engines and transmissions removed and converted to battery electric operation. The locomotives shunt at various sidings on the line. They have a pantograph fitted for use when recharging the batteries.

Built: 1998.
Builder – Mech. Parts: StLB Weiz.
Builder – Elec. Parts: WB Antriebstechnik Waltrop, Germany.
Length over Buffers: 6.68 m.
Maximum Speed: 7.5 or 15 km/h.
Wheel Diameter: 950 mm.
Weight: 25 tonnes.
Power: 32 kW (54 kW for max. 5 minutes).
Transmission: Electric.

RE 01	(2060 008-6)	RE 03	(2060 007-8)
RE 02	(2060 001-1)	RE 04	(2060 030-0)

DIESEL RAILCARS

VT 51/2 B-2

Former ÖBB Class 5047 vehicles bought by StLB in 1992.

Built: 1987.
Builder: JW.
Engine: Daimler Benz OM444LA of 419 kW.
Transmission: Hydraulic.
Weight: 45 tonnes.
Length over Buffers: 25.42 m.
Maximum Speed: 120 km/h.
Accommodation: –/62 (6) 1T.

VT 51	91 34 5047 401-4	WEIZ	VT 52	91 34 5047 402-2	GLEISDORF

▲ StLB still uses a former DR Class V 60 for shunting at Weiz station. V 61 stands at Weiz on 15 October 2011.

▼ One of the new StLB Stadler GTW DMUs has been painted in blue advertising livery for S-Bahn Steiermark. On 15 October 2011 5062 003 waits for its next turn to Gleisdorf at Weiz.

CLASS 5062 2-Bo-2

In 2011 StLB obtained three GTW 2/6 DMUs from Stadler for use on the Gleisdorf–Weiz line. Together with VT 51/2 these railcars also work through from Weiz to Graz.

Built: 2010–11.
Builder: Stadler.
Engines: MAN 1100 kW.
Transmission: Electric (ABB).
EVN: 95 81 5062 xxx-c
Weight: 68 tonnes.
Length over Couplers: 41.89 m.
Maximum Speed: 140 km/h.
Accommodation: –/91.

5062 001 | 5062 002 | 5062 003

DEPARTMENTAL STOCK

This is a track maintenance vehicle similar to ÖBB Class X 626 kept at Weiz.

X 41

2.16.3. PEGGAU–ÜBELBACH

10.25 km.

System: 15 kV AC 16.7 Hz.
Depot: Übelbach.
Timetable: 540.

ELECTRIC MULTIPLE UNITS

ET 15 Bo-Bo

A second hand acquisition from Switzerland being ex SZU BDe4/4 93. It is now kept in reserve and used on occasional mixed trains only.

Built: 1968.
Builder: SWS/MFO.
Power: 520 kW.
Accommodation: –/34.
Weight: 25 tonnes.
Maximum Speed: 70 km/h.
Length: 20.60 m.

ET 15

CLASS 4062 2-Bo-2

In 2011 StLB obtained three GTW 2/6 EMUs from Stadler for use on the Peggau-Übelbach line. These railcars also work through from Übelbach to Graz and can also be found on some ÖBB Graz–St. Michael trains.

Built: 2010.
Builder: Stadler.
Power: 1100 kW.
Accommodation: –/93.
EVN: 94 81 4062 xxx-c
Weight: 72 tonnes.
Length over Couplers: 40.89 m.
Maximum Speed: 140 km/h.

4062 001 | 4062 002 | 4062 003

DEPARTMENTAL STOCK

This is a "Motor Tower Wagon" kept at Übelbach.

X 952 06

2.16.4. MIXNITZ–ST. ERHARD

This freight-only 10.4 km line has its own standard gauge shunters for transfer work at the main-line junction.

Gauge: 760 mm.
Depot: Mixnitz.

System: 800 V DC.

DIESEL LOCOMOTIVES

VEL 1 — Bo

Built: 1956.
Builder: Gebus.
Engine:
Power: 48 kW.
Transmission: Electric.

Wheel Diameter: 950 mm.
Weight: 20 tonnes.
Length: 6.56 m.
Maximum Speed: 18 km/h.
Gauge: 1435 mm.

VEL 1

VHL 2 — B

Built: 1967.
Builder: JW.
Engine: JW 200
Power: 150 kW.
Transmission: Hydraulic.

Wheel Diameter: 950 mm.
Weight: 27 tonnes.
Length: 6.64 m.
Maximum Speed: 60 km/h.
Gauge: 1435 mm.

VHL 2

E 1/2 — Bo

Built: 1913.
Builder: AEG.
Engine: AEG.
Power: 122 kW.
Gauge: 760 mm.

Wheel Diameter: 950 mm.
Weight: 15 tonnes.
Length: 5.51 m.
Maximum Speed: 30 km/h.

E 1 | E 2

E 3/4 — Bo-Bo

Built: 1957/63.
Builder: ÖAM.
Engine: BBC.
Power: 150 kW.
Gauge: 760 mm.

Wheel Diameter: 840 mm.
Weight: 30 tonnes.
Length: 9.60 m.
Maximum Speed: 40 km/h.

E 3 | E 4

2.16.5. UNZMARKT–TAMSWEG (MURTALBAHN)

This line is 65. 5 km long and used to go through to Mauterndorf.

Gauge: 760 mm.
Depots: Murau-Stolzalpe (Main depot & works), Unzmarkt, Tamsweg (Sub-sheds).
Timetable: 630.

STEAM LOCOMOTIVES

Stainz 2 0-4-0T

As the name suggests this loco originated on the Stainz system which once connected into the GKB but became part of the StLB in the 1920s. It is currently used for footplate courses.

Built: 1892.
Builder: Krauss Linz.
Wheel Diameter: 760 mm.
Length over Buffers: 5.35 m.
Boiler Pressure: 1.00 MN/sq m. (165 lbf/sq in).
Weight: 12 tonnes.
Cylinders: 225 x 350 mm.
Maximum Speed: 25 km/h.

Stainz 2

CLASS U 0-6-2T

The "U" in the classification stands for Unzmarkt - the line for which the first locos of this type were built and all subsequent locos of the same type were classed "U". Of these locos U40 was in fact built for the Trieste–Parenzo line and also saw service in Jugoslavia before coming to the StLB lines. U43 was built for the Unzmarkt line. As far as it is known both the locos built for the line have never been withdrawn from service and simply graduated from normal service into tourist train use.

Built: 1894, 1908, 1913.
Builder: WrN, KrL.
Driving Wheel Diameter: 800 mm.
Length over Buffers: 7.54 m.
Tractive Effort: 160 kW.
Boiler Pressure: 1.00 MN/sq m. (165 lbf/sq in).
Weight: 24.5 tonnes.
Cylinders: 290 x 400 mm.
Maximum Speed: 45 km/h.

U 11 | U 40 | U 43

DIESEL LOCOMOTIVES

VL 6 B

Another import from Germany originating on the Rhein Sieg Eisenbahn (V 13) then passing to the Zillertalbahn in 1969 (for spares only) and then the StLB in 1974.

Built: 1959.
Builder: OK.
Engine: OK316V6D of 104 kW.
Transmission: Hydraulic.
Wheel Diameter: 700 mm.
Weight: 18 tonnes.
Length over Buffers: 5.50 m.
Maximum Speed: 20 km/h.

VL 6

VL 12–13 Bo-Bo

These locos were built for the StLB lines and continue to see use on what freight trains still run. Sister locomotives VL 14 and 16 operate on the Weiz–Oberfeistritz line, VL 15 has been withdrawn.

Built: 1966–67.
Builder – Mech. Parts: ÖAM.
Builder – Elec. Parts: BBC
Engine: 260 kW (315 kW*).
Transmission: Electric.
Wheel Diameter: 840 mm.
Weight: 31 tonnes.
Length over Buffers: 9.80 m.
Maximum Speed: 50 km/h.

VL 12 EHRENFRIED | VL 13 FERDINAND

DIESEL RAILCARS

CLASS VT 30 Bo-Bo

These modern railcars from which the ÖBB Class 5090 were developed reinvigorated passenger services on the line and allowed bus services to be discontinued!

Built: 1980/81 (1998*).
Builder: Knotz/BBC (JW/Adtranz*).
Engine: MAN D3256BTYVE of 250 kW.
Transmission: Electric.
Weight: 28.8 tonnes.
Length: 18.30 m.
Maximum Speed: 70 km/h.
Accommodation: –/56.

VT 31 | VT 32 | VT 33 | VT 34 | VT 35*

CLASS VS 40 2-2

Trailers to work with Class VT 30.

Built: 1980/81.
Builder: Knotz/BBC.
Maximum Speed: 70 km/h.
Weight:
Length: 17.80 m.
Accommodation: –/52 1T.

Note: Some or all of these trailers are now –/34 1T plus a bicycle stowage area.

VS 41 | VS 42 | VS 43 | VS 44

DEPARTMENTAL STOCK

X 42 | X 45 | X 52

2.16.6. WEIZ–OBERFEISTRITZ (FEISTRITZTALBAHN)

This line is 13 km long and is freight-only but with steam-hauled tourist trains in the summer. The section from Oberfeistritz to Birkfeld is owned and operated by the preservation group "Club U44".

Gauge: 760 mm.
Depot & Works: Weiz.

STEAM LOCOMOTIVES

Kh 101 0-10-0T

The K in the classification denotes the type originated on the Kühnsdorf system, the h means superheated (Heissdampf). The locomotive has wandered around the StLB lines being first used on the Unzmarkt system and was at Kapfenberg before coming to Weiz.

Built: 1926.
Builder: KrL.
Driving Wheel Diameter: 800 mm.
Length: 8.72 m.
Power: 280 kW.
Boiler Pressure: 1.00 MN/sq m. (165 lbf/sq in).
Weight: 33.3 tonnes.
Cylinders: 400 x 400 mm.
Maximum Speed: 45 km/h.

Kh 101

U 8/44 0-6-2T

U 8 is one of the original locos built for the Unzmarkt line whilst U 44 was built much later for the same system.

Built: 1894 (*1922).
Builder: Krauss L.
Driving Wheel Diameter: 800 mm.
Length: 7.54 m.
Power: 160 kW.
Boiler Pressure: 1.00 MN/sq m. (165 lbf/sq in).
Weight: 24.5 tonnes.
Cylinders: 290 x 400 mm.
Maximum Speed: 45 km/h.

U 8 | U 44*

DIESEL LOCOMOTIVES

VL 4 C

This little shunter is a former Wehrmacht HF 130C type obtained second-hand from a paper factory.

Built: 1942.
Builder: Gmeinder.
Engine: 100 kW.
Transmission: Hydraulic.
Wheel Diameter: 750 mm.
Weight: 16.5 tonnes.
Length: 5.58 m.
Maximum Speed: 25 km/h.

VL 4

VL 8 B

This locomotive came second hand from Judenburg Stahlwerk.

Built: 1966.
Builder: Jung, 13989.
Engine: 110 kW.
Transmission: Hydraulic.
Wheel Diameter:
Weight: 16 tonnes.
Length over Buffers:
Maximum Speed: 20 km/h.

VL 8

VL 14/16 Bo-Bo

Built 1967 for StLB lines. For technical details see VL 12–13 in section 2.16.5.

VL 14 | VL 16*

VL 22–24 Bo-Bo

The first two locomotives were acquired from Yugoslavia in the 1980s after that country had closed down the major parts of its 760 mm gauge lines. StLB then spent some 4–6 years converting the locos to suit their requirements. The locos have been modified for radio remote control. The third loco arrived in 1998 from Banovici coal mine but has not yet been rebuilt.

Built: 1971–1972.
Builder: Djuro Djakovic.
Engine: MTU 6V396 Tc12 of 485 kW.
Transmission: Hydraulic.
Wheel Diameter: 850 mm.
Weight: 32 tonnes.
Length: 12.85 m.
Maximum Speed: 50 km/h.

VL 22 (ex JZ 740-023) | VL 23 (ex JZ 740-024) | VL 24 (ex JZ 740-106)

RT 3 B

There is a talcum factory on the Weiz system at Oberfeistritz where this loco shunts. It was acquired in 1980 from Braubach am Rhein (Lok I).

Built: 1957.
Builder: Deutz.
Engine: 41 kW.
Transmission: Hydraulic.
Wheel Diameter:
Weight:
Length over Buffers:
Maximum Speed: 25 km/h.

RT 3

2.17 STERN & HAFFERL StH

This organisation runs several lines in Oberösterreich. Many of these lines use second-hand tramway equipment and offer a quaint way of travel through some backwater routes. The line infrastructure is owned by subsidiaries whilst trains are operated by Stern & Hafferl. Rolling stock is either owned by StH or by the subsidiaries (see Numbering System below).

NUMBERING SYSTEM

The second digit of the numbering system denotes the owning company and the third digit denotes the type as follows:

Second digit:

20000	Stern und Hafferl (StH)
22000	Linzer Lokalbahn (LILO)
23000	Gmunden–Vorchdorf (GV)
24000	Lambach–Vorchdorf (LV)
25000	Lambach–Haag (LH)
26000	Vöcklamarkt–Attersee (VA)

Third digit:

This is 0 for a locomotive, 1 for a railcar and 2 for a trailer.

Note that vehicles are often, but not always, renumbered when transferred between lines. On renumbering, the last two digits are generally unaltered unless this would cause duplication. Renumberings shown are those which have occurred since the first edition of this book was published in 1985.

Details of the lines operated, which are all electrified at 800 V DC, are as follows:

STANDARD GAUGE LINES

2.17.1. LINZER LOKALBAHN LILO

A commuter line with some freight traffic. The Neumarkt–Waizenkirchen–Peuerbach line was a separate undertaking but was absorbed into LILO in 1998. The LILO depot at Eferding is also the base for open access activities by StH. In reality these are not "true" open access activities but duties subcontracted by RCA to StH who provide diesel locos and staff.

Routes: Linz–Peuerbach, Waizenkirchen–Niederspaching–Neumarkt-Kalham.
Depots: Eferding, Waizenkirchen.
Length: 58.9 km.
Timetable: 143.

ELECTRIC LOCOMOTIVES

E 20 007 Bo-Bo

Built for LILO, this loco passed to the Bürmoos–Trimmelkam line in 1980, moving to LVE in 1994 when the Trimmelkam line became part of SVB. It is now back at Eferding.

Built: 1956.
Builder – Mech. Parts: SGP Graz.
Builder – Elec. Parts: BBC.
Power: 492 kW.
Wheel Diameter: 1000 mm.
Weight: 48 tonnes.
Length over Buffers: 12.20 m.
Maximum Speed: 40 km/h.

E 20 007

E 22 001 Bo-Bo

This loco is from Wöllersdorf which LILO acquired in 1935.

Built: 1915.
Builder – Mech. Parts: Ganz.
Builder – Elec. Parts: Ganz.
Power: 200 kW.
Wheel Diameter: 900 mm.
Weight: 30 tonnes.
Length over Buffers: 11.70 m.
Maximum Speed: 40 km/h.

E 22 001

▲ SKGB Z4 is one of the original Schafbergbahn rack locomotives. It works hard to propel a single coach passenger train uphill on 14 July 2010.

E 22 002 Bo

An original LILO loco.

Built: 1912.
Builder – Mech. Parts: Ganz.
Builder – Elec. Parts: SSW.
Power: 80 kW.
Wheel Diameter: 900 mm.
Weight: 19 tonnes.
Length over Buffers: 6.90 m.
Maximum Speed: 25 km/h.

E 22 002

E 22 005 Bo-Bo

This is a steeple cab loco. It is from the Wöllersdorf amunition factory (No. II) and was obtained in 1947.

Built: 1915/26.
Builder – Mech. Parts: Ganz.
Builder – Elec. Parts: Ganz.
Power: 200 kW.
Wheel Diameter: 900 mm.
Weight: 30 tonnes.
Length over Buffers: 11.70 m.
Maximum Speed: 40 km/h.

E 22 005

DIESEL LOCOMOTIVES

V 20 011 B-B

This loco was former Tegernseebahn (Germany) No. 14. It is used for engineering trains and on shunting duties for RCA at Lambach.

Built: 1982.
Builder: MaK (G1203 BB).
Engine: MTU 8V396 TC13 of 745 kW at 1800 rpm.
Transmission: Hydraulic, Voith L4r4zU2.
Length over Buffers: 12.50 m.
Wheel Diameter: 1000 mm.
Weight: 80 tonnes.
Maximum Speed: 70 km/h.

V 20 011   92 81 2020 011-0

V 20 012 B-B

This locomotive was the formerly GKB DH 1500.7. It is based at Eferding but usually works trip freights on behalf of RCA around Lambach.

Built: 1992.
Builder – Mech. Parts: MaK.
Transmission: Hydraulic.
Power: 1100 kW.
Wheel Diameter: 1000 mm.
Weight: 72 tonnes.
Length over Buffers: 12.80 m.
Maximum Speed: 100 km/h.

V 20 012   92 81 2020 012-8

CLASS 2016 Bo-Bo

StH started to act as subcontractor for RCA in 2007 when they provided locomotives and staff for the twice daily Wels–Eferding-–Aschach freight train. A Class 2016 is now the regular locomotive on this duty. Another RCA duty is Steyrermühl–Kleinmüpnchen sand trains for which the second Class 2016 is being used. For technical details see ÖBB Class 2016.

EVN: 92 81 2016 xxx-c

2016 910 | 2016 911

ELECTRIC RAILCARS

ET 22 105 — Bo

This wooden-bodied unit has been reinstated as a museum car having spent some time in the tramway museum at Mariazell. It is now stored at Peuerbach station.

Built: 1951.
Builder – Mech. Parts: Graz.
Builder – Elec. Parts: AEG.
Accommodation: –/55.
Power: 100 kW.
Weight: 17.5 tonnes.
Length over Buffers: 11.50 m.
Maximum Speed: 50 km/h.

ET 22 105 (25 105)

ET 22 106/7 — Bo-Bo

Built new for LILO. 22 106 also carried 20 112 and 21 106 previously.

Built: 1951.
Builder – Mech. Parts: SGP Graz.
Builder – Elec. Parts: Elin.
Accommodation: –/54.
Power: 376 kW.
Weight: 39 tonnes.
Length over Buffers: 16.90 m.
Maximum Speed: 60 km/h.

ET 22 106 | ET 22 107

ET 22 109 — Bo

An original NWP unit now classed as a museum car and retained for excursion use.

Built: 1908.
Builder – Mech. Parts: Graz.
Builder – Elec. Parts: AEG.
Accommodation: –/32.
Power: 108 kW.
Weight: 17.0 tonnes.
Length over Buffers: 17.00 m.
Maximum Speed: 50 km/h.

ET 22 109 (21 150)

ET 22 137 — Bo-Bo

This is the last survivor of a batch of units which had been acquired from KFBE in the early 1970s and had entered service on the Linz system over the next 13 years. 22 137 is a single car with two cabs and acted as a strengthening unit. It is now in departmental use.

Built: 1954.
Builder – Mech. Parts: Westwaggon.
Builder – Elec. Parts: Kiepe.
Accommodation: –/49.
Power: 240 kW.
Weight: 24.1 tonnes.
Length over Buffers: 15.75 m.
Maximum Speed: 60 km/h.

22.137 (KFBE 1289)

ET 22 151–158 — 2-Bo-2

These are new units of type GTW 2/6. 22 151 was delivered as dual voltage and the others have later been converted to dual voltage.

Built: 2000.
Power: 520 kW.
Builder – Mech. Parts: Stadler.
Builder – Elec. Parts: Bombardier.
Accommodation: –/54 (6) + –/48 (6) 1TD.
EVN: 94 81 4822 xxx-c
Systems: 800 V DC/15 kV 16.7 Hz AC.
Weight: 56 tonnes.
Length over Buffers: 38.20 m.
Maximum Speed: 80 (DC), 130 (AC) km/h.

22 151 | 22 153 | 22 155 | 22 156 | 22 157 | 22 158
22 152 | 22 154

ET 22 159–164 2-Bo-2

These are new dual voltage units of type GTW 2/6.

Built: 2005.
Power: 520 kW.
Builder – Mech. Parts: Stadler.
Builder – Elec. Parts: Bombardier.
Accommodation: –/66 + –/52 (6) 1TD.
EVN: 94 81 4822 xxx-c
Systems: 800 V DC/15 kV 16.7 Hz AC.
Weight: 60 tonnes.
Length over Buffers: 38.20 m.
Maximum Speed: 80 (DC), 130 (AC) km/h.

22 159 | 22 160 | 22 161 | 22 162 | 22 163 | 22 164

2.17.2. LAMBACH–HAAG LH

This line had always been owned by ÖBB but was maintained and operated by StH. It shared some tracks with the ÖBB main line which is electrified at 15 kV AC whilst the LH line used 800 V DC. Two transformer vehicles were included in the fleet which were attached to DC vehicles before reaching ÖBB lines and detached on the return journey. The line closed in December 2009.

Rolling stock has been transferred to other StH lines except for the two modern railcars which are in fact owned by ÖBB. The latter are now stored at Linz works and are listed below.

ELECTRIC RAILCARS

ET 25 103/104 Bo-Bo

These modern units are dual voltage thus allowing through workings to Wels on the ÖBB main line. Classified 4855 by ÖBB.

Built: 1989.
Power: 480 kW.
Builder – Mech. Parts: Bombardier Rotax.
Builder – Elec. Parts: Elin.
Accommodation: –/64.
EVN: 93 81 4855 xxx-c
Systems: 800 V DC/15 kV 16.7 Hz AC.
Weight: 58.0 tonnes.
Length over Buffers: 24.43 m.
Maximum Speed: 120 km/h.

ET 25 103 | ET 25 104

2.17.3. LAMBACH–VORCHDORF LV

Known as the "Vorchdorferbahn".

Depot: Vorchdorf Eggenberg (shared with the narrow-gauge GV line).
Length: 15.5 km.
Timetable: 160.

ELECTRIC LOCOMOTIVE

E 24 010 Bo-Bo

A good second-hand loco acquired in 1980 from Wuppertal Stadtwerke (3608).

Built: 1910.
Builder – Mech. Parts: Maffei.
Builder – Elec. Parts: SSW.
Power: 300 kW.
Wheel Diameter: 900 mm.
Weight: 33 tonnes.
Length over Buffers: 8.81 m.
Maximum Speed: 40 km/h.

E 24 010

ELECTRIC RAILCARS

ET 20 109 Bo

This rebodied unit was acquired in 1970 from the German Extertalbahn and was used on the Bürmoos–Trimmelkam line which is now part of the Salzburger Lokalbahn.

Built: 1953.
Builder – Mech. Parts: Rastatt.
Builder – Elec. Parts: AEG.
Accommodation: –/32.
Power: 203 kW.
Weight: 25.4 tonnes.
Length over Buffers: 16.75 m.
Maximum Speed: 70 km/h.

ET 20 109 (21 001, 21 150, 22 109)

ET 20 111 Bo

This rebodied unit was also acquired in 1970 from the German Extertalbahn.

Built: 1953.
Builder – Mech. Parts: Westwaggon.
Builder – Elec. Parts: AEG.
Accommodation: –/60.
Power: 320 kW.
Weight: 26.5 tonnes.
Length over Buffers: 17.30 m.
Maximum Speed: 70 km/h.

ET 20 111

▲ Two former Extertalbahn EMUs are the regular motive power on the Lambach-Vorchdorf-Eggenberg line. On 30 September 2010 ET20 109 arrives at Vorchdorf.

ET 22 133/136 Bo-Bo + 2-2

These railcars were acquired second hand from KFBE and had been used on LILO. The two remaining units have been transferred to LV and are used in peak hours.

Built: 1953–54.
Builder – Mech. Parts: Westwaggon.
Builder – Elec. Parts: Kiepe.
Accommodation: –/49 + –/49.
Power: 240 kW.
Weight: 24.1 + 18.1 tonnes.
Length over Buffers: 15.75 + 15.75 m.
Maximum Speed: 60 km/h.

ET 22 133 + ES 22 233 (KFBE 1288 + 2288) | ET 22 136 + ES 22 236 (KFBE 1290 + 2290)

ET 24 101 Bo

A museum unit.

Built: 1931.
Builder – Mech. Parts: Graz.
Builder – Elec. Parts: SSW.
Accommodation: –/46.
Power: 106 kW.
Weight: 17 tonnes.
Length over Buffers: 11.01 m.
Maximum Speed: 50 km/h.

ET 24 101

ET 24 103 Bo

A museum unit.

Built: 1912.
Builder – Mech. Parts: Graz.
Builder – Elec. Parts: SSW.
Accommodation: –/60.
Power: 108 kW.
Weight: 20 tonnes.
Length over Buffers: 12.70 m.
Maximum Speed: 50 km/h.

ET 24 103

▲ Two ex-KFBE EMUs were transferred from Eferding to Vorchdorf and are used during the morning peak hours. ET22 136 stands at Vorchdorf on 14 July 2010.

METRE GAUGE LINES

2.17.4. GMUNDEN–VORCHDORF GV

Known as the "Traunseebahn".

Length: 14.6 km.
Depot: Vorchdorf Eggenberg. **Timetable:** 161.

ELECTRIC RAILCARS

ET 23 103 Bo

A museum unit.

Built: 1921.
Builder – Mech. Parts: Graz.
Builder – Elec. Parts: AEG.
Power: 110 kW.
Accommodation: –/40.
Wheel Diameter: 850 mm.
Weight: 13 tonnes.
Length over Buffers: 10.40 m.
Maximum Speed: 30 km/h.

ET 23 103

ET 23 105/106 Bo-Bo

Acquired in 1978 from the Swiss Trogener Bahn where they were Nos. 5 and 4 respectively. No. 3 was also acquired but was used for spares. Originally built for Lausanne Tramways.

Built: 1954.
Builder – Mech. Parts: ACMV Vevey.
Builder – Elec. Parts: BBC.
Power: 320 kW.
Accommodation: –/40 (*–/38).
Wheel Diameter: 720 mm.
Weight: 28.0 tonnes.
Length over Buffers: 17.10 m (*17.40 m).
Maximum Speed: 50 km/h.

ET 23 105 (Basel BDe 4/4 5) | ET 23 106* (Basel BDe 4/4 4)

ET 23 111/112 Bo-Bo

Acquired in 1994 from WSB.

Built: 1954.
Builder – Mech. Parts: SWS.
Builder – Elec. Parts: BBC.
Power: 326 kW.
Accommodation: –/48.
Wheel Diameter:
Weight: 28.5 tonnes.
Length over Buffers: 17.15 m.
Maximum Speed: 75 km/h.

ET 23 111 (WSB Be4/4 7) | ET 23 112 (WSB Be4/4 8)

TRAM 307/320 6-AXLE ARTICULATED TRAM

In 2011 GV hired a low floor tram from Innsbruck to provide a low floor service until the arrival of new vehicles (expected 2015). In 2012 another one followed. For technical details see section 3.3.

307 | 320

TRAILERS 2-2

Various trailers

Number	*Built*	*Weight*	*Accommodation*	*Length*
20.224 (VBW 8)	1916	12.8 tonnes	–/54.	15.25 m.
20.225 (VBW 9) buffet	1926	14.0 tonnes	–/54.	15.24 m.
20.227 (VBW 10)	1942	11.3 tonnes	–/54.	14.50 m.
23.221	1899			

2.17.5. VÖCKLAMARKT–ATTERSEE VA

Known as the "Atterseebahn".

Length: 13.4 km.
Depot: Attersee.
Timetable: 180.

ELECTRIC RAILCARS

ET 20.104 Bo

A Ganz 4-wheeled railcar built for the Pressburgerbahn and regauged after acquisition in 1941, now in museum use.

Built: 1913.
Builder – Mech. Parts: Ganz.
Builder – Elec. Parts: Ganz.
Power: 108 kW.
Accommodation: –/46.
Wheel Diameter: 850 mm.
Weight: 13 tonnes.
Length over Buffers: 9.50 m.
Maximum Speed: 30 km/h.

ET 20 104

ET 26 109/110 Bo-Bo

These railcars were built for the Swiss Sernftalbahn (Schwanden–Elm) moving in 1969 to the Aigle–Ollon–Monthey–Champéry line before coming to Austria in 1985.

Built: 1949.
Builder – Mech. Parts: SWS.
Builder – Elec. Parts: MFO.
Power: 320 kW.
Accommodation: –/40.
Wheel Diameter:
Weight: 25 tonnes.
Length over Buffers: 15.92 m.
Maximum Speed: 50 km/h.

ET 26 109 (AOMC BDe 4/4 112) ST. GEORGEN AM ATTERSEE
ET 26 110 (AOMC BDe 4/4 111)

ET 26 111 Bo-Bo

This is another former Swiss railcar being built for the Birsigtalbahn (now part of Baselland Transport) and acquired by Stern & Hafferl in 1989. It was previously used on the GV line as ET 23 109.

Built: 1951.
Builder – Mech. Parts: SWP.
Builder – Elec. Parts:
Power: 320 kW.
Accommodation: –/48.
Wheel Diameter:
Weight: 25 tonnes.
Length over Buffers: 15.92 m.
Maximum Speed: 50 km/h.

ET 26 111 (BLT BDe 4/4 8)

TRAILERS

Number	*Wheel Arrangement*	*Built*	*Details*
B 20.220	2	1907	Museum stock. Ex Gmunden 7.
B 20.222	2	1907	Museum stock. Ex St. Florian 1.
B 20.223	2-2	1914	Ex VBW (Switzerland) 7. Buffet.
B 20.226	2-2	1914	Ex VBW (Switzerland) 10.
B 20.228	2-2	1914	Ex VBW (Switzerland) 15.
B 26.201	2	1912	

2.18. SÜDBURGENLÄNDISCHE REGIONALBAHN SRB

This organisation had taken over the former ÖBB lines Oberwart–Oberschützen and Unterwart–Rechnitz. It moves some freight traffic and in the tourist season operated museum trains. Oberwart–Oberschützen has been handed over to a preservation society and Unterwart–Rechnitz was temporarily closed at the end of 2011 due to the poor state of the track. The future of this railway is uncertain.

Depot: Großpetersdorf.

STEAM LOCOMOTIVE

CLASS 93 — 2-8-2T

This typical Austrian branch line locomotive spent some time as part of the Brenner & Brenner fleet before passing to the SRB. Now dumped with expired boiler certificate.

Built: 1928.
Builder: Floridsdorf.
Driving Wheel Diameter: 1140 mm.
Length over Buffers: 11.96 m.
Maximum Speed: 60 km/h.
Boiler Pressure: 1.35 MN/sq m. (195 lbf/sq in).
Weight: 66.5 tonnes.
Tractive Effort: 575 kW.
Cylinders (2): 450 x 570 mm.

93.1422

DIESEL LOCOMOTIVES

CLASS 242 — B

This shunting loco was built for the Linz steelworks who sold it to Schleppbahn Liesing (Wien) in 1982, passing it on to SRB from there early in the 1990s.

Built: 1962.
Builder: SGP F.
Engine: SGP of 182 kW.
Transmission: Hydraulic.
Wheel Diameter:
Weight:
Length over Buffers:
Maximum Speed:

242.01

CLASS M 31 — C

These are standard MAV shunters and retain their MAV numbers.

Built: 1958–60.
Builder: Ganz Mavag.
Engine: Ganz Mavag 12 Jv 17/24 of 330 kW.
Transmission: Hydraulic.
Wheel Diameter: 1225 mm.
Weight: 45 tonnes.
Length over Buffers: 10.95 mm.
Maximum Speed: 62 km/h.

M31.2013 | M31.2020

2.19. WESTBAHN MANAGEMENT GmbH WSTBA

Not counting the ÖBB part-owned City Airport Train (CAT), WESTbahn is the first new entrant in the field of open access passenger services. Trains are being operated two hourly (hourly during peak hours) on the route Wien West–Linz–Salzburg–Freilassing.

Depot: Linz Wahringer Bahnhof (on Linz steelworks site).
Website: www.westbahn.at

ELECTRIC MULTIPLE UNITS

CLASS 4010 Bo'Bo'+2'2'+2'2'+2'2'+2'2'+Bo'Bo'

These double deck EMUs are registered in Switzerland which eased certification by Swiss manufacturer Stadler. Each unit consists of six segments with driving motor coaches at each end and intermediate coaches in the middle. The latter have a small buffet compartment each. Whilst each unit carries number 4010 00x the segments are numbered as follows: 4010 10x + 4010 20x + 4010 30x + 4010 40x + 4010 50x + 4010 60x.

DMBSO–4 x TBSO–DMBSO

Built: 2011.
Builder: Stadler.
Power: 6000 kW.
Voltage: 15 kV 16.7 Hz AC.
EVN: 94 85 4010 xxx-c

Weight: 296 tonnes.
Length over Couplers: 150 m.
Maximum Speed: 200 km/h
Accommodation: 60/441.

4010 001
4010 002
4010 003
4010 004
4010 005
4010 006
4010 007

▲ Second hand EMUs from Switzerland are still being used on the StH Gmunden-Vorchdorf narrow gauge line. ET23 112 arrives at Gmunden Seebahnhof on 30 September 2010.

2.20. WIENER LOKALBAHNEN AG — WLB

A light rail line from Wien to Baden which also runs freight trains. The trams run along Wiener Linien tracks to the terminus at Wien Oper. The company is now also operating charter trains under open access rules for various preservation societies. Open access freight has been outsourced to subsidiary Wiener Lokalbahnen Cargo (WLC).

Length: 30.3 km.
Depots: Wien Wolfganggasse. Leesdorf.
Timetable: 515.
System: 850 V DC.
Works: Inzersdorf.
Website: www.wlb.at

TRAMS

3-SECTION CARS — B-2-2-B

These modern trams were built in batches between 1979 and 1993 and allowed the former KBE units which the company used to operate to be withdrawn. All these cars are named after staff on the system, but these are being removed when the trams are re-liveried.

Built: 1979–93.
Builder – Mech. Parts: SGP Simmering.
Builder – Elec. Parts: AEG, Kiepe, SSW.
Accommodation: 64 seats, 130 standees.
Power: 380 kW.
Weight: 36 tonnes.
Length over Couplers: 26.75 m.
Maximum Speed: 80 km/h.

101	Erich	111	Inge	119	Margot
102	Karl	112	Reni	120	Michaela
103	Theo	113	Vera	121	Erika
105	Toni	114	Franziska	122	Elfriede
106	Alois	115	Andrea	123	Harald
108	Ernst	116	Wilhelm	124	Claudia
109	Hans	117	Josef	125	Susanne
110	Herta	118	Adi	126	Robert

▲ Open access passenger operator WESTbahn uses seven Stadler KISS EMUs on its new Wien-Salzburg-Freilassing service. Winter sunshine catches 4010.002 as it arrives at Tullnerbach-Pressbaum on 31 December 2011.

3-SECTION CARS Bo+2+2+Bo

These trams are based on those ordered by Wiener Linien for use on line U6 (the former Stadtbahn), but have cabs at both ends and a different seating layout. They have been built in three batches: 401–406, 407–410, 411–414.

Built: 2001, 2005, 2009–2010.
Builders – Mech. Parts: Bombardier Wien.
Builder – Elec. Parts: Bombardier.
Traction motors: 4 of 100 kW.
Accommodation: 70 seats, 118 standees.
Weight: 35.7 tonnes.
Floor height: 440/525 mm.
Systems: 600/850 V DC.
Length over Couplers: 26.94 m.
Width: 2.50 m.
Maximum Speed: 80 km/h.

401	404	407	409	411	413
402	405	408	410	412	414
403	406				

DEPARTMENTAL STOCK

01/02 B

These two diesel shunting locomotives have been obtained second hand from Wien metro and have been converted to work on auxiliary trains on the WLB line. They are kept at Inzersdorf works.

01 (WVB UDD 6901) | 02 (WVB UDD 6902)

MUSEUM CARS

All these are bogie cars.

Number	*Built*	*Details*
200	Graz 1899	Imperial saloon.
223	Graz 1927	Ex 23.
231	Graz 1928.	Ex 31.

2.21. WIENER LOKALBAHNEN CARGO GmbH WLC

This is a subsidiary of WLB for open access freight. WLC hauls container trains on the Passau–Wien–Hegyeshalom and Petrzalka–Wien Spielfeld-Strass routes serving terminals at Enns, Kalsdorf and Wien-Freudenau. There is also a lot of automotive traffic between Passau and Hegyeshalom as well as plenty of spot trains. WLC has its own safety certificate in Hungary for trains proceeding to Budapest but also works in co-operation with partners from Hungary and Germany. WLC locos are used throughout Germany as well as in Hungary and conversely locos from partners often appear on WLC trains in Austria. WLC also hauls freight trains on the branch line owned by parent company WLB. Diesel locos are kept at the WLB depot at Inzersdorf whilst electric locos are serviced at ÖBB workshops as required. The latter are often stabled at Wien Donaukaibahnhof on a track hired by WLC.

▲ WLB low floor tram 408 is pictured at Wien Wolfganggasse on 15 August 2011.

▼ WLC V 83 was built by Jenbacher; it is mostly used on freight trains on WLB infrastructure. On 01 November 2006 it leads a short freight from Wien Matzleinsdorf to Inzersdorf Güterbahnhof.

DIESEL LOCOMOTIVES

V 83 C

This is a standard Jenbach shunter of a type also built for several industrial railways. The loco had been obtained by WLB and later passed to WLC. The loco usually works the local freight train on WLB infrastructure but is also used occasionally on transfer trains in the Wien area.

Built: 1980.
Builder: JW.
Engine: JW 600 of 445 kW.
Transmission: Hydraulic
Wheel Diameter: 950 mm.
Weight: 54 tonnes.
Length over Buffers: 10.50 m.
Maximum Speed: 60 km/h.

V 83 92 81 2064 403-6

V 90–92 C

The first open access locomotives acquired by WLB and now owned by WLC were former DB Class 201/202 locos modernised by Adtranz at Kassel. Unfortunately the original identifications are not known. They have Zugfunk ZFM90, Indusi I60R (PZB 90), remote radio control and automatic shunting couplers. They are used for shunting at the terminals of Wien Freudenau and Enns as well as on some trip freights.

Built/rebuilt: 19xx/2001–02.
Builder: LKM rebuilt Adtranz, Kassel.
Engine: Caterpillar BDI-TA, 12-cyl 4-stroke.
Power: 1060 kW.
Transmission: Hydraulic.
EVN: 92 81 2000 0xx-c
Wheel Diameter: 1000 mm.
Weight: 74 tonnes.
Length over Buffers: 14.36 m.
Maximum Speed: 100 km/h.

90 | 91 | 92

ELECTRIC LOCOMOTIVES

CLASS ES64U2 Bo-Bo

WLC has several Taurus locomotives leased from MRCE for use on their open access trains. ES64U2 060/064/066/068 are commissioned to work in Hungary as well. Technical details are as for ÖBB Class 1116. For full details of MRCE please refer to the Platform 5 European Handbook on German Railways – Part 2 Private Operators, a new edition of which is in preparation.

EVN: 91 80 6182 5xx-c

ES64U2-019 | ES64U2-021 | ES64U2-023 | ES64U2-027 | ES64U2-060 | ES64U2-066
ES64U2-020 | ES64U2-022 | ES64U2-024 | ES64U2-035 | ES64U2-064 | ES64U2-068

CLASS 1216/183 Bo-Bo

WLC owns five multisystem Class 1216 locomotives for use on their open access trains. These are of subtype C and are identical to ÖBB Class 1216. They are commissioned to work in Austria, Germany, Hungary and Slovakia. Interestingly three locos are registered in Austria as Class 1216 whilst two are registered in Germany as Class 183 although they are identical. For technical details please see ÖBB Class 1216.

EVN: 91 81 1216 xxx-c 91 80 6183 xxx-c

1216 950 | 1216 953 | 1216 954 | 183 704 | 183 705

▲ WLC uses its diesel locomotives for shunting at Wien Freudenau and Enns container terminals as well as on short freight trains. Loco 91 is seen at Wien Ost on 22 October 2011.

▼ WLC uses a fleet of Class ES64U2 electrics hired from MRCE which are painted in WLC colours. On 05 May 2011 ES64U2-027 + 021 pass Wien Oberlaa with an intermodal train to Hamburg.

2.22. ZILLERTALBAHN ZB

Gauge: 760 mm.
Route: Jenbach–Mayrhofen (31 km).
Timetable No. 310.
Depots: Jenbach (main), Mayrhofen (subshed).
Website: www.zillertalbahn.at

STEAM LOCOMOTIVES

2 0-6-2T

This locomotive is of the famous U type (ÖBB Class 298).

Built/rebuilt: 1900.
Builder: Krauss Linz.
Driving Wheel Diameter: 800 mm.
Length over Buffers: 7.19 m.
Maximum Speed: 35 km/h.
Boiler Pressure: 1.00 MN/sq m. (165 lbf/sq in).
Weight: 21.9 tonnes.
Power: 160 kW.
Cylinders: 290 x 400 mm.

2 ZILLERTAL

3 0-6-2T

This locomotive is of the compound Uv type (ÖBB Class 298.2).

Built: 1902.
Builder: Krauss Linz.
Driving Wheel Diameter: 800 mm.
Length over Buffers: 7.84 m.
Maximum Speed: 35 km/h.
Boiler Pressure: 1.25 MN/sq m. (180 lbf/sq in).
Weight: 25.4 tonnes.
Power: 225 kW.
Cylinders: 320/500 x 400 mm.

3 TIROL

4 0-8-2

This locomotive has been acquired on a lease from Club 760. It is in fact JZ 83-076 and has taken a vacant ZB number as the original No. 4 was sold off many years ago. The tourist traffic on the ZB was getting so heavy that double headed trains had to be run. Now this powerful loco means one engine only on these trains.

Built: 1909.
Builder: Krauss Linz.
Driving Wheel Diameter: 900 mm.
Length over Buffers: 13.70 m.
Maximum Speed: 35 km/h.
Boiler Pressure: 1.25 MN/sq m. (180 lbf/sq in).
Weight – Locomotive: 36 tonnes.
– Tender: 16 tonnes.
Cylinders: 430 x 450 mm.

4

5 0-6-2T

This locomotive is of the superheated Uh type (ÖBB Class 498).

Built: 1930.
Builder: Krauss Linz.
Driving Wheel Diameter: 800 mm.
Length over Buffers: 8.02 m.
Maximum Speed: 40 km/h.
Boiler Pressure: 1.25 MN/sq m. (180 lbf/sq in).
Weight: 28.1 tonnes.
Power: 250 kW.
Cylinders: 350 x 400 mm.

5 GERLOS

6 0-4-0T

This small locomotive was acquired from the Böhler steelworks in Kapfenberg in 1972 and is used for driving lessons for the public as part of the tourist steam operations.

Built: 1916.
Builder: Krauss München.
Driving Wheel Diameter: 600 mm.
Length over Buffers: 5.70 m.
Maximum Speed: 20 km/h.
Boiler Pressure:
Weight: 10.9 tonnes.
Power:
Cylinders: 210 x 300 mm.

6

DIESEL LOCOMOTIVES

D 8/9 D

These two locomotives were built new for the line. Following the arrival of the new Gmeinder locos they are now dumped at Jenbach shed.

Built: 1967.
Builder: OK.
Engine: JW 600 of 397 kW.
Transmission: Hydraulic.
Wheel Diameter: 750 mm.
Weight: 36 tonnes.
Length over Buffers: 9.70 m.
Maximum Speed: 50 km/h.

D 8 | D 9

▲ Zillertalbahn D12 can be radio controlled. The man in front uses the controller device to move the locomotive forward in Jenbach narrow gauge yard on 24 July 2008.

D 10 B-B

This is former JZ 740-007 acquired in 1980 and rebuilt by Jenbach to ZB requirements and in service on ZB since 1982. In 1995 it was converted to push-pull operation in order to replace railcars.

Built: 1970, rebuilt 1962.
Builder: DD JW.
Engine: JW 600 of 440 kW.
Transmission: Hydraulic.
Wheel Diameter: 850 mm.
Weight: 32 tonnes.
Length over Buffers: 12.05 m.
Maximum speed: 60 km/h.

D 10

D 11/12 B

Both bought from the Rhein-Sieg Eisenbahn (Germany) in 1969. In 1995 these locos were fitted with radio remote control. They are used for shunting at Jenbach yard.

Built: 1958/60.
Builder: OK.
Engine: OK 316U6D of 104 kW.
Transmission: Hydraulic.
Wheel Diameter: 700 mm.
Weight: 18 tonnes.
Length over Buffers: 5.50 m.
Maximum Speed: 20 km/h.

D 11 | D 12

▲ Gmeinder narrow gauge diesel locomotives are used by the Zillertalbahn and the Pinzgauer Lokalbahn. On 12 March 2010 ZB D 13 arrives at Jenbach with a freight train.

D13–16 B-B

The first two of these new locomotives were acquired in 2004 to deal with heavy freight traffic. The timber industry along the Zillertalbahn is thriving causing the diesel fleet to be augmented. The locomotives have been constructed so that they are gauge convertible should the ZB install dual gauge down to the main saw mills. As they proved successful two more were obtained in 2007. The locomotives have remote radio control for shunting operations and can work in multiple with driving trailers so that they are now also in regular use on passenger trains.

Built: 2004, 2007.
Builder: Gmeinder (Type D75 BB-SE).
Engine: Caterpillar 3412 E DI-TTA of 746 kW at 2100 rpm.
Transmission: Hydraulic, Voith L3r4zseU2.
Maximum speed: 70 km/h.
Wheel Diameter: 920 mm.
Weight: 50 tonnes.
Length: 14.53 m.

D 13 | D 14 | D 15 | D 16

DIESEL RAILCARS/MULTIPLE UNITS

VT 3–4 /VS 3–4 B-B + 2-2

Built: 1984.
Builder – Mech. Parts: Knotz.
Builder – Elec. Parts: BBC.
Engine: 228 kW.
Accommodation: –/64 + –/46.
Transmission: Electric.
Weight: 28.6 + 17.5 tonnes.
Length over Buffers: 16.875 + 16.605 m.
Maximum speed: 70 km/h.

VT 3 + VS 3
VT 4 + VS 4 RAIMUND RAINER

VT 5–8 B-B

Built: 1992/93 (VT 5/6), 1998 (VT 7/8).
Builder – Mech. Parts: JW.
Builder – Elec. Parts: ABB.
Engine: MAN D2866 LUE of 250 kW.
Accommodation: –/64.
Transmission: Electric.
Weight: 31 tonnes.
Length: 16.88 m.
Maximum speed: 70 km/h.

VT 5 ADOLF TRAPPMAIR
VT 6
VT 7
VT 8

3. TRAMWAY SYSTEMS

There are four cities in Austria which have tramway systems plus the single line in Gmunden which is advertised as the smallest tramway in the world. Trams in Austria go by the nickname of "Bim", after the sound of their bells.

Special Note: Neither tramway museums, nor the numerous historic vehicles of Wiener Linien are included within the scope of this book. For details of these please consult the book "Tramways and Light Railways of Switzerland and Austria", published by the Light Rail Transit Association. Note that historic trams from museums in Innsbruck, Graz and Wien operate over the city networks.

3.1. GMUNDEN

Line Length: 2.3 km.
Livery: Red and white.
Depot: Gmundner Keramik.

This small tramway connects the town of Gmunden with the ÖBB station and is owned by Stern und Hafferl. All trams are bidirectional.

5 MUSEUM CAR

The last surviving original Gmunden tram is used at weekends during July and August.

Built: 1911.
Builder: Graz.
Power: 62 kW.
Accommodation: 32 seats 18 standees.
Weight: 11 tonnes.
Wheel Arrangement: Bo.
Length: 9.08 m.
Maximum Speed: 30 km/h.

5

8

This is a standard Duewag design tram built under license.

Built: 1962.
Builder: Lohner
Power: 200 kW.
Accommodation: 37 seats 32 standees.
Weight: 16 tonnes.
Wheel Arrangement: Bo-Bo.
Length: 13.40 m.
Maximum Speed: 60 km/h.

8

9/10

These two cars were from the former Vestische Strassenbahn in Germany. They were obtained in 1974 and put into service in 1977 and 1983 respectively. Car 10 carries varying advertising livery.

Built: 1951–52.
Builder: Duewag.
Power: 200 kW.
Accommodation: 38 seats 52 standees.
Weight: 18 tonnes.
Wheel Arrangement: Bo-Bo.
Length: 14.30 m.
Maximum Speed: 70 km/h.

9 (VS 347)	10 (VS 341)

▲ Gmunden tram number 8 leaves the terminus at Franz Josefs Platz on 30 September 2010.

▼ Only a few of the 1965 built Graz Linien trams are still in use and these will soon be withdrawn. Tram 279 performs a test run on 7 February 2008.

100 MUSEUM CAR

This open-sided museum car was obtained from the Pöstlingbergbahn in Linz in 1995. It is used at weekends in July and August if there is no rain (otherwise tram 5 is used).

Built: 1898.
Builder: Graz.
Power: 41 kW.
Accommodation: 24 seats 2 standees.
Weight: 8.8 tonnes.
Wheel Arrangement: Bo.
Length: 6.80 m.
Maximum Speed: 14 km/h.

100 (Pöstlingbergbahn IV)

3.2. HOLDING GRAZ LINIEN

Gauge: 1435 mm.
System: 600 V DC.
System Length: 29.7 km.
Depots: Remise I (Steyrergasse), Remise III (Eggenberger Strasse).
Livery: Green and cream.

Graz has a network of six routes which are operated in traditional manner in the centre of the street. Some tracks are quite close together so the trams had to be very narrow. With the arrival of the wider Variobahn trams the operator started to rebuild the narrow sections of the network so that the new trams can be used on all routes in future. All cars are unidirectional. The Graz tram operator has undergone several name changes since 2008 (until then Grazer Verkehrsbetriebe – GVB) and since 2010 has carried the name above. The tram network continues to be extended.

200 SERIES VARIOBAHN 5-SECTION CARS

These new 100% low floor trams will spell the end for the 260 and 520 series. 45 trams are on order for delivery by 2015. Problems with vibrations led to delays in final approval of the first vehicles.

Built: 2010–.
Builder: Stadler, Pankow.
Wheel Arrangement: Bo+2+Bo.
Traction Motors: 8 of 45 kW.
Accommodation: 47 (9) seats 98 standees.
Weight: 36.6 tonnes.
Floor height: 350 mm.
Length: 27.468 m.
Width: 2.30 m.
Maximum Speed: 70 km/h.

201	203	205	207	209	211
202	204	206	208	210	212

260 SERIES 2-SECTION CARS

23 trams of this class of two-section cars were built, but only seven now survive. These will be withdrawn once all the new Stadler Variobahn trams have been delivered.

Built: 1965.
Builder – Mech. Parts: Lohner (261–265), SGP (266–273).
Builder – Elec. Parts: Siemens.
Wheel Arrangement: Bo-2-Bo.
Traction Motors: 4 Siemens of 55 kW.
Accommodation: 38 seats 70 standees.
Weight: 24.1 tonnes.
Length: 19.35 m.
Width: 2.24 m.
Maximum Speed: 60 km/h.

263	267	268	271	278	279
265					

500 SERIES — 3-SECTION CARS

This class of three-section cars was based on a Duewag design for Duisburg.

Built: 1978.
Builder – Mech. Parts: SGP.
Builder – Elec. Parts: Duewag.
Wheel Arrangement: B-2-2-B.
Traction Motors: 2 x Duewag of 150 kW.
Accommodation: 52 seats 82 standees.
Weight: 32.2 tonnes.
Length: 25.35 m.
Width: 2.26 m.
Maximum Speed: 60 km/h.

501 | 503 | 505 | 507 | 509 | 510
502 | 504 | 506 | 508

520 SERIES — 3-SECTION CARS

These trams were obtained second-hand from Duisburg and went into service in Graz in 1988–94. They have traditional diamond pantographs.

Built: 1971–74.
Builder – Mech. Parts: Duewag.
Builder – Elec. Parts: Duewag.
Wheel Arrangement: B-2-2-B.
Traction Motors: 2 Duewag of 120 kW.
Accommodation: 63 seats 164 standees.
Weight: 32.2 tonnes.
Length: 25.90 m.
Width: 2.29 m.
Maximum Speed: 60 km/h.

Former Duisberg numbers in parentheses.

521 (1077)
524 (1080)
525 (1081)
526 (1082)
527 (1083)
528 (1084)
529 (1085)
530 (1086)
531 (1087)
532 (1088)
533 (1089)
534 (1090)
535 (1091)
536 (1092)
537 (1093)

580 SERIES — 3-SECTION CARS

These four trams are rebuilds of 260 series cars with centre sections from withdrawn ex-Wuppertal cars. They have a strange appearance since the centre sections have a different type of window to the end cars.

Rebuilt: 1996–97.
Builder – Mech. Parts: SGP Graz/Duewag.
Builder – Elec. Parts: Siemens
Wheel Arrangement: Bo-2-2-Bo.
Traction Motors: 4 Siemens of 55 kW.
Accommodation: 58 seats 97 standees.
Weight: 26.9 tonnes.
Length: 26.20 m.
Width: 2.24 m.
Maximum Speed: 60 km/h.

The first number in parentheses is the former 260 series number whilst the second number is the GVB number of the ex-Wuppertal car from which the centre section was taken with the number in square brackets being its former Wuppertal number.

581 (273/552[3809])
582 (270/570[3819])
583 (276/559[3808])
584 (266/560[3807])

600 SERIES 3-SECTION CARS

These trams were built as 2-section cars but all were fitted with new low-floor centre sections in 1999 with bogies from withdrawn ex-Wuppertal cars.

Built: 1986.
Builder – Mech. Parts: SGP Graz.
Builder – Elec. Parts: Siemens
Wheel Arrangement: B-2-2-B.
Traction Motors: 2 Duewag of 150 kW.
Accommodation: 40 seats 126 standees.
Weight: 33.95 tonnes.
Floor Height of Low-Floor Section: 300 mm.
Length: 26.30 m.
Width: 2.24 m.
Maximum Speed: 60 km/h.

601	603	605	607	609	611
602	604	606	608	610	612

650 SERIES CITYRUNNER 5-SECTION CARS

These 100% low floor cars brought about the demise of the 260 series.

Built: 2000–01.
Builder – Mech. Parts: Bombardier Wien.
Builder – Elec. Parts: Kiepe.
Wheel Arrangement: Bo+2+Bo.
Traction Motors: 6 Kiepe of 145 kW.
Accommodation: 53 (4) seats 93 standees.
Weight: 32 tonnes.
Floor Height: 290 mm.
Length: 27.00 m.
Width: 2.20 m.
Maximum Speed: 70 km/h.

651	654	657	661	664	667
652	655	658	662	665	668
653	656	659	663	666	

▲ The Innsbruck tramway and Stubaitalbahn are now entirely operated by a fleet of Bombardier Flexity Outlook trams. Tram 301 is seen near Innsbruck Hauptbahnhof on 12 October 2009.

3.3 INNSBRUCKER VERKEHRSBETRIEBE UND STUBAITALBAHN GmbH IVB

Gauge: 1000 mm.
System Length: 35.8 km.
Livery: Red and beige.
System: 600 V DC.
Depot: Wilten.

Innsbruck has three city tram lines plus the former AC Stubaitalbahn which was incorporated into the city undertaking in 1997. The city routes had used unidirectional cars, whilst the Stubaitalbahn, a single-track route to Fulpmes, always used bi-directional cars. In 1999 a decision was taken to extend the tram network instead of closing it and to order a new fleet of low-floor trams. A total of 32 trams have been delivered of which six are earmarked for the Stubaitalbahn. The older vehicles have now all been withdrawn from regular service but one of each type has been preserved in working order.

300 SERIES FLEXITY OUTLOOK 5-SECTION CARS

These 100% low floor cars are now used on all lines including the Stubaitalbahn. Six trams have been adapted by fitting ATP equipment which is required on the Stubaitalbahn. These are numbered 351–356. Trams 325 and 326 were subsequently retrofitted with this equipment as well. 307 and 320 are on hire to StH.

Built: 2007–10.
Builder – Mech. Parts: Bombardier Wien.
Builder – Elec. Parts: Elin.
Wheel Arrangement: Bo+2+Bo.
Traction Motors: 4 of 105 kW.
Accommodation: 58 seats 149 standees.
Weight: 36.8 tonnes.
Floor Height: 290 mm.
Length: 27.60 m.
Width: 2.40 m.
Maximum Speed: 70 km/h.

301	306	311	315	319	323
302	307	312	316	320	324
303	308	313	317	321	325
304	309	314	318	322	326
305	310				

351	352	353	354	355	356

HISTORIC VEHICLES

Number	*Built*	*Type*	*Builder*	*Remarks*
2	1909	Bo-Bo	Graz	built for Lokalbahn Innsbruck-Hall in Tirol
3	1909	Bo-Bo	Graz	built for Lokalbahn Innsbruck-Hall in Tirol
19	1909	Bo	Schlieren	ex Zürich 147
39	1962	B-2-B	Duewag	ex Bielefeld 805
75	1966	B-2-B	Lohner	
83	1960	B-2-B	Duewag	ex Hagen 63
88	1961	B-2-B	Duewag	ex Hagen 68, for sale

3.4. LINZ AG LINIEN

Gauge: 900 mm.
System Length: 41.5 km.
System: 600 V DC.
Depots: Kleinmünchen, Weingartshof.
Livery: White with orange lower bodyside band. Only a few trams actually carry the fleet livery. The second series of Cityrunners is in silver livery.

The main tramway in Linz has the unusual gauge of 900 mm. A new subway was built to serve the main station. All trams are unidirectional.

3.4.1. MAIN SYSTEM

CITYRUNNER 7-SECTION CARS

These new 100% low floor cars have brought about the demise of the older three-section cars.

Built: 2002–08.
Builder – Mech. Parts: Bombardier Wien.
Builder – Elec. Parts: Elin.
Wheel Arrangement: 1A+Bo+Bo+A1.
Traction Motors: 6 of 100 kW.
Accommodation: 68 (3) seats 156 standees.
Weight: ? tonnes.
Floor Height: 320 mm.
Length: 40.00 m.
Width: 2.30 m.
Maximum Speed: 70 km/h.

001	007	013	019	024	029
002	008	014	020	025	030
003	009	015	021	026	031
004	010	016	022	027	032
005	011	017	023	028	033
006	012	018			

THIRD SERIES 4-SECTION CARS

Four-section cars. Upon delivery of the latest series of Cityrunners these trams will all be withdrawn.

Built: 1985–86.
Builder – Mech. Parts: Rotax.
Builder – Elec. Parts: Siemens.
Wheel Arrangement: B-2-2-2-B.
Traction Motors: 2 x Duewag of 150 kW.
Accommodation: 54 seats 141 standees.
Weight: ? tonnes.
Length: 31.78 m.
Width: 2.30 m.
Maximum Speed: 70 km/h.

All are thought to be in advertising livery.

41	44	46	50	53	55
42	45	48	52	54	56
43					

CITYRUNNER SECOND SERIES 7-SECTION CARS

This is a new series of low-floor vehicles. A total of 23 are due to be delivered by the end of 2012.

Built: 2011–2012.
Builder – Mech. Parts: Bombardier Wien.
Builder – Elec. Parts: Elin.
Wheel Arrangement: 1A+Bo+Bo+A1.
Traction Motors: 6 of 105 kW.
Accommodation: 68 (3) seats 156 standees.
Weight: 49.9 tonnes.
Floor Height: 320 mm.
Length: 40.80 m.
Width: 2.30 m.
Maximum Speed: 70 km/h.

060	064	068	072	076	080
061	065	069	073	077	081
062	066	070	074	078	082
063	067	071	075	079	

▲ Tramway operator Linz Linien is increasing its fleet of Bombardier Flexity Outlook trams. On 01 October 2011 tram 063 is seen on the new route 3 extension at Gaumberg.

▼ The regauged Pöstlingberg tram line uses some rebuilt vintage tram cars on summer weekends. Trams VIII and XI working in multiple are seen near the Hauptplatz terminus on 01 October 2011.

HISTORIC VEHICLES (bidirectional unless otherwise stated)

Number	*Built*	*Type*	*Builder*	*Remarks*
6	1950	Bo	Simmering	
12	1962	Bo	Simmering	
25	1957	Bo	Gräf und Stift	
32	1880	2-axle horse car	Graz	
45	1920	Bo	Graz	
64	1971	Bo-2-Bo	Lohner	unidirectional
109	1950	2-axle trailer	Simmering	
111	1950	2-axle trailer	Simmering	
140	1954	2-axle trailer	Gräf und Stift	
141	1954	2-axle trailer	Gräf und Stift	

3.4.2. PÖSTLINGBERGBAHN

Gauge: 900 mm.
System Length: 2.9 km.
Livery: Cream.
Voltage: 600 V DC.
Depot: Urfahr.

This adhesion mountain tramway has the second steepest gradient in the world at 10.6% (1 in 9.5). The old cars were numbered using Roman numerals to distinguish them from the city trams. These were 4-wheeled and bidirectional. The line has been completely renovated and re-gauged to 900 mm so that trams are able to run into the main square in Linz. New low-floor cars have been built but three of the original 4-wheelers have been modernised and re-gauged. They usually work in a pair at weekends June–September complementing the new vehicles.

VIII

Built: 1898, rebuilt 1950/2010.
Builder: Graz, rebuilt ESG.
Accommodation: 22 seats 7 standees.
Length: 6.86 m.

VIII

X

Built: 1912, rebuilt 1960/2010.
Builder: Graz, rebuilt ESG.
Accommodation: 22 seats 7 standees.
Length: 8.08 m.

X

XI

Built: 1948, rebuilt 2010.
Builder: ESG, rebuilt ESG.
Accommodation: 22 seats 7 standees.
Length: 9.09 m.

XI

CITYRUNNER 3-SECTION CARS

These new 100% low-floor cars have been built for the re-gauged line. Their interior is in a retro design resembling the old cars.

Built: 2009–11.
Builder – Mech. Parts: Bombardier Wien.
Builder – Elec. Parts: Elin.
Wheel Arrangement: Bo+Bo.
Traction Motors: 4 of 105 kW.
Accommodation: 33 (6) seats 55 standees.
Weight: 27.6 tonnes.
Floor Height: 320 mm.
Length: 19.16 m.
Width: 2.30 m.
Maximum Speed: 50 km/h.

501 | 502 | 503 | 504

HISTORIC VEHICLES (1000 mm gauge)

Two trams have been preserved in original condition in working order. They are kept at Urfahr depot where there is a short demonstration track of 1000 mm gauge. The old Urfahr Bergbahnhof station is now a museum which is open at weekends in summer.

Number	*Built*	*Type*	*Builder*
I	1898	Bo	Graz
XII	1948	Bo	ESG

▲ Wiener Linien are slowly replacing their ageing type E1 trams with new ultra low floor models. Tram car 4748 + trailer 1318 are seen at Westbahnhof on 19 July 2011.

3.5. WIENER LINIEN GmbH

Gauge: 1435 mm.
System Length: 230 km.
System: 600 V DC.
Livery: Red and white (standard cars); red and silver (ultra low floor cars).

Although St. Petersburg used to have the largest tram system in the world, Wien (Vienna) was second, but is now probably the largest since many routes in St. Petersburg have now closed due to them having fallen into disrepair. All Wiener Linien trams are unidirectional.

DEPOT CODES

FD	Floridsdorf (Sub-sheds: Brigittenau, Kagran)
HN	Hernals (Sub-shed: Gürtel)
RH	Rudolfsheim (Sub-sheds: Ottakring, Speising)
FA	Favoriten (Sub-shed: Simmering)

CLASS A — 5-SECTION ULTRA-LOW-FLOOR CARS

Built: 1995–2003.
Builder – Mech. Parts: SGP/Siemens.
Builder– Elec. Parts: Elin.
Wheel Arrangement: 1-A-A-A-1.
Traction Motors: 6 of 36 kW.
Weight: 29.3 tonnes.
Accommodation: 42 seats 94 standees.
Length: 24.01 m.
Width: 2.40 m.
Maximum speed: 70 km/h.
Floor Height: 197 mm.

1	FD	10	FA	19	RH	28	HN	36	HN	44	HN
2	FD	11	FA	20	RH	29	HN	37	HN	45	HN
3	FD	12	FA	21	HN	30	HN	38	HN	46	HN
4	FA	13	FA	22	HN	31	HN	39	HN	47	HN
5	FA	14	FA	23	HN	32	HN	40	HN	48	HN
6	FA	15	FA	24	HN	33	HN	41	HN	49	HN
7	FA	16	RH	25	HN	34	HN	42	HN	50	HN
8	FA	17	RH	26	HN	35	HN	43	HN	51	HN
9	FA	18	RH	27	HN						

CLASS A_1 — 5-SECTION ULTRA-LOW-FLOOR CARS

This class is a development of class A, the most significant change being that there is now air conditioning for the whole vehicle. Technical details are as Class A except:

Built: 2007–2011, 40 more on order.

52	RH	59	RH	66	RH	73	RH	80	RH	86	RH
53	RH	60	RH	67	RH	74	RH	81	RH	87	RH
54	RH	61	RH	68	RH	75	RH	82	RH	88	RH
55	RH	62	RH	69	RH	76	RH	83	RH	89	RH
56	RH	63	RH	70	RH	77	RH	84	RH	90	RH
57	RH	64	RH	71	RH	78	RH	85	RH	91	RH
58	RH	65	RH	72	RH	79	RH				

LASS B 7-SECTION ULTRA-LOW-FLOOR CARS

uilt: 1995–2005.
uilder – Mech. Parts: SGP/Siemens.
uilder – Elec. Parts: Elin.
heel Arrangement: 1-A-A-A-A-1.
action Motors: 8 of 36 kW.
eight: 42.45 tonnes.
ccommodation: 66 seats 141 standees.
Length: 35.47 m.
Width: 2.40 m.
Maximum Speed: 70 km/h.
Floor height: 197 mm.

01	FA	618	FA	635	FA	652	FD	669	FD	686	FD
02	FA	619	FA	636	FA	653	FD	670	FD	687	FD
03	FA	620	FA	637	FA	654	FD	671	FD	688	FD
04	FA	621	FA	638	FA	655	FD	672	FD	689	RH
05	FA	622	FA	639	FA	656	FD	673	FD	690	RH
06	FA	623	FA	640	FA	657	FD	674	FD	691	RH
07	FA	624	FA	641	FA	658	FD	675	FD	692	RH
08	FA	625	FA	642	FA	659	FD	676	FD	693	RH
09	FA	626	FA	643	FA	660	FD	677	FD	694	RH
10	FA	627	FA	644	FA	661	FD	678	FD	695	RH
11	FA	628	FA	645	FA	662	FD	679	FD	696	RH
12	FA	629	FA	646	FA	663	FD	680	FD	697	RH
13	FA	630	FA	647	FA	664	FD	681	FD	698	RH
14	FA	631	FA	648	FA	665	FD	682	FD	699	RH
15	FA	632	FA	649	FA	666	FD	683	FD	700	RH
16	FA	633	FA	650	FA	667	FD	684	FD	701	RH
17	FA	634	FA	651	FD	668	FD	685	FD		

▲ Tram operator Wiener Linien operates a growing fleet of ultra low floor trams. A long ULF of Type B passes Zentralfriedhof on 13 September 2008.

CLASS B_1 7-SECTION ULTRA-LOW-FLOOR CAR

This class is a development of class B, the most significant change being that there is now a conditioning for the whole vehicle. Technical details are as Class B except:

Built: 2009–2012, 28 more on order.

702	RH	710	RH	717	HN	724	HN	731	HN	738	HN
703	RH	711	RH	718	HN	725	HN	732	HN	739	HN
704	RH	712	RH	719	HN	726	HN	733	HN	740	HN
705	RH	713	RH	720	HN	727	HN	734	HN	741	HN
706	RH	714	RH	721	HN	728	HN	735	HN	742	HN
707	RH	715	HN	722	HN	729	HN	736	HN	743	HN
708	RH	716	HN	723	HN	730	HN	737	HN	744	HN
709	RH										

CLASS E_1 2-SECTION CAR

Built: 1967–1976.
Builder – Mech. Parts: Lohner/Rotax or SGP.
Builder – Elec. Parts: Siemens, Elin.
Wheel Arrangement: B-2-B.
Traction Motors: 2 of 150 kW.
Accommodation: 39 seats 66 standees.
Weight: 23.3 tonnes.
Length: 20.335 m.
Width: 2.20 m.
Maximum Speed: 60 km/h.

4500 Series (built by Lohner/Rotax)

4501	FA	4512	FA	4523	FA	4536	RH	4544	RH	4552	RH
4502	FA	4513	FA	4524	FA	4537	RH	4545	RH	4553	RH
4505	FA	4515	FA	4526	FA	4538	RH	4546	RH	4554	RH
4506	FA	4518	FA	4528	FA	4539	RH	4547	RH	4555	RH
4507	FA	4519	FA	4530	FA	4540	RH	4548	RH	4556	RH
4508	FA	4520	FA	4532	FA	4541	RH	4549	RH	4558	RH
4509	FA	4521	FA	4534	RH	4542	RH	4550	RH	4559	RH
4510	FA	4522	FA	4535	RH	4543	RH	4551	RH	4560	RH
4511	FA										

4700 Series (built by SGP)

4729	RH	4752	FD	4786	FD	4809	FD	4830	FD	4849	HN
4730	RH	4755	FD	4787	FD	4811	FD	4831	FD	4850	HN
4732	RH	4756	FD	4788	FD	4812	FD	4832	FD	4851	HN
4733	RH	4762	FD	4789	FD	4813	FD	4833	HN	4852	HN
4734	RH	4763	FD	4790	FD	4814	FD	4834	HN	4853	HN
4735	RH	4768	FD	4791	FD	4815	FD	4835	HN	4854	HN
4736	RH	4769	FD	4792	FD	4816	FD	4836	HN	4855	HN
4737	RH	4771	FD	4793	FD	4817	FD	4837	HN	4856	HN
4738	RH	4772	FD	4794	FD	4819	FD	4838	HN	4857	HN
4739	RH	4774	FD	4795	FD	4820	FD	4839	HN	4858	HN
4740	RH	4775	FD	4797	FD	4821	FD	4840	HN	4859	HN
4741	RH	4776	FD	4798	FD	4822	FD	4841	HN	4861	HN
4742	RH	4777	FD	4799	FD	4823	FD	4842	HN	4862	HN
4743	RH	4778	FD	4800	FD	4824	FD	4843	HN	4863	HN
4744	RH	4779	FD	4801	FD	4825	FD	4844	HN	4864	HN
4745	RH	4780	FD	4803	FD	4826	FD	4845	HN	4865	HN
4747	RH	4781	FD	4804	FD	4827	FD	4846	HN	4866	HN
4748	FD	4782	FD	4807	FD	4828	FD	4847	HN	4867	FA *
4749	FD	4783	FD	4808	FD	4829	FD	4848	HN	4868	FA *
4750	FD	4784	FD								

* carries yellow livery and is used on excursions around the Ringstraße (Vienna Raing Tram).

LASS E_2 — 2-SECTION CARS

uilt: 1977–1990. Based on a design for Mannheim with electronic control.
uilder – Mech. Parts: SGP Simmering, Rotax.
uilder – Elec. Parts: Siemens, Elin.
heel Arrangement: B-2-B.
action Motors: 2 of 150 kW.
ccommodation: 43 seats 59 standees.
Length: 19.765 m.
Width: 2.265 m.
Maximum Speed: 60 km/h.
Weight: 24.5 tonnes.

000 Series (built by SGP)

001	HN	4018	HN	4034	HN	4050	RH	4066	FA	4082	FA
002	HN	4019	HN	4035	HN	4051	RH	4067	FA	4083	FA
003	HN	4020	HN	4036	RH	4052	RH	4068	FA	4084	FA
004	HN	4021	HN	4037	RH	4053	RH	4069	FA	4085	FA
005	HN	4022	HN	4038	RH	4054	RH	4070	FA	4086	FA
006	HN	4023	HN	4039	RH	4055	RH	4071	FA	4088	FA
007	HN	4024	HN	4040	RH	4056	RH	4072	FA	4089	FA
008	HN	4025	HN	4041	RH	4057	RH	4073	FA	4090	FA
009	HN	4026	HN	4042	RH	4058	RH	4074	FA	4091	FA
010	HN	4027	HN	4043	RH	4059	RH	4075	FA	4092	FA
011	HN	4028	HN	4044	RH	4060	RH	4076	FA	4093	FA
012	HN	4029	HN	4045	RH	4061	RH	4077	FA	4094	FA
013	HN	4030	HN	4046	RH	4062	RH	4078	FA	4095	FA
014	HN	4031	HN	4047	RH	4063	RH	4079	FA	4096	FA
015	HN	4032	HN	4048	RH	4064	RH	4080	FA	4097	FA
016	HN	4033	HN	4049	RH	4065	FA	4081	FA	4098	FA
017	HN										

300 Series (built by Rotax)

301	FA	4305	FA	4309	FA	4313	FA	4317	FA	4321	FA
302	FA	4306	FA	4310	FA	4314	FA	4318	FA	4322	FA
303	FA	4307	FA	4311	FA	4315	FA	4319	FA	4323	FA
304	FA	4308	FA	4312	FA	4316	FA	4320	FA	4324	FA

LASS c_3 — TRAILER CARS

uilt: 1959–1962.
ength: 14.70 m.
eight: 11.6 tonnes.
ccommodation: 32 seats 43 standees.
Builder: Lohner.
Width: 2.20 m.
Maximum Speed: 60 km/h.

116	RH	1211	RH	1234	RH	1252	FA	1269	FA	1278	FA
119	RH	1213	RH	1235	RH	1260	FA	1270	FA	1280	FA
187	RH	1214	RH	1238	RH	1261	FA	1272	FA	1282	FA
190	RH	1217	RH	1240	RH	1264	FA	1273	FA	1283	FD
200	RH	1222	RH	1242	RH	1265	FA	1274	FA	1284	FD
205	RH	1227	RH	1244	FA	1266	FA	1275	FA	1285	FD
207	RH	1228	RH	1247	FA	1267	FA	1276	FA	1286	FD
209	RH	1229	RH	1249	FA	1268	FA	1277	FA	1288	FD
210	RH	1233	RH	1250	FA						

CLASS c_4 TRAILER CAR

This class has three doors and wider windows than Class c_3

Built: 1974–1977. **Builder**: Rotax.
Length: 14.70 m. **Width**: 2.20 m.
Weight: 11.5 tonnes. **Maximum Speed**: 60 km/h.
Accommodation: 31 seats 43 standees.

1301	FD	1313	FD	1325	FD	1337	FD	1350	HN	1362	HN
1302	FD	1314	FD	1326	FD	1338	FD	1351	HN	1363	HN
1303	FD	1315	FD	1327	FD	1339	FD	1352	HN	1364	HN
1304	FD	1316	FD	1328	FD	1340	FD	1353	HN	1365	HN
1305	FD	1317	FD	1329	FD	1341	FD	1354	HN	1366	HN
1306	FD	1318	FD	1330	FD	1342	FD	1355	HN	1367	HN
1307	FD	1319	FD	1331	FD	1343	FD	1356	HN	1368	RH
1308	FD	1320	FD	1332	FD	1344	FD	1357	HN	1369	RH
1309	FD	1321	FD	1333	FD	1345	FD	1358	HN	1370	RH
1310	FD	1322	FD	1334	FD	1346	FD	1359	HN	1371	RH
1311	FD	1323	FD	1335	FD	1348	FD	1360	HN	1372	RH
1312	FD	1324	FD	1336	FD	1349	FD	1361	HN	1373	RH

CLASS c_5 TRAILER CARS

These trailers work with Class E_2 motors.

Built: 1977–1980/1985–90. **Builder**: Rotax.
Length: 13.00 m. **Width**: 2.30 m.
Weight: 11.94 tonnes. **Maximum Speed**: 60 km/h.
Accommodation: 32 seats 59 standees.

1401	HN	1421	HN	1441	RD	1461	RD	1480	FA	1499	FA
1402	HN	1422	HN	1442	RD	1462	RD	1481	FA	1500	FA
1403	HN	1423	HN	1443	RD	1463	RD	1482	FA	1501	FA
1404	HN	1424	HN	1444	RD	1464	FA	1483	FA	1502	FA
1405	HN	1425	HN	1445	RD	1465	FA	1484	FA	1503	FA
1406	HN	1426	HN	1446	RD	1466	FA	1485	FA	1504	FA
1407	HN	1427	HN	1447	RD	1467	FA	1486	FA	1505	FA
1408	HN	1428	HN	1448	RD	1468	FA	1487	FA	1506	FA
1409	HN	1429	HN	1449	RD	1469	FA	1488	FA	1507	FA
1410	HN	1430	HN	1450	RD	1470	FA	1489	FA	1508	FA
1411	HN	1431	HN	1451	RD	1471	FA	1490	FA	1509	FA
1412	HN	1432	HN	1452	RD	1472	FA	1491	FA	1510	FA
1413	HN	1433	HN	1453	RD	1473	FA	1492	FA	1511	FA
1414	HN	1434	HN	1454	RD	1474	FA	1493	FA	1512	FA
1415	HN	1435	RD	1455	RD	1475	FA	1494	FA	1513	FA
1416	HN	1436	RD	1456	RD	1476	FA	1495	FA	1514	FA
1417	HN	1437	RD	1457	RD	1477	FA	1496	FA	1515	FA
1418	HN	1438	HN	1458	RD	1478	FA	1497	FA	1516	FA
1419	HN	1439	RD	1459	RD	1479	FA	1498	FA	1517	FA
1420	HN	1440	RD	1460	RD						

I. WIENER U-BAHN

he Wiener U-Bahn is operated by Wiener Linien who also operate the trams. Lines U1, U2, U3 nd U4 are traditional third-rail Metro lines. Depots are at Erdberg, Hütteldorf, Leopoldau and Vasserleitungswiese. Heavy maintenance is carried out at the Simmering works of Wiener inien which is rail connected to ÖBB, as are the depots at Erdberg and Wasserleitungswiese. letro units are transferred via ÖBB on special transporter wagons owned by Wiener Linien.

LASS U/U$_2$ — 2-CAR UNITS

riginal monomotor design. Used on lines U1, U3 and U4.

uilt: 1972–82.
System: 750 V DC bottom contact third rail.
uilder – Mech. Parts: SGP Wien.
Wheel arrangement: B-B + B-B.
uilder – Elec. Parts: AEG/Elin/AEG/Siemens.
raction Motors: 2 BBC type GM200 of 200 kW per car (r 4 Elin MCF-031 M06 Z9Z-9 of 75 kW per car).
ength: 18.40 + 18.40 m.
Width: 2.80 m.
Veight: 52.60 tonnes.
Maximum speed: 80 km/h.
ccommodation: 49 seats 91 standees each car.

Rebuilt with AC asynchronous traction motors (Class U$_2$).

001	3001	2016	3016	2029	3029	2041	3041
005	3005	2018	3018	2030	3030	2042	3042
006	3006	2019	3019	2031	3031	2043	3043
007	3007	2020	3020	2032	3032	2044	3044
008	3008	2021	3021	2033	3033	2045	3045
009	3009	2022	3022	2034	3034	2046	3046
010	3010	2023	3023	2036	3036	2047	3047
011	3011	2024	3024	2037	3037	2048	3048
013	3013	2025	3025	2038	3038	2049	3049
014	3014	2027	3027	2039	3039	2050	3050
015	3015	2028	3028	2040	3040	2051	3051

▲ A Class U2 set headed by Wiener Linien 3318 + 2218 is seen near Schwedenplatz on metro line J4 on 13 May 2010.

2052 3052
2053 3053
2054 3054
2055 3055
2056 3056
2058 3058
2059 3059
2060 3060
2061 3061
2062 3062
2063 3063 r
2064 3064 r
2065 3065 r
2066 3066 r
2067 3067 r
2068 3068 r
2069 3069 r
2070 3070 r
2071 3071 r
2072 3072 r
2073 3073 r
2074 3074 r
2075 3075 r
2076 3076 r
2077 3077 r
2078 3078 r
2079 3079 r
2080 3080 r
2081 3081 r
2082 3082 r
2083 3083 r
2084 3084 r
2085 3085 r
2086 3086 r
2087 3087 r
2088 3088 r
2089 3089 r
2090 3090 r
2091 3091 r
2092 3092 r
2093 3093 r
2094 3094 r
2095 3095 r
2096 3096 r
2097 3097 r
2098 3098 r
2099 3099 r
2100 3100 r
2101 3101 r
2102 3102 r
2103 3103 r
2104 3104 r
2105 3105 r
2106 3106 r
2107 3107 r
2108 3108 r
2109 3109 r
2110 3110 r
2111 3111 r
2112 3112 r
2113 3113 r
2114 3114 r
2115 3115 r
2116 3116 r
2117 3117 r
2118 3118 r
2119 3119 r
2120 3120 r
2121 3121 r
2122 3122 r
2123 3123 r
2124 3124 r
2125 3125 r
2126 3126 r
2127 3127 r
2128 3128 r
2129 3129 r
2130 3130 r
2131 3131 r
2132 3132 r
2133 3133 r
2134 3134 r
2135 3135 r
2136 3136 r

CLASS U_1 — 2-CAR UNITS

Development of Class U with three-phase drive. Used on lines U1, U2, U3 and U4.

Built: 1986–97.
Builder – Mech. Parts: SGP/Siemens.
Builder – Elec. Parts: AEG/Elin/ABB/Siemens.
Traction Motors: Four Elin MCF-425 V06 Z9Z of 125 kW per car.
Length: 18.48 + 18.48 m.
Weight: 56.00 tonnes.
Accommodation: 49 seats 91 standees each car.
System: 750 V DC bottom contact third rail.
Wheel arrangement: Bo-Bo + Bo-Bo.
Width: 2.80 m.
Maximum speed: 80 km/h.

2201 3201
2202 3202
2203 3203
2204 3204
2205 3205
2206 3206
2207 3207
2208 3208
2209 3209
2210 3210
2211 3211
2212 3212
2213 3213
2214 3214
2215 3215
2216 3216
2217 3217
2218 3218
2219 3219
2220 3220
2221 3221
2222 3222
2223 3223
2224 3224
2225 3225
2226 3226
2227 3227
2228 3228
2229 3229
2230 3230
2231 3231
2232 3232
2233 3233
2234 3234
2235 3235
2236 3236
2237 3237
2238 3238
2239 3239
2240 3240
2241 3241
2242 3242
2243 3243
2244 3244
2245 3245
2246 3246
2247 3247
2248 3248
2249 3249
2250 3250
2251 3251
2252 3252
2253 3253
2254 3254
2255 3255
2256 3256
2257 3257
2258 3258
2259 3259
2260 3260
2261 3261
2262 3262
2263 3263
2264 3264
2265 3265
2266 3266
2267 3267
2268 3268
2269 3269
2270 3270
2271 3271
2272 3272
2273 3273
2274 3274
2275 3275
2276 3276
2277 3277
2278 3278
2279 3279
2280 3280
2281 3281
2282 3282
2283 3283
2284 3284
2285 3285
2286 3286
2287 3287
2288 3288
2289 3289
2290 3290
2291 3291
2292 3292
2293 3293
2294 3294
2295 3295
2296 3296
2297 3297
2298 3298
2299 3299
2300 3300
2301 3301
2302 3302
2303 3303
2304 3304
2305 3305
2306 3306
2307 3307
2308 3308
2309 3309
2310 3310
2311 3311
2312 3312
2313 3313
2314 3314
2315 3315
2316 3316
2317 3317

CLASS V 6-CAR UNITS

6-car units featuring through gangways and air conditioning. The end cars are classified v (lower case), this being usual Wiener Linien practice for unpowered vehicles. Used on lines U1, U2, U3 and U4. A total of 60 units are on order; 41 had been delivered up to the beginning of 2012. Delivery is to be concluded in 2017.

Built: 2000–.
System: 750 V DC bottom contact third rail.
Builder – Mech. Parts: Siemens.
Builder – Elec. Parts: Siemens.
Wheel arrangement: 2-2 + Bo-Bo + Bo-Bo + Bo-Bo + Bo-Bo + 2-2.
Traction motors: 4 Elin MCF-725 W04 Z9Z of 160 kW per car.
Length: 19.11 + 18.25 + 18.25 + 18.25 + 18.25 + 19.11 m.
Accommodation: 38 (4) + 44 + 44 + 44 + 44 + 38 (4). 1100 standees per train.
Width: 2.85 m.
Weight: 162.60 tonnes.
Maximum speed: 80 km/h.

3801	2401	2801	2802	2402	3802
3803	2403	2803	2804	2404	3804
3805	2405	2805	2806	2406	3806
3807	2407	2807	2808	2408	3808
3809	2409	2809	2810	2410	3810
3811	2411	2811	2812	2412	3812
3813	2413	2813	2814	2414	3814
3815	2415	2815	2816	2416	3816
3817	2417	2817	2818	2418	3818
3819	2419	2819	2810	2410	3810
3821	2421	2821	2822	2422	3822
3823	2423	2823	2824	2424	3824
3825	2425	2825	2826	2426	3826
3827	2427	2827	2828	2428	3828
3829	2429	2829	2820	2420	3820
3831	2431	2831	2832	2432	3832
3833	2433	2833	2834	2434	3834
3835	2435	2835	2836	2436	3836
3837	2437	2837	2838	2438	3838
3839	2439	2839	2840	2440	3840
3841	2441	2841	2842	2442	3842
3843	2443	2843	2844	2444	3844
3845	2445	2845	2846	2446	3846
3847	2447	2847	2848	2448	3848
3849	2449	2849	2850	2450	3850
3851	2451	2851	2852	2452	3852
3853	2453	2853	2854	2454	3854
3855	2455	2855	2856	2456	3856
3857	2457	2857	2858	2458	3858
3859	2459	2859	2860	2460	3860
3861	2461	2861	2862	2462	3862
3863	2463	2863	2864	2464	3864
3865	2465	2865	2866	2466	3866
3867	2467	2867	2868	2468	3868
3869	2469	2869	2870	2470	3870
3871	2471	2871	2872	2472	3872
3873	2473	2873	2874	2474	3874
3875	2475	2875	2876	2476	3876

▲ Class V is the most recent addition to the fleet of Wien metro cars. A set led by car 3807 arrives at Längenfeldgasse station on 26 August 2010.

3877	2477	2877	2878	2478	3878
3879	2479	2879	2880	2480	3880
3881	2481	2881	2882	2482	3882
3883	2483	2883	2884	2484	3884
3885	2485	2885	2886	2486	3886
3887	2487	2887	2888	2488	3888
3889	2489	2889	2890	2490	3890
3891	2491	2891	2892	2492	3892
3893	2493	2893	2894	2494	3894
3895	2495	2895	2896	2496	3896
3897	2497	2897	2898	2498	3898
3899	2499	2899	2900	2500	3900
3901	2501	2901	2902	2502	3902
3903	2503	2903	2904	2504	3904
3905	2505	2905	2906	2506	3906
3907	2507	2907	2908	2508	3908
3909	2509	2909	2910	2510	3910
3911	2511	2911	2912	2512	3912
3913	2513	2913	2914	2514	3914
3915	2515	2915	2916	2516	3916
3917	2517	2917	2918	2518	3918
3919	2519	2919	2920	2520	3920

STADTBAHN (LINE U6)

The Wiener Stadtbahn is a segregated light rail system with low platforms which uses bi-directional cars. It is classified as "U-Bahn" and is known as line U6. Trains are formed of four cars.

System: 750 V DC overhead.
Depots: Michelbeuern, Rösslergasse.

CLASS T — 3-SECTION CARS

These bi-directional low-floor cars have a cab at one end only and can therefore only operate in pairs.

Built: 1993–1995, 1999–2000.
Builder – Mech. Parts: Bombardier, Wien.
Builder – Elec. Parts:
Traction motors: 4 of 100 kW.
Accommodation: 58 seats 136 standees.
Floor height: 440/525 mm.
Wheel arrangement: Bo-2-2-Bo.
Length: 26.80 m.
Width: 2.65 m.
Weight: 34.7 tonnes.
Maximum speed: 80 km/h.

2601
2602
2603
2604
2605
2606
2607
2608
2609
2610
2611
2612
2613
2614
2615
2616
2617
2618
2619
2620
2621
2622
2623
2624
2625
2626
2627
2628
2629
2630
2631
2632
2633
2634
2635
2636
2637
2638
2639
2640
2641
2642
2643
2644
2645
2646
2647
2648
2649
2650
2651
2652
2653
2654
2655
2656
2657
2658
2659
2660
2661
2662
2663
2664
2665
2666
2667
2668
2669
2670
2671
2672
2673
2674
2675
2676
2677
2678

CLASS T_1 — 3-SECTION CARS

To get rid of the last Class E_6 cars (all now withdrawn) 46 more new 3-section cars were ordered from Bombardier. The new Class T_1 is based on Class T but has air conditioning and a more modern interior. Class T and T_1 can work in multiple. 20 more vehicles are on order for delivery from 2013. Technical details are the same as for Class T.

Built: 2007–2009, 20 on order.

2679
2680
2681
2682
2683
2684
2685
2686
2687
2688
2689
2690
2691
2692
2693
2694
2695
2696
2697
2698
2699
2700
2701
2702
2703
2704
2705
2706
2707
2708
2709
2710
2711
2712
2713
2714
2715
2716
2717
2718
2719
2720
2721
2722
2723
2724

5. MUSEUMS AND MUSEUM LINES

Preservation in Austria has settled down after considerable expansion at the turn of the century. There have been additions to the number of diesel and electric locomotives preserved but some steam locomotives have been scrapped and others sold out of the country. The major collections of ÖGEG and Strasshof have taken over some locomotives previously with ÖBB Nostalgie/ÖBB Erlebnisbahn.

As always there are regular steam operations on the rack railways and private lines with NÖVOG as a new independent railway now operating the narrow gauge lines around Gmünd and to Mariazell which have some steam trains. The Salzburger Lokalbahn has taken over the former ÖBB line from Zell am See and reopened it through to Krimml. Steam trains are to continue here.

The list of museums and museum lines is grouped into provinces and arranged in alphabetical order and also includes steam operations on the private lines as a convenient way of giving the reader as much detail as possible. The numbers in brackets are post codes.

The websites www.erlebnisbahn.at and www.erlebnis-bahn-schiff.at have useful links to most Austrian museum lines.

BURGENLAND

Oberschützen (7432)

Freunde der Bahnlinie Oberwart–Oberschützen (FrOWOS).

The society has taken over the closed Oberwart–Oberschützen line and operates it with several small diesel trolleys (Motorbahnwagen, former ÖBB classes X 614 and X 626) on Sundays and public holidays May to October. Diesel trains with former ÖBB classes 2060 and 2062 operate only occasionally. Some rolling stock is kept at Friedberg shed.

4 diesel locomotives, 3 diesel trolleys and 1 diesel railcar.

Website: www.frowos.com

KÄRNTEN

Bad Bleiberg (9530)

The former Bleiberger Bergswerk Union mine has an 800 metre tourist railway of 600 mm gauge.

3 battery electric locomotives.

Treibach Althofen (9330)

Kärntner Museumsbahnen (KMB).
Gurkthalbahn.
Treibach Althofen–Pöckstein.
3 km.

The KMB saved part of the Gurkthalbahn after its closure in 1969 and this became the first Austrian museum line. The main depot is at Pöckstein but some locos are often found stored at Treibach-Althofen station. The line operates Sundays only late June to early September

8 steam and 3 diesel locomotives.

Website: www.gurkthalbahn.at

Klagenfurt (9020)

The Bergbau Museum Klagenfurt (Kinkstrasse 6) includes a diesel and an electric loco from industrial concerns.

Nostalgiebahnen in Kärnten (NBiK)

This organisation is responsible for six operations:

- Museum trains are operated over the Weizelsdorf–Ferlach line on summer Saturdays and Sundays (6 km).
- Kärntner Museum for Technik und Verkehr – Historama. This is located in a former factory in Ferlach and is open MX July and August.
- HISTO-Tram, the former industrial line to the KESTAG factory has been partially electrified and is used by historic trams from near Ferlach station to the Historama museum.
- Eurotramway in Klagenfurt between Landcanal and the Stadtverkehrsmuseum.
- Nostalgic ship on the Wörthersee (MV LORETTO, 1924).
- Workshop in the old ÖBB depot at St. Veit an der Glan (West).

Most of the railway items are at St. Veit but there are some at Historama and there is a locomotive depot at Weizelsdorf. Most of the trams are at Ferlach. The St. Veit site is considered a workshop and is not normally open to the public but there is usually one open day a year whilst responsible enthusiasts are not likely to be turned away on a working day.

7 steam, 2 electric and 19 diesel locomotives, 6 electric railcars, 1 diesel railcar and 23 trams. Further 6 trams at Eurotramway.

Website: www.nostalgiebahn.at

▲ 298.52 was amongst the regular motive power when ÖBB closed the Steyrtalbahn and is now used again since the line became a museum operation. On 06 September 2009 it is seen at the head of a freight train at Aschach.

NIEDERÖSTERREICH

Freiland (3183)

Feld und Industriemuseum.

This museum is now well established at its site at Freiland station. It is open on the last Sunday of the month May to September 10.00–16.00.

Gauges: 600, 700, 760 mm. 4 steam, 41 diesel, 3 electric and 3 battery electric locomotives.

Website: www.feldbahn.at

Etsdorf-Strass (3492)

Österreichischer Club für Diesellokgeschichte (ÖCD).

The ÖCD is a new organisation interested in preserving diesel traction. They own a shed at Etsdorf-Strass which is also the base of the NÖVOG Krems–Emmersdorf excursion trains. Several ÖCD vehicles are stored at Amstetten shed.

Gmünd (3950)

Niederösterreichische Verkehrsorganisationsgesellschaft mbH (NÖVOG).

This organisation has taken over the former ÖBB lines from Gmünd to Gross Gerungs and Litschau. The normal train service has been withdrawn and only tourist trains run in the season. The Gross Gerungs line sees virtual daily operation in the peak season but not all trains get through to Gross Gerungs which is principally served at weekends May to October, with steam operation on the first Saturday of the month otherwise trains are diesel hauled. The Litschau line operates on Wednesdays June to September with some weekend operations. Steam tends to run on alternate Saturdays with other weekend trains diesel hauled. (see page 84 for details of the locomotive fleet)

Heidenreichstein (3860)

Waldviertler Schmalspurverein.
760 mm gauge.
Kursbuch Table 802.

This group operates between Heidenreichstein and Alt Nagelberg. Operations are Wednesday, Saturday and Sunday in the peak tourist season plus a few other dates.

3 steam and 7 diesel locomotives (but some are understood to have left for the Czech Republic).

Website: www.wsv.or.at

Hirschwang (2651)

Museumsbahn Payerbach–Hirschwang (Höllentalbahn).
760 mm gauge.
5.3 km.

This line was known as the Lokalbahn Payerbach–Hirschwang (LBPH) and was electrified from opening in 1918. It is now operated by the Österreichische Gesellschaft für Lokalbahnen (ÖGLB). When the line at Kienberg Gaming was acquired as a museum line most of the former steam fans here decamped to Kienberg and the present day group concentrates on the electric traction which is what the line was all about. One of the original railcar trailers has been converted to a power car and is in effect a true version of the original rolling stock.

2 steam, 3 electric and 2 diesel locomotives, 2 electric railcars.

Website: www.lokalbahnen.at

Kienberg Gaming (3291)

Ybbstalbahn Bergstrecke (YB).
Kienberg Gaming–Lunz–Göstling.
760 mm gauge.
27.1 km.

In 1988 ÖBB closed the eastern section of the Ybbstalbahn; the section between Kienberg Gaming and Lunz was subsequently taken over by Österreichische Gesellschaft für Lokalbahnen (ÖGLB). In 2012 they took over Lunz–Göstling as well. The previous facilities at Kienberg Gaming had to be enlarged to take in the new museum stock which came from other parts of Austria. Trains operate Saturdays and Sundays June to September and are mostly steam hauled but there are some diesel only days.

3 steam and 5 diesel locomotives.

Website: www.lokalbahnen.at

Mistelbach (2130)

Verein Neue Landesbahn.

The old loco shed at Mistelbach Loklabahnhof is the home base of Verein Neue Landesbahn. It promotes the Mistelbach–Hohenau branch line which is under threat of closure. It owns a steam loco and two diesels and is the home of several steam locomotives owned by other operators.

1 steam and 2 diesel locomotives.

Website: www.landesbahn.at

Obergrafendorf (3200)

Club Mh6.

Part of the locomotive depot at Obergrafendorf has been handed over to a preservation group. Some NÖVOG rolling stock is kept here as well for use on the Mariazell line.

3 steam and 1 diesel locomotives.

Puchberg (2734)

Puchberg am Schneeberg–Hochschneeberg.
1000 mm gauge.
9 km.
Kursbuch Table 523.

This rack railway is now owned by NÖSBB and operated by NÖVOG. Most trains are now worked by diesels with steam in use at peak times or as nostalgia trains at weekends. Operates May to November.

Website: www.schneebergbahn.at

Sigmundsherberg (3751)

Waldviertler Eisenbahnmuseum.

This museum is located in the old ÖBB depot close to Sigmundsherberg station. Open daily May to October.

3 steam, 6 diesel and 1 electric locomotives, and 1 diesel railcar.

Website: www.eisenbahnmuseum-waldviertel.at

Waidhofen an der Ybbs (3340)

Club 598.

Following privatisation and closure of the Ybbstalbahn sections east of Gstadt, Club 598 had to stop running steam excursions. The locos are kept at Waidhofen Lokalbahnhof but will probably soon move to another narrow gauge line.

2 steam and 1 diesel locomotives.

Website: www.ybbstalbahn-club598.at

Zwettl (3910)

Martinsberger Lokalbahnverein (MLV).

This group has been established to operate trains over the freight only line from Zwettl to Martinsberg and has set up shop in the old loco depot at Zwettl.

2 steam and 3 diesel locomotives.

Website: www.lokalbahnverein.at

▲ Most of the ÖBB Nostalgia electric locomotives have been passed on to various museums. 1040.01 is kept at Strasshof museum and is used on occasional charter trains. On 28 September 2008 it leaves Wien Ost station with a charter to Ernstbrunn.

OBERÖSTERREICH

Ampflwang (4843)

Österreichische Gesellschaft für Eisenbahn Geschichte (ÖGEG).
Ampflwang–Timelkam.
11 km.

ÖGEG has grown considerably and seems to have enormous financial resources judging by the number of additional locomotives that have been purchased. It had to move out of the old premises in the main ÖBB works at Linz and instead built a replica Austrian roundhouse and workshop at Ampflwang. The collection has grown fast in the last few years as ÖBB disposed of old locomotives and opportunities arose to purchase locomotives abroad. With the changes to ÖBB Erlebnisbahn, ÖGEG managed to obtain several locomotives from their fleet. ÖGEG also owns paddle steamer SCHÖNBRUNN which is kept at Linz and is used on excursion cruises.

The Ampflwang–Timelkam line is operated on summer weekends with either steam or diesel locomotives.

42 steam, 25 diesel and 46 electric locomotives, 7 diesel railcars and 1 EMU.

Website: www.oegeg.at

Bad Ischl (4820)

Museum Fahrzeug–Technik–Luftfahrt.

A private museum which includes some railway exhibits.

2 steam and 1 diesel locomotives.

Grünburg (4594)

Steyrtal Museumsbahn.
Steyr Lokalbahnhof–Grünburg.
760 mm gauge.
17 km.

When ÖBB closed the Garsten–Grünburg line, ÖGEG was quick to step in and by 1985 was already operating trains on this well loved line. Several former ÖBB narrow gauge locomotives have been restored with others being imported from Romania after lines closed there.

10 steam and 6 diesel locomotives.

Website: www.oegeg.at

Linz (4020)

Dora – Club für Industriebahngeschichte.

This club was formed to restore the preserved Linz steelworks loco DORA (0-4-0T, Jung 3237/1922). Trips around the steelworks with this locomotive are operated several times a year with a diesel railcar also being used from time to time.

1 steam locomotive and 1 railcar.

Mondsee (5310)

Salzkammergut Lokalbahn Museum.

The old SKGLB depot in Mondsee has been restored as a museum. The line closed in 1957 but some original locomotives were located and saved with one being repatriated from Jugoslavia. The museum is open Saturdays and Sundays, June–September. Some of the locomotives are operational and are being used on the Taurachbahn at Mauterndorf museum line which is operated by Club 760.

4 steam locomotives.

;t. Florian (4490)

lub Florianerbahn.
t. Florian–Pichling Ort.
00 mm gauge.

tern & Hafferl used to operate this line which closed down in 1974. ÖGEG then took it over but s their main line operations grew a separate group formed Club Florianerbahn and took over ıe line. It is no longer operational and the vehicles are stored at St. Florian depot, where they an be visited.

diesel and 4 electric locomotives, 12 trams.

/ebsite: www.florianerbahn.at/CFB/

;ALZBURG

3öckstein (5645)

;asteiner Heilstollenbahn.
00 mm gauge.
.4 km.

ourist trains operate into this former gold mine.

battery electric locomotives.

/lauterndorf (5570)

:lub 760.
Taurachbahn).
/lauterndorf–St. Andrä.
60 mm gauge.
0 km.

his line is the western end of the Murtalbahn which was closed by StLB in 1980 and later aken over by Club 760. After a period of restoration of the track and structures, tourist train perations started in 1988. The line normally operates at weekends June–September.

steam and 4 diesel locomotives.

/ebsite: www.club760.at

t. Wolfgang (5360)

;t. Wolfgang–Schafbergspitze.
000mm gauge.
km.
,ursbuch Table 173.

'his line has now been privatised and is operated by SKGB. This rack railway climbs from 40 metres to 1734 metres above sea level and operates May to October. Normally the new oil-red rack locomotives are in use with the railcars as back up. The coal fired steam locos operate mited services which are now marketed as nostalgia trains.

/ebsite: www.schafbergbahn.at

;chwarzach St. Veit. (5620)

'auernbahn Museum.

'his new museum is located at the station.

steam and 1 electric locomotives.

Zell am See (5700)

Pinzgauer Lokalbahn.
760 mm gauge.
54 km.

This line is now operated by SLB and operates steam trains every Thursday June–Septembe plus on some summer Sundays. Ds 3 (ex-ÖBB 399.03) is the regular locomotive but ex-JZ 73-01 (owned by Club 760) is now under repair at Ceske Velenice works and is expected to b operational from summer 2012. It has been leased to Pinzgauer Lokalbahn for a ten year period

Website: www.pinzgauer-lokalbahn.at

STEIERMARK

Eisenerz (8790)

Schaubergwerk.
900 mm gauge.
14 km.

The "Iron Mountain" is well known but less well known is that tourist trains operate over part o the old mining network and there is a museum.

2 steam, 1 diesel and 20 electric locomotives.

Website: www.abenteuer-erzberg.at

▲ Former Südbahn locomotive 17c372 is kept in working order at Strasshof museum. On 7 Octobe 2007 it provided the power for an excursion from Korneuburg to Ernstbrunn; it is seen arriving a Harmannsdorf-Rückersdorf.

Frojach (8841)

Club 760 Museum.

Club 760 has a museum at Frojach which is located on the Murtalbahn. The museum is not normally open except for a couple of weeks in the summer. However special arrangements can be made for groups.

5 steam and 2 diesel locomotives.

Website: www.club760.at

Graz. (8010)

Tramway Museum.

This museum is open Friday, Saturday and Sunday afternoons, June–September.

16 trams.

Graz (8010)

Montan und Werksbahnmuseum, Grazer Schlossberg.

Little is known about this museum located in or under the local castle but it has a large number of locomotives!

1 steam, 64 diesel, 7 electric and 25 battery electric locomotives.

Knittelfeld (8720)

Eisenbahnmuseum.

Some of the old buildings no longer needed for ÖBB use have been converted into a railway museum for the area. One building houses what is reputed to be the largest collection in the world of railway caps! The locomotives and rolling stock are mostly displayed in the open and subject to winter weather conditions. The museum is open Tuesdays, Thursdays and weekends May to October. The locomotives can be seen at any time with the permission of depot staff.

5 electric and 7 diesel locomotives.

Website: www.eisenbahnmuseum-knittelfeld.at

Mariazell (8630)

Museumstramway Mariazell–Erlaufsee.
2.5 km.

A purpose built standard gauge tramway open at weekends, July–September.

3 steam, 3 diesel and 2 electric locomotives, 28 trams and 3 electric railcars

Website: www.museumstramway.at

Murau (8850)

StLB Unzmarkt–Tamsweg "Murtalbahn".
760 mm gauge.
Kursbuch Table 630.

The Murtalbahn is 65 km long and has its operating base at Murau (km 27). On Tuesdays and Wednesdays June to September steam train excursions run on the Murau to Tamsweg section. This is not a museum railway but a very active narrow gauge railway running passenger and freight trains.

5 steam locomotives.

Mürzzuschlag (8680)

Kulturbahnhof Südbahn.

In connection with the 150th anniversary of the Semmering line (a UNESCO World Heritage site the depot at Mürzzuschlag has been converted into a museum.

6 steam and 4 electric locomotives.

Stainz (8510)

Stainzer Lokalbahn.
Stainz–Preding Wieselsdorf.
760 mm gauge.
11.4 km.

This line lost its passenger traffic as long ago as 1951 and freight finished in 1980. The line was saved and today the "Flascherlzug" runs once again.

2 steam and 4 diesel locomotives.

Website: www.flascherlzug.at

Vordernberg (8794)

Verein Erzbergbahn.
Vordernberg Markt–Eisenerz.
18.5 km.

The famous "Iron Mountain" rack railway must be known to many enthusiasts. It closed in 1988 but the rack rail had been removed earlier as diesel traction was used latterly. The Verein Erzbergbahn used to run tourist trains over the route on Sundays July–September using some of the diesel railcars that were once in normal service on the route. However, due to a landslip the line is blocked at present.

1 steam and 4 diesel locomotives, 6 diesel railcars.

Website: www.erzbergbahn.at

Weiz (8160)

Feistritztalbahn Weiz–Birkfeld.
760 mm gauge.
24 km.

This StLB line once ran through from Weiz to Ratten but was cut back to Birkfeld in 1980 and the track lifted. In 1993 StLB cut back its operation to Anger but this time no tracks were lifted and the Anger to Birkfeld section became a museum line. Club U44 is the supporting organisation but as elsewhere a company was set up to run the museum operation – the Freistritztalbahn. StLB still operate freight trains from Weiz to the talc loading point at Oberfeistritz but steam hauled tourist trains operate Weiz to Birkfeld on Thursday and Sundays in the main tourist season June–September, but there are some additional Saturday workings in September and October. Club U44 now has the old locomotive depot at Birkfeld but also rents space in the StLB depot at Weiz. In addition to their own locomotives they also use the StLB steam locomotives which are based at Weiz.

3 steam and 4 diesel locomotives.

Website: www.club-u44.at

TIROL

Innsbruck (6020)

Tiroler Museumsbahn (TMB).
1000 mm gauge.

The old Stubaitalbahn depot is now home to this society and its collection. The collection has ten Innsbruck trams, three old Stubaitalbahn cars and one electric rack locomotive from the Rittnerbahn in Bozen, Italy.

Website: www.tmb.at

Jenbach (6200)

Achenseebahn.
Jenbach–Achensee.
1000 mm gauge.
7 km.
Kursbuch Table 311.

This line had a surprise for visitors in 2010 – a brand new steam locomotive! Many years ago the AB had four steam locomotives but No. 4 was scrapped. Over the years new parts have been provided for the other three locomotives including new frames etc. AB decided they needed a fourth steam loco again and so began searching through their stores and recovered a set of frames and wheels. A boiler was obtained from a narrow gauge locomotive in Poland. The whole package has now been assembled and a new No. 4 entered service in 2010! A "phoenix" arises from the back of the depot! Operates daily May to October. In addition a fifth locomotive has been assembled using various used spare parts and a spare boiler but this is not operational and just acts as a monument.

4 (5) steam and 1 diesel locomotives.

Website: www.achenseebahn.at

Jenbach (6200)

Zillertalbahn.
Jenbach–Mayrhofen.
760 mm gauge.
32 km.
Kursbuch Table 310.

This narrow gauge line continues to thrive and steam tourist trains are a feature of its operations. There are two return trips with steam in the peak season otherwise just one return May to October.

Jochberg (6373)

Schaubergwerke Kupferplatte.
600 mm gauge.

This copper mine near Kitzbühel runs tourist trains into the mine daily May to October with departures on the hour 09.00–16.00 except at 12.00.

Website: www.schaubergwerke.at/kupferplatte

Lienz (9900)

IG Tauernbahn/Verein der Eisenbahnfreunde Lienz.
This group is housed in the old ÖBB depot at Lienz which dates from 1871. Local excursions operate a few times each year.

2 steam, 3 electric and 2 diesel locomotives.

Website: bahnbilder.warumdenn.net/1020-news.html

VORARLBERG

Bezau (6870)

Bregenzerwald Museumsbahn.
Bezau–Bersbuch.
760 mm gauge.
6 km.

This former ÖBB line closed in 1980 after a severe rockfall damaged and blocked the line. A preservation group was formed and reopened part of the line in 1987. In 1999 another storm caused a bridge to be washed away. The preservation group raised funds and got the military involved and the bridge was reconstructed in time for trains to operate again in 2000. The line now operates at weekends plus other odd days June–October with steam traction alternating with diesel.

3 steam and 4 diesel locomotives.

Website: www.waelderbaehnle.at

Lustenau (6893)

Verein Rheinschauen.
750 mm gauge.

Verein Rheinschauen operates excursion trains over part of the network of Internationale Rheinregulierung (IRR). The IRR was an industrial railway which used to transport materials to strengthen and maintain the banks of the Rhein. This is now no longer the case. Verein Rheinschauen operates steam trains most weekends May to September with some Friday operations as well. The whole operation is now under threat as a bridge across the river Rhein needs repairs.

2 steam, 4 electric and 6 diesel locomotives.

Website: www.rheinschauen.at

WIEN AREA

Gross Schwechat (2320)

Eisenbahn Museum Schwechat, Verband der Eisenbahnfreunde (VEF).

The VEF is a well established society having been founded in 1950. Their base at Gross Schwechat is in the old Pressburgerbahn depot where they have preserved an interesting selection of rolling stock. Apart from various standard gauge items the museum has a 600 mm gauge Feldbahn with lots of vehicles. The latter operates on all open days whilst there are some steam days each year when a standard gauge loco is steamed. Open Sundays May to October.

Standard gauge: 6 steam, 6 electric, 1 battery electric and 26 diesel locomotives, 2 diesel railcars.
Narrow gauge: 4 steam, 45 diesel, 5 electric, 1 battery electric and 1 compressed air locomotives.

Website: www.eisenbahnmuseum.at

ıödling (2340)

ıödlinger Stadtverkehrs Museum (MStM).

. small museum has been established near Mödling railway station. The collection concentrates n trams, since Mödling once had a narrow gauge tram line to Hinterbrühl as well as a line from Vien (route 360) which have long since closed. Open Sunday mornings May to September.

trams.

/ebsite: www.dr-peter-standenat.at/museum/index.html

;trasshof (2231)

as Heizhaus. 1. Österreichische Strassenbahn und Eisenbahn Klub (1ÖSEK) and sterreichisches Eisenbahnmmuseum.

his is the former ÖBB locomotive depot at Strasshof but note that the nearest station is ilberwald and not Strasshof! 1ÖSEK saved the depot when ÖBB closed it in 1978 and opened as a museum six years later. In recent years, co-operation with the Technische Museum, Vien, has seen most of the locomotives from that museum moved to Strasshof. Also here now re some of the former ÖBB Nostalgia locomotives which are now either owned by 1ÖSEK or y Österreichisches Eisenbahnmuseum (owned by the republic of Austria).

0 steam, 20 diesel and 26 electric locomotives, 4 electric railcars and 6 diesel railcars.

/ebsite: www.eisenbahnmuseum-heizhaus.com

The 381 mm gauge Liliputbahn in Wien uses steam at weekends. On 11 October 2008 loco umber 2 is seen in the Prater recreation area.

Wien Rudolfsheim (1150)

Technical Museum, Mariahilfstrasse 212.

This museum having been closed for many years for rebuilding is now open again but th railway collection has been reduced with many locomotives remaining at Strasshof as part c the collection there.

3 steam and 2 electric locomotives.

Wien Heiligenstadt (1190)

Brenner und Brenner.

B&B steam locomotives operate on special trains all over Austria but especially in the greate Wien area. Besides some enthusiast tours there are private charters for weddings or firm' outings. Most coaches and some of the locomotives are kept at Wien Heiligenstadt station bu others are kept at various locations.

10 steam locomotives.

Website: www.bb-bluetrain.com

Wien Prater (1020)

Lilliputbahn im Prater.
381 mm gauge.
2.5 km.

The Wien Prater park and its big wheel are world famous and the same probably applies to it miniature railway. The railway operates April to October but steam is only used at weekends.

2 steam and 5 diesel locomotives.

Website: www.liliputbahn.com

Wien Erdberg (1030)

Strassenbahn Museum.
Ludwig Kössler Platz, Wien 3.

This former Wien tramway depot is now the Wiener Strassenbahn Museum and involves no only the operator, Wiener Linien but also the VEF society and Wien Tramway Museum.

1 steam locomotive and 43 trams.

Website: www.wienerlinien.at/eportal/ep/channelView.do/channelId/-31304/pageTypeId/9424

Wiener Lokalbahn (1120)

Wolfganggasse, Wien 12.

The Wiener Lokalbahn has restored three of its old cars with the Hofsalonwagen dating back t 1900. They are normally kept at the depot at Wolfganggasse.

6. PRESERVED LOCOMOTIVES & RAILCARS

STATUS CODES

A Active (location could vary).
P Plinthed ('Denkmal').
M Museum or Museum line locomotive.
R Under restoration (sometimes at another location).
S Stored or retained for spares.

Note: Quotation marks around locomotive numbers indicate that the number is fictitious and never carried when the loco was in regular service.

6.1. ÖBB STEAM LOCOMOTIVES

Standard gauge

Number	*Type*	*Built*	*Status*	*Location.*
12.10	2-8-4	1936	M	EM Strasshof.
15.13	2-6-2	1910	M	EM Strasshof.
16.08	2-6-4	1911	MA	EM Strasshof. Preserved as KKStB 310.23.
30.33	2-6-2T	1897	MA	EM Strasshof.
30.109	2-6-2T	1900	MR	EM Strasshof.
33.102	4-8-0	1923	M	EM Strasshof.
"33.132"	4-8-0	1925	MA	Brenner & Brenner, Heiligenstadt (Ex JZ 10-005).
35.233	2-6-2	1916	M	EM Strasshof.
38.4101	4-6-0	1912	MA	EM Strasshof. Preserved as Sudb 109.13.
42.2708	2-10-0	1946	M	EM Strasshof.
42.2721	2-10-0	1947	MA	Luxembourg.
50.685	2-10-0	1940	M	Technikmuseum Speyer, Germany.
50.1171	2-10-0	1942	M	Brenner & Brenner, Linz.
52.100	2-10-0	194x	MA	EM Strasshof ex JZ 33-044.
52.221	2-10-0	1943	MR	St. Sulpice, Switzerland.
52.855	2-10-0	1944	M	Sigmundsherberg.
52.1198	2-10-0	1943	MA	ÖGEG, Ampflwang.
52.1227	2-10-0	1944	MA	Brenner & Brenner, Linz.
52.2436	2-10-0	1943	P	Kyoto, Japan.
52.3314	2-10-0	1944	MR	CFV3V Treignes, Belgium.
52.3316	2-10-0	1944	MS	ÖGEG, Ampflwang.
52.3504	2-10-0	1943	MR	Luxembourg.
52.3517	2-10-0	1943	MA	ÖGEG, Ampflwang.
52.3816	2-10-0	1944	M	Lienz.
52.3879	2-10-0	1944	MA	VSM, Beekbergen, Netherlands.
52.4984	2-10-0	1944	MA	Mistelbach.
52.5804	2-10-0	1943	M	Neuenmarkt Wirsberg, Germany.
52.7046	2-10-0	1943	P	Selzthal.
52.7102	2-10-0	1943	M	ÖGEG, Ampflwang.
52.7409	2-10-0	1943	MA	Würzburg Zell, Germany.
52.7593	2-10-0	1944	P	Strasshof (Bundestrasse 205).
52.7594	2-10-0	1944	M	EM Strasshof.
52.7596	2-10-0	1944	MA	EFZ Tübingen. Germany.
52.7612	2-10-0	1944	MA	Brenner & Brenner, Mistelbach.
152.3109	2-10-0	1942	M	TM Speyer, Germany.
152.4552	2-10-0	1944	MS	ÖGEG, Ampflwang.
152.4867	2-10-0	1942	MA	H.E. Frankfurt/M, Germany.
53.7101	0-6-0	1868	M	EM Strasshof (as KEB 106 FUSCH).
153.7114	0-6-0	1869	M	EM Strasshof (as Südbahn 852).
54.14	2-6-0	1899	M	EM Strasshof.
55.5708	0-8-0	1887	M	EM Strasshof.
56.3115	2-8-0	1913	M	GKB Lieboch.
56.3255	2-8-0	1919	M	Jaroměř, Czech Republic.
156.3423	2-8-0	1920	M	EM Strasshof.
57.223	0-10-0	1916	M	EM Strasshof.

257.601	0-10-0	1921	M	EM Strasshof.
58.744	2-10-0	1923	M	EM Strasshof.
258.902	2-10-0	1912	M	EM Strasshof.
69.02	2-2-2T	1898	M	EM Strasshof.
770.86	2-4-0T	1913	MR	ÖGEG, Ampflwang.
175.817	2-6-2T	1912	M	EM Strasshof.
77.28	4-6-2T	1920	MA	ÖGEG, Ampflwang.
77.66	4-6-2T	1913	MA	EM Strasshof (restored as Südbahn 629.01).
77.244	4-6-2T	1927	MA	Brenner & Brenner, Heiligenstadt (restored as "77.250")
77.250	4-6-2T	1927	MA	Schaan Vaduz, Lichtenstein.
78.606	4-6-4T	1931	P	Amstetten Eggersdorferstrasse.
78.618	4-6-4T	1938	MA	ÖGEG, Ampflwang.
86.476	2-8-2T	1943	M	ÖGEG, Ampflwang.
088.01	0-4-0T	1906	M	EM Strasshof.
789.837	0-6-0T	1921	M	BEM Nördlingen, Germany.
989.01	0-6-0T	1944	P	Probstdorf.
91.32	2-6-0T	1900	M	Mürzzuschlag.
91.107	2-6-0T	1908	MA	Gross Schwechat.
92.2220	0-8-0T	1898	P	Puchberg (near station).
92.2231	0-8-0T	1909	MS	Gross Schwechat.
92.2234	0-8-0T	1910	S	EM Strasshof.
"92.2271"	0-8-0T	1919	MA	Zwettl (Ex WLB 72).
392.2510	0-8-0T	1927	MS	ÖGEG, Ampflwang.
392.2530	0-8-0T	1927	MA	ÖGEG, Ampflwang (restored as WTK No.4).
93.1326	2-8-2T	1927	MR	ÖGEG, Ampflwang.
93.1332	2-8-2T	1927	MA	Weizelsdorf.
93.1335	2-8-2T	1927	M	Sigmundsherberg.
93.1360	2-8-2T	1927	MA	Eurovapor – Fützen, Germany.
93.1364	2-8-2T	1927	P	Ernstbrunn.
93.1378	2-8-2T	1927	MA	Eurovapor – Kandern,Germany.
93.1379	2-8-2T	1927	P	Bhf Schwarzach St. Veit.
93.1394	2-8-2T	1927	M	ÖGEG, Ampflwang.
93.1403	2-8-2T	1927	P	Korneuburg.
93.1410	2-8-2T	1928	MS	Bahnpark Augsburg, Germany.
93.1420	2-8-2T	1928	MA	Neue Landesbahn, Mistelbach.
93.1421	2-8-2T	1928	MA	Sigmundsherberg.
93.1422	2-8-2T	1928	M	Grosspetersdorf.
93.1434	2-8-2T	1928	MR	Zwettl.
93.1455	2-8-2T	1931	MR	ÖGEG, Ampflwang.
694.503	0-10-0T	1913	MS	ÖGEG, Ampflwang.
95.112	2-10-2T	1922	P	Bhf Payerbach.
97.201	0-6-2T	1890	M	Vordernberg shed (Dismantled and sectioned).
97.203	0-6-2T	1890	P	Grosspetersdorf.
97.208	0-6-2T	1892	MA	EM Strasshof.
97.210	0-6-2T	1893	M	Darmstadt Kranichstein, Germany.
97.217	0-6-2T	1908	P	Vordernberg Markt Hauptplatz.
197.301	0-12-0T	1912	MR	EM Strasshof.
297.401	2-12-2T	1941	P	Bhf Vordernberg Markt.
3071.07	2-4-2T	1935	MA	EM Strasshof (restored as DT 1.07).

760 mm gauge

Number	*Type*	*Built*	*Status*	*Location*
298.05	0-6-2T	1898	P	Knittelfeld museum.
298.14	0-6-2T	1898	MR	Bieringen. Germany.
298.24	0-6-2T	1902	P	Bezau.
298.25	0-6-2T	1902	MA	Bezau.
298.51	0-6-2T	1898	MA	ÖGLB Kienberg Gaming.
298.52	0-6-2T	1898	MA	Grünburg.
298.53	0-6-2T	1898	MA	Grünburg.
298.54	0-6-2T	1898	MR	Obergrafendorf.
298.55	0-6-2T	1898	P	Kaprun.
298.56	0-6-2T	1899	MA	Stainz.
298.102	0-6-2T	1888	MA	Grünburg.

98.104	0-6-2T	1890	MA	ÖGLB Kienberg Gaming.
98.106	0-6-2T	1914	MA	Grünburg.
98.205	0-6-2T	1902	MR	ÖGLB Kienberg Gaming.
98.206	0-6-2T	1902	P	Langschlag Bhf.
98.207	0-6-2T	1902	MR	NÖVOG Obergrafendorf.
98.01	0-6-2T	1905	A	Murau (as StLB Bh1).
98.03	0-6-2T	1929	P	Bregenz.
98.04	0-6-2T	1929	MR	ÖGLB Grunburg.
98.06	0-6-2T	1930	P	St. Veit a.d. Glan (as 498.04).
98.07	0-6-2T	1931	MR	Tischlerhäusl.
98.08	0-6-2T	1931	MA	Bezau.
98.01	0-6-4T	1896	P	Eichgraben.
98.02	0-6-4T	1896	MR	Club 598, Waidhofen a.d. Ybbs (as Yv2).
98.03	0-6-4T	1896	MS	Club 598, Waidhofen a.d. Ybbs.
98.01	0-4-0T	1941	M	Bad Ischl.
98.101	0-6-0TT	1941	MR	Mühlenstroth, Germany.
98.01	0-6-0T	1941	MR	KMB, Treibach Althofen.
99.02	0-8-2T	1926	M	KMB, Treibach Althofen.
99.03	0-8-2T	1926	P	Izola, Slovenia.
99.01	0-8+4	1906	MR	NÖVOG Gmünd.
99.02	0-8+4	1906	MR	NÖVOG Gmünd.
99.03	0-8+4	1906	A	Tischlerhäusl (as Ds 03).
99.04	0-8+4	1906	A	NÖVOG Gmünd.
99.05	0-8+4	1908	M	Sommerhubermühle.
99.06	0-8+4	1908	MA	Club Mh6 Obergrafendorf (restored as Mh.6).
99.01	0-10-0T	1924	M	KMB, Treibach Althofen.
99.01	0-8-0	1944	MA	Mauterndorf.
99.02	0-8-0	1944	M	TM Berlin, Germany.
99.101	0-8-0T	1944	MA	KMB. Treibach Althofen.
99.103	0-8-0T	1944	MA	Grünburg.

000 mm gauge

umber	*Type*	*Built*	*Status*	*Location*
99.01	0-4-2RT	1896	MR	NÖSBB Puchberg.
99.02	0-4-2RT	1897	MA	NÖSBB Puchberg.
99.03	0-4-2RT	1897	MR	NÖSBB Puchberg.
99.04	0-4-2RT	1899	MA	NÖSBB Puchberg.
99.05	0-4-2RT	1900	MR	NÖSBB Puchberg.
99.101	0-4-2RT	1893	MR	SKGB St. Wolfgang (Z 1).
99.102	0-4-2RT	1893	M	Freizeitwelt Abersee.
99.103	0-4-2RT	1893	M	Lokwelt Freilassing, Germany.
99.104	0-4-2RT	1893	MA	SKGB St. Wolfgang (Z 4).
99.105	0-4-2RT	1894	P	St. Wolfgang.
99.106	0-4-2RT	1894	MA	SKGB St. Wolfgang (Z 6).
99.201	0-4-2RT	1992	A	SKGB St. Wolfgang (Z 11).
99.202	0-4-2RT	1996	A	SKGB St. Wolfgang (Z 12).
99.203	0-4-2RT	1996	A	SKGB St. Wolfgang (Z 13).
99.204	0-4-2RT	1996	A	SKGB St. Wolfgang (Z 14).

.2. ÖBB ELECTRIC LOCOMOTIVES

umber	*Type*	*Built*	*Status*	*Location*
010 002	Co-Co	1955	MS	EM Strasshof.
010 003	Co-Co	1955	MA	Wien FJB (ÖBB Erlebnisbahn).
010 004	Co-Co	1955	MS	ÖGEG, Ampflwang.
010 009	Co-Co	1956	MS	ÖGEG, Ampflwang.
010 010	Co-Co	1956	MA	Wien FJB (ÖBB Erlebnisbahn).
010 011	Co-Co	1956	MS	Knittelfeld.
010 013	Co-Co	1956	MS	ÖGEG, Ampflwang.
010 015	Co-Co	1956	MS	ÖGEG, Ampflwang.
110 009	Co-Co	1958	MS	ÖGEG, Ampflwang.

1110 015	Co-Co	1958	MS	Knittelfeld.
1110 018	Co-Co	1959	MS	ÖGEG, Ampflwang.
1110 020	Co-Co	1960	MS	ÖGEG, Ampflwang.
1110 023	Co-Co	1960	MS	EM Strasshof.
1110 025	Co-Co	1960	MS	ÖGEG, Ampflwang.
1110 505	Co-Co	1957	MA	Innsbruck (ÖBB Erlebnisbahn).
1110 522	Co-Co	1960	MA	ÖGEG, Ampflwang.
1110 524	Co-Co	1960	MA	MBS Schruus.
1110 526	Co-Co	1960	MS	ÖGEG, Ampflwang.
1110 529	Co-Co	1961	MS	ÖGEG, Timelkam.
1110 530	Co-Co	1961	S	Innsbruck (ÖBB Erlebnisbahn).
1018 002	1Do1	1940	MS	ÖGEG, Ampflwang.
1018 004	1Do1	1940	M	Prora, Germany.
1018 005	1Do1	1940	MS	Club 1018, Bruck/Leitha.
1018 007	1Do1	1940	MS	ÖGEG, Ampflwang.
1018 008	1Do1	1940	MS	ÖGEG, Ampflwang.
1020 003	Co-Co	1941	MS	ÖGEG, Ampflwang.
1020 010	Co-Co	1943	MS	Stuttgart, Germany.
1020 012	Co-Co	1943	MS	ÖGEG, Bahnpark Augsburg, Germany.
1020 017	Co-Co	1944	M	Nördlingen, Germany.
1020 018	Co-Co	1940	A	EC Lienz.
1020 022	Co-Co	1940	MS	ÖGEG, Ampflwang.
1020 024	Co-Co	1941	MS	ÖGEG, Ampflwang.
1020 037	Co-Co	1943	MA	ÖGEG, Ampflwang.
1020 038	Co-Co	1943	MS	EM Strasshof.
1020 042	Co-Co	1943	MS	Bludenz (owned by Roco models).
1020 044	Co-Co	1945	MS	Bludenz.
1020 047	Co-Co	1954	MS	EM Strasshof.
1040 001	Bo-Bo	1950	MA	EM Strasshof.
1040 008	Bo-Bo	1951	MA	EM Strasshof.
1040 009	Bo-Bo	1951	MR	Sigmundsherberg.
1040 013	Bo-Bo	1953	MS	Club 1018, Wien FJB.
1040 015	Bo-Bo	1953	MS	ÖGEG, Ampflwang.
1041 001	Bo-Bo	1952	MS	EM Strasshof.
1041 005	Bo-Bo	1952	MS	ÖGEG, Ampflwang.
1041 006	Bo-Bo	1952	MS	ÖGEG, Ampflwang.
1041 015	Bo-Bo	1953	MA	Arge 1041 015 Gross Schwechat.
1141 003	Bo-Bo	1956	S	Bahnpark Augsburg.
1141 007	Bo-Bo	1956	MS	ÖGEG, Ampflwang.
1141 016	Bo-Bo	1956	MS	Knittelfeld.
1141 021	Bo-Bo	1957	MA	ÖGEG, Ampflwang (Active as 1141.21).
1141 022	Bo-Bo	1957	MS	EM Strasshof.
1141 028	Bo-Bo	1957	MS	EM Strasshof.
1042 005	Bo-Bo	1963	M	Mürzzuschlag.
1042 023	Bo-Bo	1964	A	Wien FJB (ÖBB Erlebnisbahn).
1042 518	Bo-Bo	1967	MS	ÖGEG, Ampflwang.
1044 501	Bo-Bo	1974	MS	EM Strasshof.
1045 001	Bo-Bo	1927	MS	ÖGEG, Ampflwang.
1045 003	Bo-Bo	1927	MS	ÖGEG, Ampflwang.
1045 009	Bo-Bo	1928	MA	EM Strasshof.
1045 012	Bo-Bo	1927	P	Attnang Puchheim.
1045 014	Bo-Bo	1928	MS	Gross Schwechat.
1145 002	Bo-Bo	1929	MA	EM Strasshof.
1145 009	Bo-Bo	1931	MS	EM Strasshof.
1245 001	Bo-Bo	1934	MS	EM Strasshof.
1245 002	Bo-Bo	1934	MS	ÖGEG, Ampflwang.
1245 004	Bo-Bo	1934	MS	EM Strasshof.
1245 005	Bo-Bo	1934	MR	St. Veit an der Glan.
1245 514	Bo-Bo	1938	M	Schwarzach St. Veit.
1245 516	Bo-Bo	1938	MS	ÖGEG, Ampflwang.
1245 518	Bo-Bo	1938	MA	ÖGEG, Ampflwang.
1245 522	Bo-Bo	1938	MR	Lienz.
1245 525	Bo-Bo	1938	MA	Knittelfeld.
1046 001	Bo-Bo	1956	MS	ÖGEG, Ampflwang.

1046 005	Bo-Bo	1956	MS	EM Strasshof.
1046 007	Bo-Bo	1956	MS	ÖGEG, Ampflwang.
1046 016	Bo-Bo	1959	MR	EM Strasshof.
1046 019	Bo-Bo	1959	MR	EM Strasshof.
1046 020	Bo-Bo	1959	MA	ÖGEG, Ampflwang.
1060.01	1C	1911	M	EM Strasshof.
1061.02	D	1926	MS	ÖGEG, Ampflwang.
1161 012	D	1932	MR	St. Veit an der Glan.
1161 017	D	1932	P	Bischofshofen.
1161 019	D	1940	MS	EM Strasshof.
1161 020	D	1940	MR	ÖGEG, Ampflwang.
1062 007	C	1954	MA	EM Strasshof.
1062 012	C	1955	MS	ÖGEG, Ampflwang.
1067 003	C	1963	M	Knittelfeld.
1067 004	C	1964	M	ÖGEG, Ampflwang.
1570.01	1A-Bo-A1	1926	M	EM Strasshof.
1670.09	1A-Bo-A1	1928	MA	ÖGEG Linz.
1670.25	1A-Bo-A1	1929	MA	EM Strasshof.
1670.102	1A-Bo-A1	1932	MS	ÖGEG, Ampflwang.
1670.104	1A-Bo-A1	1932	MS	Bludenz.
1072.01	1B1	1913	MS	EM Strasshof.
1072.05	1B1	1913	S	Stockerau.
1073.08	1C1	1923	MS	ÖGEG, Ampflwang.
1073.20	1C1	1925	MS	ÖGEG, Ampflwang.
1080 001	E	1924	MA	EM Strasshof.
1080 011	E	1924	MS	ÖGEG, Ampflwang.
1180 004	E	1926	MS	ÖGEG, Ampflwang.
1180 009	E	1927	MA	Bludenz.
1280.14	E	1929	MS	ÖGEG, Ampflwang.
1985.02	Bo	1913	MA	Gross Schwechat (restored as Eg 2).
1089.06	1C-C1	1924	M	ATM Sinsheim, Germany.
1189.02	1C-C1	1926	MA	ÖGEG, Ampflwang.
1189.05	1C-C1	1927	MS	EM Strasshof.
1189.09	1C-C1	1927	P	ÖGEG, Ampflwang.

6.3. ÖBB DIESEL LOCOMOTIVES

Standard gauge

Number	*Type*	*Built*	*Status*	*Location*
2020.01	B-B dh	1959	MS	ÖCD Amstetten.
2043.01	B-B dh	1964	MA	Knittelfeld.
2045.01	Bo-Bo de	1952	MS	ÖCD Etsdorf-Strass.
2045 002	Bo-Bo de	1952	S	Mistelbach Lokalbahn.
2045 009	Bo-Bo de	1953	MS	ÖCD Etsdorf-Strass.
2045 012	Bo-Bo de	1954	MS	ÖGEG, Ampflwang.
2045.15	Bo-Bo de	1954	M	Lienz.
2045 019	Bo-Bo de	1954	MS	ÖGEG, Ampflwang.
2045 020	Bo-Bo de	1954	MA	Mistelbach Lokalbahn.
2050 002	Bo-Bo de	1958	MA	EM Strasshof.
2050 003	Bo-Bo de	1958	S	ÖGEG, Ampflwang.
2050 004	Bo-Bo de	1958	MA	Wien FJB (ÖBB Erlebnisbahn).
2050 005	Bo-Bo de	1958	MA	ÖGEG, Ampflwang.
2050 008	Bo-Bo de	1959	MS	ÖGEG, Ampflwang.
2050 009	Bo-Bo de	1959	MA	Wien FJB (ÖBB Erlebnisbahn).
2050 012	Bo-Bo de	1961	MS	ÖGEG, Ampflwang.
2050 015	Bo-Bo de	1962	MS	ÖGEG, Ampflwang.
2050 016	Bo-Bo de	1962	MS	ÖGEG, Ampflwang.
2050 017	Bo-Bo de	1962	MS	ÖGEG, Ampflwang.
2050 018	Bo-Bo de	1962	M	Knittelfeld.

2060 004	B dh	1954	MA	EM Strasshof.
2060 011	B dh	1955	M	Sigmundsherberg.
2060 013	B dh	1955	MS	Friedberg.
2060 014	B dh	1955	MA	Friedberg.
2060 022	B dh	1955	MS	ÖGEG, Ampflwang.
2060 037	B dh	1955	MA	EM Strasshof.
2060 055	B dh	1956	MS	Ferlach.
2060 057	B dh	1956	M	Knittelfeld.
2060 058	B dh	1956	MA	ÖGEG, Ampflwang.
2060 064	B dh	1956	MS	Ferlach.
2060 074	B dh	1956	MS	EM Strasshof.
2060 091	B dh	1962	MA	Mistelbach Lokalbahn.
2060 092	B dh	1962	MS	ÖGEG, Ampflwang.
2060 099	B dh	1962	MS	ÖGEG, Ampflwang.
2061.01	B dh	1940	MS	Gross Schwechat.
2062 002	B dh	1958	MR	Ferlach.
2062 003	B dh	1958	MR	ÖCD Amstetten.
2062 012	B dh	1959	MR	Ferlach.
2062 029	B dh	1960	MA	ÖCD Amstetten.
2062 033	B dh	1961	MS	EM Strasshof.
2062 034	B dh	1961	MS	ÖGEG, Ampflwang.
2062 036	B dh	1961	MS	Friedberg.
2062 038	B dh	1961	MS	ÖGEG, Ampflwang.
2062 053	B dh	1961	MS	Friedberg.
2062 055	B dh	1961	MS	EM Strasshof.
2065.01	C dh	1940	MS	ÖCD Amstetten.
2066.01	C dh	1940	MA	Mistelbach Lokalbahn.
2067.04	C dh	1959	MA	EM Strasshof.
X110.02	B dm	1935	MA	Ebermannstadt, Germany.
X111.04	B dm	1944	M	EM Strasshof.
X112.01	B dh	1934	MS	St. Veit an der Glan.
X112.02	B dh	1934	M	TM Berlin, Germany.
X112.06	B dh	1935	MR	EM Strasshof.
X112.07	B dh	1935	M	Knittelfeld.
X130.01	Bo de	1934	MR	EM Strasshof.
X130.02	Bo de	1935	M	Ferlach.
X130.03	Bo de	1935	M	Ferlach.
X150.01	B dh	1943	P	Bhf Erbach/Odenwald, Germany.
X150.03	B dh	1943	M	Vordernberg.
X150.04	B dh	1943	M	Vordernberg.
X150.05	B dh	1943	M	Sigmundsherberg.
X150.09	B dh	1944	MS	ÖGEG Ampflwang.

760 mm gauge

Number	*Type*	*Built*	*Status*	*Location*
2090 001	Bo de	1930	MA	Obergrafendorf.
2190.01	Bo de	1934	MA	ÖGLB Kienberg Gaming.
2190.02	Bo de	1934	MS	WSV Litschau.
2190.03	Bo de	1936	MA	Obergrafendorf.
2091.01	1Bo1 de	1936	MR	Lunz am See.
2091.02	1Bo1 de	1936	MR	Litschau.
2091.03	1Bo1 de	1936	MA	Mauterndorf.
2091 004	1Bo1 de	1936	MS	Bezau.
2091.07	1Bo1 de	1936	MR	NÖVOG Gmünd.
2091.08	1Bo1 de	1940	MA	Bezau.
2091.09	1Bo1 de	1940	MR	NÖVOG Gmünd.
2091.10	1Bo1 de	1940	MR	Döllnitzbahn, Germany (199.030).
2091.11	1Bo1 de	1940	MR	Obergrafendorf.
2091.12	1Bo1 de	1940	MR	Döllnitzbahn, Germany (199.031).
2092 001	C dh	1944	P	Puchenstuben.
2092 003	C dh	1943	MR	Obergrafendorf.
2092 004	C dh	1943	MR	Obergrafendorf.
2093.01	Bo-Bo de	1930	MA	ÖGLB Kienberg Gaming.

6.4. ÖBB ELECTRIC RAILCARS

Number	Type	Built	Status	Location
4010.009	Bo-Bo	1967	MR	ÖGEG, Ampflwang.
4030.210	Bo-Bo	1962	MA	Gross Schwechat.
4041.01	Bo-2	1929	MS	ÖGEG, Ampflwang.
4041.03	Bo-2	1929	MS	EM Strasshof.
4042.01	Bo-2	1936	MS	St. Veit an der Glan.
4042.02	Bo-2	1936	MR	St. Veit an der Glan.
4060.02	Bo-Bo	1936	MR	Strasshof.
4061.13	Bo-Bo	1958	MA	Club 1018, Wien FJB.

6.5. ÖBB DIESEL RAILCARS

Number	Type	Built	Status	Location
5029.01	A-1 dm	1927	S	Stockerau.
5041.03	Bo-2 de	1933	M	Gross Schwechat.
5042.14	1A-A1 de	1937	MA	Wien FJB (ÖBB Erlebnisbahn).
5044.06	B-2 dh	1938	MR	ÖCD Etsdorf-Strass.
5144 001	B-2 dh	1951	P	Semmering.
5144 003	B-2 dh	1951	MS	Sigmundsherberg.
5144 004	B-2 dh	1951	MS	ÖCD Amstetten.
5145 001	B-2 dh	1952	MA	EM Strasshof.
5145 009	B-2 dh	1954	MR	ÖGEG Ampflwang.
5145 011	B-2 dh	1954	MA	EM Strasshof.
5145 014	B-2 dh	1956	MA	EM Strasshof.
5046 201	B-2 dh	1954	MS	EM Strasshof.
5046 204	B-2 dh	1955	MS	EM Strasshof.
5046 206	B-2 dh	1955	MS	EM Strasshof.
5046 214	B-2 dh	1955	MS	ÖGEG Ampflwang.
5046 215	B-2 dh	1955	MS	ÖGEG Ampflwang.
5046 216	B-2 dh	1955	MS	ÖGEG Ampflwang.
5146 201	B-2 dh	1959	MR	ÖGEG Ampflwang.
5146 205	B-2 dh	1961	M	Bad Tatzmannsdorf.
5146 206	B-2 dh	1961	M	Budapest, Hungary (as GySEV 5146 02).
5146 207	B-2 dh	1961	MS	ÖGEG Ampflwang.
5146 208	B-2 dh	1961	MS	ÖGEG Ampflwang.
5081 001	A-A dh	1964	MA	EM Strasshof.
5081 002	A-A dh	1964	MS	ÖGEG Ampflwang.
5081 003	A-A dh	1964	MS	Bielefeld, Germany.
5081 013	A-A dh	1965	P	Bhf Eisenerz.
5081 014	A-A dh	1965	MS	EM Strasshof.
5081 015	A-A dh	1965	MA	ÖGEG Ampflwang.
5081 019	A-A dh	1965	MA	Linz Steelworks.
5081 021	A-A dh	1965	MA	ÖGEG Ampflwang.
5081 051	A-A dh	1965	MA	NÖVOG Etsdorf-Strass.
5081 054	A-A dh	1965	M	BEM Nördlingen, Germany.
5081 055	A-A dh	1965	MA	Eisenerz.
5081 561	A-A dh	1965	MS	Zarrentin, Germany.
5081 562	A-A dh	1965	MA	Vordernberg.
5081 563	A-A dh	1967	MA	Vordernberg.
5081 564	A-A dh	1967	MA	Vordernberg.
5081 565	A-A dh	1967	MA	Vordernberg.

6.6. ÖBB DEPARTMENTAL STOCK

Number	*Type*	*Gauge*	*Built*	*Status*	*Location*
X512.08	B dm		1963	MR	EM Strasshof.
X534.60	1A de		19xx	M	Sigmundsherberg.
X610 913	B dm	760 mm	1925	MR	Hirschwang.
X614.10	B dm		1954	MR	Ferlach.
X614.12	B dm		1954	MR	Sigmundsherberg.
X614.16	B dm		1955	MA	Ferlach.
X614.30	B dm		1955	MA	Weizelsdorf.
X614.33	B dm		1955	MR	Oberschützen.
X614.38	B dm		1955	MR	Mürzzuschlag.
X614.80	B dm		1955	MR	Lambach.
X616 003	B dm		19xx	M	Vordernberg.
X616 010	B dm		19xx	M	Unter Retzbach.
X616 084	B dm		19xx	M	Vordernberg.
X616 901	B dm	760 mm	195x	MA	Grünburg.
X616 902	B dm	760 mm	1952	MR	Kienberg Gaming.
X616 903	B dm	760 mm	195x	MA	Grünburg.
X616 909	B dm	760 mm	1955	MR	Kienberg Gaming.
X616 910	B dm	760 mm	195x	M	Mauterndorf.
X616 912	B dm	760 mm	195x	M	Birkfeld.
X626 102	B dm		19xx	M	Knittelfeld.
X626 120	B dm		19xx	M	Schwarzach-St. Veit.
X626 126	B dm		19xx	M	Vordernberg.

6.7. OTHER RAILWAYS' STEAM LOCOMOTIVES

Note: Standard gauge unless shown otherwise.

Number	*Rly*	*Gauge*	*Type*	*Built*	*Status*	*Location*
465[60]	BDZ	600 mm	0-8-0T	1917	MR	Gross Schwechat
16.18	BDZ		2-10-0	1949	MS	ÖGEG Ampflwang.
16.19	BDZ		2-10-0	1949	MS	ÖGEG Ampflwang.
ADELE	BHEV		0-4-0Tm	1888	MA	Ferlach.
764.219	CFF	760 mm	0-8-0T	1917	MR	Club 760 Frojach.
764.222	CFF	760 mm	0-8-0T	1910	MR	FIM Freiland.
764.224	CFF	760 mm	0-8-0T	1910	MR	FIM Freiland.
764.403R	CFF	760 mm	0-8-0T	1984	MR	Heidenreichstein.
764.411R	CFF	760 mm	0-8-0T	1986	MR	Stainz.
764.480	CFF	760 mm	0-8-0T	1957	MR	Grünburg.
764.007	CFI	760 mm	0-8-0T	1953	MA	Grünburg.
142.063	CFR		2-8-4	1939	MA	ÖGEG Ampflwang (as "12.14").
230.174	CFR		4-6-0	1933	MS	ÖGEG Ampflwang (as "638.2174").
230.301	CFR		4-6-0	1935	MA	ÖGEG Ampflwang (as "638.1301").
50.459	CFR		0-10-0	1930	MS	ÖGEG Ampflwang (as "657.3459").
50.519	CFR		0-10-0	1931	MS	ÖGEG Ampflwang (as "657.2519").
50.770	CFR		0-10-0	1938	MA	ÖGEG Ampflwang (as "657.2770").
01 533	DR		4-6-2	1934	MA	ÖGEG Ampflwang.
44 661	DR		2-10-0	1941	MR	ÖGEG Ampflwang.
44 1595	DR		2-10-0	1943	MS	ÖGEG Ampflwang.
44 1614	DR		2-10-0	1943	MS	ÖGEG Ampflwang.
50 1002	DR		2-10-0	1940	MS	ÖGEG Ampflwang.
50 3506	DR		2-10-0	1940	MS	ÖGEG Ampflwang.
50 3519	DR		2-10-0	1940	MR	ÖGEG Ampflwang.
50 3670	DR		2-10-0	1941	MS	Klein Schwechat.
50 3689	DR		2-10-0	1940	MS	ÖGEG Ampflwang.
52 8003	DR		2-10-0	1944	MS	ÖGEG Ampflwang.
52 8096	DR		2-10-0	1943	MS	ÖGEG Ampflwang.
52 8124	DR		2-10-0	1943	MS	ÖGEG Ampflwang.

52 8186	DR		2-10-0	1944	MS	ÖGEG Ampflwang.
52 8196	DR		2-10-0	1944	MS	ÖGEG Ampflwang.
86 056	DR		2-8-2T	1932	MS	ÖGEG Ampflwang.
86 501	DR		2-8-2T	1942	MR	ÖGEG Ampflwang.
8	DTKC		0-4-0Tm	1884	MA	Mariazell museum tram.
11	DTKC		0-4-0Tm	1884	MR	Wien Tramway Museum.
31	DTKC		0-6-0T	1904	MA	Mariazell museum tram.
4 GMUNDEN	EÖEG	1106 mm	4-4-0T	1854	M	Mürzzuschlag.
1	GB	1000 mm	0-4-0RT	1886	M	Mürzzuschlag.
372	GKB		4-4-0	1891	MA	EM Strasshof.
406	GKB		4-4-0	1896	MS	Ljubljana, Slovenia.
415	GKB		4-4-0	1897	MR	Brenner & Brenner, St. Pölten.
674	GKB		0-6-0	1860	M	TM Budapest, Hungary.
680	GKB		0-6-0	1860	MS	TM Berlin.
1851	GKB		0-6-0T	1898	P	Bärnbach.
17	GySEV		0-6-0	1885	M	Budapest, Hungary.
121	GySEV		2-6-2T	1914	P	Neufeld/Leitha.
122	GySEV		2-6-2T	1916	P	Bad Neusiedl.
123	GySEV		2-6-2T	1925	P	Marz Rohrbach.
124	GySEV		2-6-2T	1950	MA	Gross Schwechat.
324,1518	GySEV		2-6-2	1910	P	Sopron, Hungary.
424,140	GySEV		4-8-0	1941	MS	Fertöboz, Hungary.
520,030	GySEV		2-10-0	1943	MS	Fertöboz, Hungary.
28-053	JZ		0-10-0	1914	P	Knittelfeld.
33-240	JZ		2-10-0	1943	MS	EM Strasshof (DRB 52 460).
33-329	JZ		2-10-0	1943	MS	Mürzzuschlag, Kulturbahnhof (DRB 52 5422).
73-019	JZ	760 mm	2-6-2	1913	MR	Tischlerhäusl (o/h Ceske Velenice).
83-180	JZ	760 mm	0-8-2	1949	MA	Club U44, Weiz.
97-029	JZ	760 mm	0-6-4RT	1914	M	Club 760, Frojach.
37 AJAX	KFNB		0-4-2	1841	MR	EM Strasshof
94 LICAON	KFNB		2-4-0ST	1851	MR	EM Strasshof (TM Wien store).
1.20	KKStB		4-4-0	1883	MS	EM Strasshof (Partially sectioned).
494.62	KKStB		0-6-0T	1887	P	Rohrbach-Berg.
97.73	KKStB		0-6-0T	1894	MR	EM Strasshof.
180.1	KKStB		0-10-0	1900	MS	Mürzzuschlag.
229.222	KKStB		2-6-2T	1918	M	EM Strasshof.
377,247	MAV		0-6-0T	1895	P	Wulkaprodersdorf (as "377.943").
377,262	MAV		0-6-0T	1895	M	Historama, Ferlach.
1 N	ÖLB		0-4-0T	1905	M	Mariazell.
Pt47-138	PKP		2-8-2	1949	MA	Brenner & Brenner, Heiligenstadt, (as "919.138").
S 4	SKGLB	760 mm	0-6-2T	1890	M	Mondsee.
S 5	SKGLB	760 mm	0-6-2T	1890	M	Mondsee.
S 9	SKGLB	760 mm	0-6-2T	1893	M	Mondsee.
S 12	SKGLB	760 mm	0-6-2T	1906	MA	Mauterndorf.
HELLBRUNN	SLB		0-4-0Tm	1902	MA	Mariazell museum tram.
Kh 111	StLB	760 mm	0-10-0T	1930	M	Club 760, Frojach.
S 7	StLB	760 mm	0-6-2T	1893	M	Club 760, Frojach.
S 11	StLB	760 mm	0-6-2T	1894	MR	Club 760, Frojach.
U 7	StLB	760 mm	0-6-2T	1894	P	Birkfeld.
U 9	StLB	760 mm	0-6-2T	1894	P	St. Pölten Hbf (as "298.09").
Z 6	StLB	760 mm	0-6-0T	1893	MA	Mauterndorf.
699.01	StLB	760 mm	0-8-0T	1944	MA	Llanfair, United Kingdom.
11810	StLB	760 mm	0-6-0	1944	MA	Abreschwiller, France.
827	Sudb		4-4-0	1848	MS	EM Strasshof.
1665	Sudb		0-6-0	1895	M	EM Strasshof (MAV 333,002).
290c	Sulm		0-6-0T	1907	MS	Lienz.
1	ZB	760 mm	0-6-2T	1900	MR	Jenbach.

6.8. OTHER RAILWAYS' DIESEL & ELECTRIC

Note: Standard gauge unless shown otherwise.

Number	*Rly*	*Gauge*	*Type*	*Built*	*Status*	*Location*
VT 10.01	GKB		A-1 dm	1953	MA	Ferlach.
VT 10.02	GKB		A-1 dm	1953	MR	Graz.
VT 10.05	GKB		A-1 dm	1955	M	Bayerische Eisenstein, Germany.
VT 10.08	GKB		A-1 dm	1962	M	Nördlingen, Germany.
VT 10.09	GKB		A-1 dm	1962	M	GKB Museum, Lieboch.
D 1	LBPH	760 mm	0-6-0 dh	1943	MS	Bezau.
E I	LBPH	760 mm	Bo E	1903	MA	Hirschwang.
E II	LBPH	760 mm	Bo E	1903	MA	Hirschwang.
E III	LBPH		Bo E	1903	P	Reichenau.
V 10.012	MBS		C dh	1944	MS	ÖCD Etsdorf-Strass.
V 10.015	MBS		B dh	1942	MS	ÖCD Etsdorf-Strass.
L 4	RB	1000 mm	Bo RE	1909	M	Innsbruck. RB = Rittnerbahn.
13257	SBB		1C-C1 E	1919	M	EM Strasshof.
ET 11	StLB		Bo-2 er	1936	MS	St. Veit an der Glan (ÖBB 4042.01)
ET 12	StLB		Bo-2 er	1936	MS	St. Veit an der Glan (ÖBB 4042.02)
RT 2	StLB	760 mm	B dm	1941	A	KMB Treibach Althofen.
Te 2	StLB		Bo-Bo er	1928	MR	Mariazell.
VL 01	StLB	760 mm	D dh	1942	MA	Mauterndorf (restored as SKGLB D40).
VL 3	StLB	760 mm	C dh	1943	MA	Bieringen, Germany
VL 5	StLB	760 mm	B dm	1938	MS	Frojach.
ET 4	SVB		Bo er	1908	MA	Mariazell.
ET 5	SVB		Bo er	1908	M	Bayerische Eisenstein, Germany.
ET 16	SVB		Bo er	1911	MR	Mariazell.
1	STB	1000 mm	Bo-Bo er	1904	MR	Innsbruck.
2	STB	1000 mm	Bo-Bo er	1904	MR	Innsbruck.
4	STB	1000 mm	Bo-Bo er	1905	MR	Innsbruck.
E 20 001	StH		Bo-Bo E	1915	R	Gross Schwechat.
E 22 002	StH		Bo-Bo E	1916	MS	Bratislava vychod, Slovakia.
E 22 003	StH		Bo-Bo E	1916	MR	Mariazell.
ET 22 105	StH	1000 mm	Bo er	1921	MR	Peuerbach.
ET 23 101	StH	1000 mm	Bo er	1912	R	Historama, Ferlach.
ET 25 105	StH		Bo er	1921	MR	Mariazell.
ET 26 101	StH	1000 mm	Bo er	1912	R	Historama, Ferlach.
ET 26 106	StH	1000 mm	Bo-Bo er	1936	MR	Hilden, Germany.
ET 26 107	StH	1000 mm	Bo-Bo er	1936	M	Ferlach.
ABmot 12	GySEV	760 mm	A-1 dm	1926	S	Fertöboz, Hungary.
D 7[I]	ZB	760 mm	Bo-Bo de	1940	MR	Kienberg Gaming.
D 7[II]	ZB	760 mm	B-B dh	1961	MR	Stainz (ex MAV Mk48 2019).

APPENDIX I. VEHICLE TYPE CODES FOR RAILCARS & MULTIPLE UNITS

The abbreviations in common use in Austria are used, with the normal British codes in brackets. The Austrian codes are:

Code	Meaning	Code	Meaning
ET	Electric power car	A	First Class
ES	Driving trailer for above	B	Second Class
VT	Diesel power car	AB	Composite
VS	Driving trailer for above	D	Vehicle with luggage compartment
T	Trailer	4	Vehicle with 4 axles (instead of 2)
h	Electric heating	BR	Buffet Car
l	Control wired	WR	Restaurant Car

Note: The continental system does not differentiate between open and compartment stock nor indicate toilet facilities.

British codes are also shown in brackets as follows:

Code	Meaning	Code	Meaning	Code	Meaning
D	Driving	F	First	RB	Buffet
M	Motor	S	Second	O	Open
T	Trailer	C	Composite	K	Side Corridor
L	Lavatory	U	Unclassified	B	Brake

Under 'accommodation' are shown the number of first and second class seats with tip-up seats in saloons in parentheses, followed by the number of toilets, e.g. 24/49(3) 1T indicates 24 first class seats, 49 second class seats, three additional tip-up seats and one toilet. TD indicates a toilet suitable for disabled people, W indicates a wheelchair space.

APPENDIX II. DEPOT & LIVERY CODES

ÖBB DEPOT CODES

P5 Code	*ÖBB Code*	*Servicestelle (depot)*
AM	Ams	Amstetten
BL	Bl	Bludenz
FD	F	Floridsdorf
GM	Gm	Gmünd
GZ	G	Graz
IN	I	Innsbruck
KD	Kd	Knittelfeld
KR	Kr	Krems
LZ	Lz	Linz
MH1		München (DB, Germany).
NS	Nb	Wiener Neustadt
SB	Sb	Salzburg
SL	Sl	Selzthal
SP	Pb	St. Pölten
VH	Vf	Villach
WE	We	Wels
WF	Wf	Wien FJB
WM	Mat	Wien Hauptbahnhof
WW	Ws	Wien West

ÖBB LIVERY CODES

Since the founding of ÖBB there have only been a few livery schemes. The immediate post WWII period saw all electric and diesel locomotives painted dark green with railcars in blue and cream. A change took place in the late 1960s when the Class 1042s were being delivered and these locos, having started off in green, changed over to blood-orange with yellow lining whilst the railcar livery remained the same.

The 1990s saw the blood orange replaced by red (verkehrsrot) with a wide cream band at the base of the body side which continued around the cab. This was later changed to a white band. At the same time white replaced cream on the railcars. Classes 1014 and 1822 had a variant on this livery in that the two prime colours were reversed over the cabs.

For the 21st century ÖBB now has the red as a standard livery on locomotives but with no lining whilst railcars are starting to appear in red, grey and white (the white being the sliding doors). Like many other countries departmental stock is in yellow but some Klima snowploughs having started off in green and changed to red are now appearing in orange!

ÖBB locos are assumed to be the new red (*verkehrsrot*) livery unless otherwise noted. Livery codes used are as follows:

A Advertising livery.
C DMU livery 1 (cream/blue/red).
G Green.
GR DMU livery 2 (grey/blue/red).
J Railjet livery (dark red/black/grey)
O Blood orange.
M Mariazellerbahn locomotive livery (red/cream).
N Non standard livery – see note.
R New DMU/EMU livery (grey with red areas at ends and white doors).
RB Red and beige.
S S-bahn livery (white/blue).
V Valousek design (red, light grey, dark grey).
Y Yellow.
YR Yellow/red.

APPENDIX III. ABREVIATIONS

1ÖSEK	1. Österreichischer Strassenbahn und Eisenbahn Klub
AB	Achenseebahn
AC	Alternating Current
AOMC	Aigle–Ollon–Monthey–Champéry (Swiss Private Railway)
ATM	Auto und Technik Museum
ATP	Automatic Train Protection
Bh	Bauhof
Bhf	Bahnhof
Bm	Bahnmeister
BBÖ	Bundesbahnen Österreich (pre war)
BDZ	Bulgarski Durzhavni Zheleznitsi (Bulgarian Railways)
BEM	Bayerisches Eisenbahnmuseum (Germany)
CD	Ceské Dráhy (Czech Railways)
CFF	Caile Ferrate Forestiere (Romanian Forestry Railways)
CFI	Caile Ferrate Industrie (Romanian Industrial Railways)
CFR	Caile Ferrate Romane (Romanian State Railways)
CSD	Ceskoslovenské Státní Dráhy (Czechoslavakian State Railways)
CFV3V	Chemin de Fer à Vapeur des 3 Vallés (Belgium)
DB	Deutsche Bundesbahn (German Federal Railway)
DC	Direct Current
DMU	Diesel Multiple Unit
DR	Deutsche Reichsbahn (in former East Germany)
DRB	Deutsche Reichsbahn
EAB	Elektro Anlagenbau
EBS	Elektro Betriebsstelle
EC	Eisenbahn Club or Eurocity (type of train service)
EFZ	Eisenbahnfreunde Zollernbahn (Germany)
EM	Eisenbahnmuseum
EMU	Electric Multiple Unit
EVN	European Vehicle Number
FrOWOS	Freunde der Bahnlinie Oberwart-Oberschützen
FS	Ferrovie dello Stato (Italian State Railways)
GKB	Graz Köflacher Bahn
GV	Lokalbahn Gmunden-Vorchdorf
GySEV	Györ–Sopron–Ebenfurti Vasút
HE	Historische Eisenbahn
hp	Horse power
HW	Hauptwerkstätte
Hz	Hertz
IVB	Innsbrucker Verkehrsbetriebe und Stubaitalbahn
JZ	Jugoslovenske Zeleznice (Yugoslavian State Railways)
KFN	Kaiser Ferdinands Nordbahn
kkStB	kaiserlich-königliche Österreichische Staatsbahnen
KMB	Kärtner Museumsbahnen
kN	Kilonewtons
km/h	Kilometres per hour
kV	Kilovolts
kW	Kilowatts
LBB	Lavamünder Bahnbetriebs GmbH
LBPH	Lokalbahn Payerbach–Hirschwang
LH	Lokalbahn Lambach-Haag
LILO	Linzer Lokalbahn
LOGS	Logserv
LTE	LTE Logistik und Transport
LV	Lokalbahn Lambach-Vorchdorf
m	Metres
MÁV	Magyar Államvasútak (Hungarian State Railways)
MBS	Montafoner Bahn AG
MLV	Martinsberger Lokalbahnverein
mm	Millimetres

MStM	Mödlinger Stadtverkehrs Museum
NBiK	Nostalgiebahnen in Kärnten
NÖSBB	Niederösterreichische Schneebergbahn
NÖVOG	Niederösterreichische Verkehrsorganisationsgesellschaft
NWP	Neumarkt–Waizenkirchen–Peuerbach (Now part of Linzer Lokalbahn)
OBL	Oberbaulager (Track department store)
ODK	Österreichische Draukraftwerke
ÖBB	Österreichische Bundesbahnen
ÖCD	Österreichischer Club für Diesellokgeschichte
ÖGEG	Österreichische Gesellschaft für Eisenbahngeschichte
ÖGLB	Österreichische Gesellschaft für Lokalbahnen
PKP	Polskie Koleje Panstwowe (Polish State Railways)
R	Reserve
RB	Rittner Bahn
RL	Regionalleitung
rpm	Revolutions per minute
RPS	Rail Professionals Stütz
RTS	Rail Transport Service
SB	Südbahn
SBB	Schweizerische Bundesbahnen
SKGB	Salzkammergutbahn
SKGLB	Salzkammergut Lokalbahn
SLB	Salzburger Lokalbahn
Sm	Signalmeister
SOB	Südostbahn
SS	Südliche Staatsbahnen
StH	Stern & Hafferl
SRB	Südburgenländische Regionalbahn
StLB	Steiermärkische Landesbahnen
STB	Steiermarkbahn
Sudb	Südbahn
Sulm	Sulmtalbahn
SUZ	Schnellumbauzug
SVB	Salzburger Verkehrsbetriebe
SZ	Slovenske Zeleznice (Slovenian Railways)
SZU	Sihltal–Zürich–Uetliberg–Bahn (Switzerland)
TMB	Tiroler Museumsbahn
TS	Technische Services
TSI	Technical Specifications for Interoperability
TM	Technical Museum
V	Volts
VA	Lokalbahn Vorchdorf-Attersee
VBW	Vereinigte Bern Worb Bahnen (Switzerland)
VEF	Verband der Eisenbahnfreunde
VKM	Vehicle Keeper Marking
VSM	Veluwsche Stoomtrein Maatschappij, Beekbergen, Netherlands
WLB	Wiener Lokalbahnen
WLC	Wiener Lokalbahnen Cargo
WSB	Wynetal und Suhrentalbahn, Switzerland
WSTBA	Westbahn Management GmbH
WSV	Waldviertler Schmalspur Verein
WTK	Wolfsegg-Trauntaler Kohlengrube
Z	Stored
ZB	Zillertalbahn
ZSSK	Zeleznicná Spolocnost Slovensko, a.s. (Slovak Railways)

APPENDIX IV. BUILDERS

ABB	Asea Brown Boveri
ACMV	Ateliers de Constructions Méchaniques SA, Vevey, Switzerland
Adtranz	ABB Daimler Benz Transportation – various plants
AEG	Allgemeine Elektrizitätsgesellschaft, Berlin or Wien
ASEA	Allmänna Svenska Elekriska AB, Västerås, Sweden
BBC	Brown Boveri et Cie, Baden, Switzerland and Mannheim, Germany
Beilhack	Martin Beilhack, Rosenheim, Germany
BMAG	Berliner Maschinenenfabrik A.G. vormals L. Schwartzkopff, Berlin-Wildau
Bombardier	Bombardier Transportation (Various plants e.g. Bombardier Aachen)
Büssing	Büssing Fahrzeug- und Motorenbau, Braunschweig, Germany
CAT/Caterpillar	Caterpillar Inc. Illinois USA but plants worldwide
DD/Djuo Djakavic	Djuro Djakovic Industrija Lokomotive, Strjeva I Mostova, Slavonski Brod, Yugoslavia
Demag	Demag AG, Duisburg, Germany
Deutz	See KHD
Duewag	Düsseldorfer Waggonfabrik AG, Düsseldorf, Germany
Elin	Elecktrische Industrie A.G. Weiz, Austria
ESG	Elektrizitats und Strassenbahngesellschaft, Linz, Austria
Falun	AB Svenska Järnvägsverkstäderna, Falun, Sweden
FFA	Flug und Fahrzeugewerke AG, Altenrhein Switzerland
Floridsdorf	Wienerlokomotivfabrik, Wien Floridsdorf
Ganz	Ganz Waggon und Machinenfabrik, Budapest, Hungary
Ganz Mavag	Ganz Mavag Mozdony-, Vagon, és Gépgyár, Budapest, Hungary
Ganz Hunslet	Ganz Hunslet, Budapest, Hungary
Gebus	Gelinck und Judtmann, Wien
GM	General Motors, La Grange, Illinois, USA
Gmeinder	Gmeinder & Co. Gmbh, Mosbach, Baden, Germany
Graff	Niedersachsisches Waggonfabrik, Josef Graff, Elze, Germany
Graz	Johann Weitzer, Waggonfabrik, Graz
Györ	Waggon és Gépgyár, Budapest, Hungary
Hagglund	Hagglund & Söner, Örnsköldsvik, Werk Falun, Sweden
Henschel	Henschel & Sohn, Kassel, Germany
Hunslet Barclay	Hunslet Barclay Ltd, Kilmarnock, Scotland
Jung	Arn.Jung Lokomotivfabrik GmbH, Jungenthal bei Kirchberg an der Sieg, Germany
JW/Jenbach	Jenbacher Werke, Jenbach, Tirol, Austria
Kable Gmeinder	see Gmeinder
KHD	Klöckner Humboldt Deutz AG, Köln, Germany
Knotz	Franz Knotz KG, Stahl & Kesselbau, Wien (now Bombardier-Rotax)
Krauss, Linz (KrL)	Lokomotivfabrik Krauss & Co., Linz
Krauss-Maffei	Krauss-Maffei AG, München Allach, Germany
Krauss, München (KrM)	Lokomotivfabrik Krauss & Co. Werk München, Germany
Kiepe	Th. Kiepe, Düsseldorf, Germany
Layritz	Elisabeth Layritz GmbH, Penzberg, Bayern, Germany
LEW	VEB Lokomotivbau Elektrotechnische Werke "Hans Beimler", Berlin-Hennigsdorf, East Germany
LKM	VEB Lokomotivebau und bahnbedarf "Karl Marx", Potsdam-Babelsberg, East Germany
Lindner	Gottfried Lindner AG, Ammendorf, Halle, Germany
Linz	Elektrobau, Linz
Lohner	Karosseriewerk Lohner, Wien, Austria
Lugansk	Lugansker Lokomotivfabrik, Oktoberrevolution, Lugansk, USSR (Ukraine)
Maffei	J.A. Maffei AG, München, Germany
MaK	Maschinenbau Kiel, Germany
MAN	Maschinenfabrik Augsburg-Nürnberg, Nürnberg, Germany
MFO	Maschinenfabrik Oerlikon, Zürich Oerlikon, Switzerland
Mavag	Mávag Mozdony és Gépgyár, Budapest, Hungary
MTU	Motoren und Turbinen Union, Friendrichshafen, Germany

Nohab	Nydqvist & Holm, AB, Trollhättan, Sweden
ÖAM	Österreichische Alpin Montageselleschaft, Zeltweg
OK	Orenstein & Koppel, Berlin Drewitz, Germany (Steam) Orenstein-Koppel und Lübecker Maschinenbau AG, Dortmund Dorstfeld, Germany (Diesels)
Plasser	Plasser und Theurer, Bahnbaumaschinen, Purkersdorf and Linz, Austria
Rotax	Rotax, Wien, Austria
RTM	Rotterdamsche Tramweg Maatschappij
Schöma	Christoph Schöttler Maschinenfabrik GmbH, Diepholz, Germany
SGP G (or W or F)	Simmering Graz Pauker, Graz (or Wien Simmering or Wien Floridsdorf)
SIG	Schweizerische Industrie Gesellschaft, Neuhausen am Rheinfall, Switzerland
Siemens	Siemens Transportation Systems, various works in Austria and Germany
Simmering	Maschinen und Waggonbau AG Wien Simmering
Skoda	Skoda Werke, Plzen, Czechoslovakia (now Czech Republic)
SLM	Schweizerische Lokomotive und Maschinenfabrik, Winterthur, Switzerland
SSW	Siemens Schuckertwerke, Wien + elsewhere
Stadler	Stadler Rail AG. Bussnang and Altenrhein Switzerland; Berlin-Pankow, Germany
SWS	Schweizerische Waggons und Aufzugefabrik AG, Schlieren, Switzerland
SWP	Schindler Waggon AG, Pratteln, Switzerland
StEG	Maschinenfabrik der Staatseisenbahngesellschaft, Wien, Austria
Tobisch	Franz Tobisch, Wien, Austria
U23A	Uzinele 23 August, Bucuresti, Romania
Uerdingen	Waggonfabrik Uerdingen AG, Krefeld-Uerdingen Germany
VOEST	Voest Alpine, various plants, Austria
VSFT	Vossloh Schienenfahrzeugetechnik GmbH, Kiel, Germany
Westwaggon	Vereinigte Westdeutsche Waggonfabrik AG, Köln, Germany
Windhoff	Rheiner Maschinenfabrik Windhoff AG, Rheine, Westfalen, Germany
WrN	AG der Lokomotivfabrik, formerly G. Sigl, Wiener Neustadt
WMD	Waggon und Machinenbau Gmbh, Donauworth, Germany
Voith	J.M. Voith Gmbh, Heidenheim (Brenz), Germany, and St. Pölten, Austria